This piece of work is as profound as it is elegant. Exploring what might seem like simple concepts into depths of discovery and understanding that should be requisite of anyone working in education. Many educators will go through full careers without considering some of these areas. With this work as a guide, the education landscape could be irrevocably changed for the better.

— **Lewis Ames**, Director—Children of the Forest

These books immediately—no fooling around—challenge whether you are even learning, and then help you understand how to know if you are learning anything at all!

Book I: Outer Work, is a challenging book to help those who want to think for themselves. *Book II: Inner Work*, is about thoughts and perceptions: Are you the creator of your own problems? Avoid group think even when you feel compelled to conform. Hear your fear and deal with it! Intuition favors the quiet mind. When you are unclear, you are wrong. Where did you lose your intuition? These are all such important parts of intelligence.

Here are the most useful questions you will ever ask yourself; crucially important for self-inquiry, self-understanding, and self-esteem. They will help your mind strengthen through your own self-work. These books provide landmarks to gain, to hold, and to refer to in the project of deeply understanding who you are. *Becoming Supergenius* is outstanding! This is definitely genius.

— **Ann Hallock**, MSW, LCSW, ACSW

2020 presented a pivot point in life for most of us. The pandemic has caused us to be incredibly introspective in our thinking. Enter *Becoming Supergenius*. It has a calming influence when used as a meditation and it has the ability to spark deep thinking.

After reading *Becoming Supergenius*, I think I have found my inner voice! It has been sleeping for a very long time. After reading the first few sections, I found myself popping to different sections as my pandemic experience brought on different situations and emotions in life. Other times, when I would start reading, I just needed more and kept reading.

I judge a book by how it grabs me emotionally and intellectually and, indeed, *Becoming Supergenius*, locked me in and opened my thinking. Life may never find its 'normal' for a very long time. So, hold on tight. Reach out for some sage wisdom that will grow your new genius from within.

— **Rose. L. Colby**, award winning author of *Competency-Based Education: A New Architecture for K-12 Schooling*

Becoming Supergenius: Creativity and Transformation is an engaging and inspiring book that is composed in a way that can be revisited often. No story lives unless someone wants to listen, and Lincoln has developed great skill as a listener and investigator. Sapient, incisive, perceptive, and enlightened.

— **Darren Saare**, RSW, Leader—Community Health Services, Vancouver Island Health

In *Becoming Supergenius: Creativity and Transformation*, Lincoln Stoller explores the concept—and importance—of degrees of intelligence. Just as transcendent athletes and musicians can forever elevate their respective crafts, 'supergeniuses' also have the potential to do the same for society.

Stoller carefully lays out the modern sociocultural/sociodigital context for the application of creativity and intelligence. In doing so, he illustrates not just the ability of exceptional genius to affect change, but our collective dire need for them to do exactly that.

— **Terry Heick**, Founder and Director of TeachThought.com, author of *10 Ideas in Pursuit of a Global Curriculum*

On exceptional occasions at best, a work is produced that gives the world a glimpse at an explanation of it all, some grand analysis in an otherwise incomprehensible world. Stoller has done just that with *Becoming Supergenius: Creativity and Transformation*. By combining the experiences and words from thirty-five "supergeniuses" and then weaving them together in his own authentic classifications, he has created a comprehensive guide to being.

— **Alexander Khost**, Founder of Voice of the Children NYC, and Flying Squads, and organizer at Alliance for Self-Directed Education

Becoming Supergenius

Creativity and Transformation

328 secrets from 1,600 years of experience

Part 1: The Outer World

by

Lincoln Stoller, PhD, CHt

MindStrengthBalance.com

"To live is to think."

— Marcus Tillius Cicero

"The most pressing task is to teach people how to learn."
— Peter Drucker

BECOMING

SUPERGENIUS

PART I: THE OUTER WORLD

First Edition.
Published 2021 by Mind Strength Balance
Victoria, British Columbia, Canada
https://www.mindstrengthbalance.com

Stoller, Lincoln, 1956- author.
becoming supergenius, part I: the outer world, creativity and transformation / Lincoln Stoller.
Includes bibliographic references.
ISBN 978-1-7774204-3-7 (mobi) | ISBN 978-1-7774204-2-0 (epub)
ISBN 978-1-7774204-0-6 (paper) | ISBN 978-1-7774204-1-3 (hard cover) ISBN 978-1-7774204-4-4 (audio)

Subjects: LCSH: Creative Ability. | Self-actualization. | Wisdom. | Genius. | Learning.

Cover Art:
etching Albrecht Dürer
tinting Polina Hrytskova

To my sons.

Table of Contents

2 – Attitudes 29

The Landscape

The Future

3 – Actors 64

Introduction

Teachers

Students

Agents

Part II: The Inner World

Preface to Part 2

I – Thoughts and Perceptions

Acknowledgments

Thanks to all those who contributed to *The Learning Project*. I am beholden to the elders, most of whom have passed on; and to the younger ones—still being formed in the crucible of adulthood—who may not realize the importance of their feelings and their voices. I hope these books will help you become strident in your wisdom.

Those contributors of middle age probably understand the importance of their insights. By bringing our voices together they are amplified. I consider you all mentors, and I think of you often.

Guide To The Reader

Becoming Supergenius consists of 328 indications about learning, thinking, and seeing the world that are drawn from my experience, the wisdom of others, and the 35 interviews in my previous book, *The Learning Project*. The purpose of *Becoming Supergenius* is to reveal, condense, and clarify true thinking in an inclusive and instructive format. It's your genius that is at issue.

This material applies scientific thinking, the psychology of mind, and many people's experience; all the ways and means of our minds: intellect, emotion, personality, gender, body, spirit, self-confidence, groupthink, power, fallacy, and prejudice. The work roughly divides into our relationship to the world and the world within us.

The opposite of any deep truth is another deep truth, and my object is to present both in each case. I don't claim to be complete, I aim to be comprehensive. I don't aim for certainty, I aim for clarity, but it comes at a cost: you have to think about it. If you reach contrary conclusions, you are succeeding.

Preface to Part I

Where We Start

We remember traumatic events, sometimes so clearly we have to forget them. To help in forgetting them, we mix them up. Memory is malleable and that's important. We don't remember in order to know what happened; we remember in order to know what to do.

I remember standing on the sidewalk, looking toward the long, low building that was Midland School. At the far left end was the sixth grade, and at the far right end was the kindergarten where I was headed in my first year of school. I remember it as my first day but it was probably some other day. In any event, it's the first day of school that I remember.

As I looked at the building, I wondered why school had to be so awful. I wished I could go to Summerhill, the English boarding school where kids could do whatever they wanted. It actually would have been possible, but I was only five and I didn't know. I have no idea how I knew about Summerhill.

That was one of my earliest memories of asking why things were how they were, and why they couldn't be otherwise. The deeper question was how to find satisfaction. The answer I was heading toward—but didn't know at the time—was that I was only satisfied by learning.

I learned stuff in the subsequent forty-five years, but I still wondered what to make of it. I wondered why I learned, and how I learned, and what fundamental thing learning was. I made learning about learning into a project, and, since I had met a number of people whom I really admired, I resolved to ask them.

That was the start of a project whose thirty-five interviews I gathered into a book titled *The Learning Project, Rites of Passage*. It was clear that through all my reading and experience, no one knew how learning was done, what it meant, or why it was important. It was clear that there was and should not be one answer to each of these questions.

In *The Learning Project* I asked accomplished people of all ages, interests, and backgrounds what these questions meant to them. I asked not for answers but stories: how each person learned and how it's been important to them. Thirty-five people, ranging in age from 16 to 94, with over 1,600 years of accumulated learning.

Learning means different things to different people, and it is not my right to extract just one meaning. The best answer I've found is that learning is the pursuit of the meaningful. Meaning has a different texture for every person. The stories told in *The Learning Project* are fully textured. The 328 points given in here are conceptual, sterilized. They are easier to understand but, because they are disconnected from a person's life, each must be fit into your life's story.

The Learning Project is a diamond with thirty-five facets. The question of learning enters like a beam to be reflected into the rays of different people's opinions. The image created within the space of these rays— inside the diamond—is the hero's journey.

Where We Go

The steps in this journey are the things we learn in order to recognize our full potential, the means for discovering our full nature. They comprise things that can be put into words and practical steps that we can take. I suggest that many of these things we either don't know or don't know well. The path to self-discovery has been hidden from us, and it's hidden for interesting reasons.

The process of learning what to do to manifest our full potential is related to learning how to think. It requires that we explore where our thinking comes from, and how much control we have over what we think. We find that much of our thinking and many of our conclusions are not our own. Ways of thinking are hammered into us through repetition, trauma, need, denial, frustration, enticement, and reward. They are the cultural ideas and attitudes that hold the culture together. They don't serve us individually; they serve the culture.

The universe evolves through the oscillation of action and potential. The increase in potential appears as structures condense and evolve. You take the energy of action, learn from it, arrange with it and create things of greater complexity. We create structures in our minds and harvest energy to hammer them together. Energy is released in the destruction of existing things, as the exploitation of resources is an action of disassembly. You've got to both assemble and disassemble, and this is a guide for surviving the process.

The Paths We Take

Thinking is a complicated process, more complicated than we understand. There is truth to every thought and some context in which every thought makes some sense. Every structure exists for some reason, but we are nowhere near understanding the full truth of things. We learn by examining how things are put together.

We don't want to examine every idea as many are not important, but we don't want to only focus on the important few because we need the background. We want somewhat reliable directions in how to think about things. We're not looking to be enlightened—a concept that's always beyond what we know—but a schematic for right thought and action.

This schematic breaks the learning process into the learning situations of our lives. There are places we learn in, people we learn from, situations we are subjected to, and resources we learn with. There is a chaos of forces and, in this forest of possibilities, there are trail markers and compass bearings.

There are many ways to prepare and many places at which to start. There is what we remember of the thoughts and feelings we started with as children. There is where we were when we began to think for ourselves and the role models we had, if we were lucky enough to have any. And there are the obstacles we encountered and what we learned from them. We can be constantly beginning if we choose to. Every new tool deserves our greatest respect.

This book draws ideas from *The Learning Project* and organizes them into chapters. Other ideas have come to mind in the process, and still others came in on the wind of their own accord by reference or investigation.

Each idea is explored in its own right without any attempt to build it into a larger structure. Things are left in their generality for you to apply or reject. This is a toolbox, not a lesson plan; an armamentarium for all occasions.

Becoming Supergenius has grown like a forest on fire scorched land. The barren land is the current state of learning, teaching, and education. This is not a small matter; this shapes the future of our species.

I have roped off certain areas for reforestation and I've called them chapters, but there is an element of arbitrariness to the lines I've drawn.

All these ideas are related, even if they seem out of place. Ideas sprout from other ideas and ideas far removed complete them. These ideas share the relationships between living things: some are mutualistic and strengthen each other, others are parasitic and destroy each other, and others are saprophytic in their being the outgrowth of failure. Think of learning as building an ecology.

Each chapter is an attitude toward learning, and each learning secret is a world of its own. Some will nourish you, some you might find tasteless, and still others might poison you. They are ingredients. Combine them into your own recipe and don't feel obliged to use them all.

The closer you scrutinize how I've divided the subject into chapters, the more collaborations, competitions, and contradictions you'll find. Because learning happens at all levels and in all directions, I try not to over-explain it.

Where We Arrive

You might expect all these secrets will lead to a learning paradise, but they don't; the hero's journey leads back home. We come back to where we started. We don't learn, protected in hallowed halls at the feet of masters; we learn in the real world, as it is, full of contradictions.

There are a million journeys. Some are glorious and some are terrible, as *The Learning Project* demonstrates. The object is not happiness, it's more than that.

This book does not give you the map for your journey. It only tells you how to rig and trim the sails, and the obligations of a sailor. No matter how glorious or miserable you feel about your journey, it's your journey, and you were made for it.

It's you that changes, in the end, not the landscape. You arrive back in the same family and culture that you left. It's your odyssey, and you are changed by it, but when you change, you change others. When called to make this journey you really have no choice. You have to go, and you can complete it.

The Supergenius

A supergenius is not an expert. Supergeniuses are not welcome in expert society. A supergenius is a loner, outsider, and disrupter, and such a person is rarely recognized for what they know or rewarded for what they do. Some supergeniuses lived to participate in the revolutions they started, such as Confucius, Newton, and Picasso. Others did not, like Vincent van Gogh, Leonardo da Vinci, and Giordano Bruno. And there are thousands, I am sure, who will never be known at all.

That the work of most supergeniuses goes unrecognized until well after his or her death underlies the "100 monkey theory." According to this theory, it takes one hundred of the same discovery before an idea can gain a footing in the collective mind. It is only then that a novel idea can achieve the subliminal resonance, metaphoric importance, and social interest that's required to support a community of experts.

John Taylor Gatto, a supergenius in the field of education, says geniuses are as common as dirt. Supergeniuses appear to be less common because they frequently go unrecognized. Practicing the ideas in this book will help you become a supergenius, if that's what you're inclined to do, but it won't help you become famous or successful. Those accomplishments require a more common mentality.

The Structure of the Books

These learning secrets are drawn from interviews I present in *The Learning Project, Rites of Passage*, as well as the others I encountered along the way. The task of listing all the major aspects of learning, which seems impossible, was made possible by filtering the experiences in *The Learning Project*.

That book presented the insights of 35 people of all ages, and interests, coming from all social, cultural, and political perspectives. Not fully all but close enough. And while none of those interviewed were attempting to explain all their secrets, they all focused on how they learned what was most important. This allowed me to extract the important points, as I understood them. This gave me an outline, which I then filled in.

This book is presented in two volumes whose content comprises a whole that has been split down the middle. The first volume, subtitled *The Outer World*, addresses the learning situation and the environment in which we find ourselves. It addresses the basic definitions of education, learning, teaching, as well as the structures of the institutions that provide these. These are the practical issues.

The titles of the chapters are: Definitions, Attitudes, Actors, Context, Paths, Encounters, and Behaviors. I address the attitudes people have about learning, the actors and agents we encounter in our attempts to learn, where we find these people, and how they behave. Overall, people don't think much about thinking, or what makes them think and act the way they do.

This division into the outer and inner worlds is not hard and fast, it's rather a turning inwards. At first there is the situation in which you find yourself, what you perceive, and how you react. Then, there is the issue of how you think about what you encounter, how you react, and the extent to which you're aware of yourself.

The second volume, subtitled *The Inner World*, leans toward the how, what, and why of our inner thoughts and feelings. The goal is to understand ourselves. The chapters in the second volume are titled: Thoughts, Perception Bias, Presentation Bias, Gender, Journey, Arriving, and Looking Ahead. The focus is reflective: thinking about ourselves, what we're doing, how we're thinking, and why.

A few years ago I gave a public lecture titled "Learn To Think," and invited sixty psychotherapy colleagues. Two people attended: a mother and her 13-year old son. This accurately reflected the greater self-awareness of young people, and the lesser self-awareness of adults. Most adults are frightened by the chaos of deep learning. Most adults won't admit they think poorly.

Learning is relevant for everyone, but it's mostly adolescents who recognize that what they learn is constrained by how they think. Distilling this material down to a single phrase yields, "Think like a child."

> *"The first half of life is learning to be an adult—the second half is learning to be a child."*
> — **Pablo Picasso**, artist

1. Read a book like you would do exploratory surgery.

Many people who have something valuable to say are poor at saying it. Don't let the way someone puts together the ideas you need keep you from finding them. Follow your intuition. Scan pages and let words pop out at you.

Look for what might be of use to you with some idea in your mind of what you're looking for. You see much more than you're aware of and you'll find things will light up if you keep your mind clear of extraneous thoughts. The more clearly you have things in mind, the more likely these things will find you as you page through the book.

Writing a book is a responsibility and having a reader is a privilege. Don't struggle with a book that fails to cooperate. If the section you're reading is dense, frustrating, or unenlightening, skip it. Ask yourself how you might use the material. Many of the ideas you're looking for will be your own. Read lightly and give yourself space to think.

1 – Definitions

Introduction

Language emerged from emotional awareness and we use it to fight an uphill battle to achieve and maintain clarity. Most of what we talk about we refer to, point at, and hold separate from us. For this reason, when it comes to what we hold close, we rarely know what we're talking about.

Moments of clarity are an epiphany that allows us to feel a deep truth... but we still don't know how to talk about it and, the more deeply we experience something, the harder it is to communicate. If you think about how well you can communicate a deep thought you'll appreciate that words don't communicate well.

There is then the question of whether we've been understood, and that is even more uncertain and unpredictable. Here, I'm writing a book, and I have no idea what you're thinking. I have to make myself clear, consistent, and gradually include deeper and more meaningful ideas. I don't have to be right, and I don't have to make sense, but I do have to be transparent so that you can understand me. I will do that.

Thoughts are a like pictures, they have many perspectives, varying levels of detail, and rest on presumptions about what and how another person sees. The chapters in this book rest on definitions that clarify, even if they don't fully describe the contents of the chapters.

If you get a chance, listen to the song of the hummingbird. The song of the ruby-throated hummingbird sounds like it's built of words, but even if we knew the words, I don't believe we could ever fathom their meaning.

Learning

We overlook the big things—like love and humanity. Learning is such a thing, it has many aspects. Learning, in general, is the process through which we grow and change in all respects. This book is about learning as it affects us most deeply.

> *"The more we know and the more skilled we are, the more we can learn."*
> — **Nils Nilsson**, PhD, computer scientist

2.   If your understanding isn't growing with your learning, then you're not learning, you're training.

Learning is about the relationships between things, not facts. If you're learning new facts but they're not creating in you a better understanding, then either you're simply accumulating data, or you're wasting your time. Distinguish how much of each is happening in order to accept what's useful and avoid what's not. If it's just data, store it in a machine; if it's not just data, then reflect on the insights and opportunities it will avail.

No one knows how to teach the important things. These things are too deeply rooted below the level of thought and language: love, trust, and insight, for example. We're supposed to learn by instinct, in the way we learn how to walk, but when it comes to applying our intellect, learning is not innate and not assured.

> *"I learned so much about myself from being there, just from lying in that heap of leaves…"*
> — **Ella Gerazuk**, student, from *The Learning Project*

"To ask for an explanation is to explain the obscure by the more obscure."
— **Maurice Merleau-Ponty**, PhD, philosopher

Motivation underlies learning, and people are motivated by comfort and curiosity. Comfort aims for pleasure and sedation, while curiosity aims for excitement and stimulation. They are not exclusive—the greatest rewards come when we achieve the two together—but we pursue them separately. These two motivations underlie most of our reasons for learning anything.

The poles of sedation and stimulation define our sympathetic and parasympathetic nervous systems. These opposing poles are, in part, mediated by sedating and activating hormones as well as inhibitory and excitatory neurotransmitters. Relaxation and stimulation form the foundation of our behavior. When the structure of our learning is not built to satisfy sedation and stimulation, it works against our nature.

Modern schooling fails in this regard. It is largely sedating and inhibitory. It more discourages than encourages our expansion. Natural play, as well as the exploration of nature and other complex systems, engages both our attractive and defensive drives. Learning lies somewhere in the resonance between expression and restraint.

New thoughts form as old ones fall away. If training is holding all things constant and changing one aspect of behavior, then learning is letting many things readjust and reform into a new whole, a new understanding.

"The best education consists in immunizing people against systematic attempts at education."
— **Paul K. Feyerabend**, PhD, philosopher

Schooling

In addition to extinguishing curiosity, traditional schooling fails in five other measures, as well. First, its emphasis on reading, writing, and arithmetic is antiquated.

Second, shoehorning everyone toward a level of minimal competence that suits no one reflects the 18th-century prerequisites of the early industrial age. These are not necessary skills for an individual or for the future, they reflect a level of skill that was lacking and needed in the past.

Third, school fails massively in fostering creative intellectual skills. This includes the entrepreneurial skills of money, marketing, enterprise, investment, information, and authority management. It also includes the creative skills of science and engineering.

Even today, art class remains focused on visual effusion. Forty years ago, people ridiculed basket weaving classes, which were a first step in recognizing the art in engineering. Only recently, with the expansion of STEM curricula (Science, Technology, Engineering, and Math), has education grown up to see the need for art in everything. Even now, art continues to exist outside of academics, as if there was no place for art in reading, writing, and arithmetic; as if music and math were unrelated.

> *"There were no sex classes. No friendship classes. No classes on how to navigate a bureaucracy, build an organization, raise money, create a database, buy a house, love a child, spot a scam, talk someone out of suicide, or figure out what was important to me. Not knowing how to do these things is what messes people up in life, not whether they know algebra or can analyze literature."*
> — **William Upski Wimsatt**, author and activist

Fourth, school works to disintegrate the organic relationships that exist between individuals within families, communities, and cultures. In a natural environment, learning emerges from one's role in these groups so that learning emerges from, and in the service of, sustainable relationships.

And finally, fifth, traditional schooling is oblivious to the difference between outward attention, in recognition of the environment, from inward attention, which serves the development of the self. The segregation of self-awareness from schooling continues the perennial misidentification of spirit with religion, which reflects people's own misunderstanding of spirit within themselves.

The focus of traditional education has been, and largely remains, the creation of human-based automation: training people to do what machines could not do in the industrial age. These tasks are now done by machines, or soon will be, making these limited, basic skills insufficient and sometimes unnecessary.

> *"I am beginning to suspect all elaborate and special systems of education. They seem to me to be built up on the supposition that every child is a kind of idiot who must be taught to think."*
> — **Anne Sullivan**, teacher and companion of Helen Keller

3.   Self-awareness lies at the root of all learning.

Self-awareness grows as your environment grows and you see yourself playing a larger part in it. Many things that have a great impact on who we are and how we operate are obscure and uncertain: deep emotions, early life memories, questions that we don't know how to ask. Reflect on your own thinking process and appreciate that how you think sets the context for what you see.

Self-awareness is one of the few activities that cannot be automated and remains outside the scope of traditional education. Traditional education is based on the model of an automated classroom. Personal development has a limited social aim, and teachers are trained to model their own limited self-awareness.

Learning is transformative when it focuses on more than acquiring knowledge. What you learn directs who you become, or who you feel you can become. Learning can be a process of bringing into existence something in yourself that does not yet exist. We might call this curiosity, empowerment, inspiration, or maturity.

There are socially acceptable ways to express enthusiasm and appreciation is given to those who most express what other people want. Your personal experience, which is unique to you, will not be as well appreciated. Expressing ever more personal values, which develop along with your self-knowledge, generates increasingly less social rewards. Self-learning is only rewarded as a personal passion.

> *"To keep working towards that, day by day. Allow life to be the fabric of a giant, potential canvas: life as theater, to cast ourselves in new roles, to write new stories for ourselves."*
> — **Phantom Street Artist**, graffiti artist, from *The Learning Project*

Education

All schools that are designed within the context of what we now call schools will fail in the current global environment. It is necessary to distinguish this failed model, which I call school, with the model's aim, which I call education. In the current environment, curiosity and exploration will be critical skills.

> *"It is a miracle that curiosity survives formal education."*
> — **Albert Einstein**, PhD, physicist

Education describes something smaller than learning. The process of educating is one of providing material that is, or will be, useful for growth. Learning is the transformation that this material might foster. One might get an education in ancient Greek literature without learning much. In contrast, I know people who have learned much without any formal education.

4. There is nothing wrong with schools and they can't be fixed.

There is nothing wrong with horses, and they can't be fixed, either. Both current schools and horses are now obsolete as vehicles in the domains where they were introduced. Schools were designed to automate training at a time when many people needed to be trained. People were needed to run and maintain machines, and schools were designed to produce those people. Leaders and creative people—the few that were needed—were cultivated through other means.

Since its inception, modern schooling was, and still is, a feeder mechanism for an unbalanced and unsustainable human-dominated ecology. These hierarchical schools only succeed in the hierarchical model. Institutions outside this school model—such as home, free, democratic schools, wilderness, apprentice, real-life, on-the-job, and leadership training—do not look like schools. While they develop skills to varying degrees, their focus is on growth, individuality, self-sufficiency, social balance, and creativity.

People who create the most opportunities for themselves are forward-thinking people. Forward thinking people recognize that the road they're on may end at any moment, or that circumstances may prevent them from traveling further. These people are not just working to build the road on which they're traveling, they're also building vehicles to take them beyond the end of the road.

Being forward-thinking is a mind-set. It's not usually something that you are at one point and then retire from being. Similarly, if you want to be forward-thinking but you have not been, then don't expect circumstances will arrange themselves to enable you to become forward-thinking in the future. It may seem like "the chicken and the egg" paradox, but in this case, the egg comes first: create forward thoughts first, only then can you create an environment to support them.

> *"I've concluded that genius is as common as dirt. We suppress our genius only because we haven't yet figured out how to manage a population of educated men and women. The solution, I think, is simple and glorious. Let them manage themselves."*
> — **John Taylor Gatto**, teacher

The expression, "The best time to plant a tree is twenty years ago; the second-best time is now," is an expression that applies to lost opportunities. The forward-thinking person is not worried about the best time to plant a tree because they already planted one twenty years ago. Now, that person is trying to figure out what new tree to plant, and where to plant it. The expression is really about the future, not the past. It is saying that you want to be taking steps now to put you where you want to be in twenty years. Only you can properly execute this responsibility.

> *"Eleven different schools... and there's not one that I've enjoyed. Their memory chafes like a slipping rope against the flesh of childhood... Why should I continue studying to pass examinations to get into a life I don't want to lead—a life of factories, and drawing boards, and desks? In the first half of my sophomore year I left college to learn to fly..."*
> — **Charles A. Lindbergh**, aviator, from *The Spirit of St. Louis* (Lindbergh, 2003)

Hierarchical systems are not cyclic, they are consumptive. They have consumption at their foundation. They consume basic resources and build towering organizations. A hierarchy is only sustainable if it's periodically torn down and rebuilt anew.

Eventually, at the top where there should be growth, there is only debris. Progress, such as it is, is based on needs the system has itself generated; there is no vision, and the system consumes itself. All the energy of the system, and all of the products of the hierarchy, have been used up, worn out, or dissipated. The goal of our modern world economy is comfortable survival. The end product of the modern world economy is heat and garbage, much of it toxic.

Just as the modern world economy exists by exploiting the natural environment, modern schooling exploits humans by creating human machines whose purpose is limited to the work they've been trained to do. They have no planned purpose beyond this goal. In the industrial model, people, as machines, are discarded, recycled, or retooled when obsolete. The purpose of people is a means of production.

There are sustainable alternatives. These are systems in which balance and continuity are higher goals than profit, such as community organization, network learning, and personal growth.

In community organizations, different specialists from the community work together to gather resources for future needs. The range of opportunities depends on the community's openness to change and the resources available to it. Community organization involves community planning and moves toward that plan. Some examples of organizations that can be communal are the legal system, law enforcement, insurance, and healthcare.

Network learning grows within a bounded network of resources, producers, and consumers. A network becomes sustainable when it includes recyclers to decompose outputs and supply new resources. Network learning exploits collaboration but depends on opportunities from outside the network. In it, human resources push outward toward new skills, territories, and relationships. Hunters, gatherers, explorers, and scientists follow the network learning model.

Personal growth is, ultimately, the system to which we all subscribe. If personal growth is your aim, then purpose and meaning are your guides. Since these are not ends that one can achieve and your search for them is not a parasitic use of resources, the path of personal growth does not end and the resources available are never exhausted.

It is unclear whether a community based on personal growth can succeed. Most utopian organizations make personal growth a top priority, but none have lasted more than a few generations. Most religious communities consider personal growth a top priority and have the most success when they leave the means and goals up to each individual.

5.   Learn through networks.

Today's ever more global environment is a feedback network in which each actor must understand both the patterns of things and the patterns of thoughts. It's not enough to have skills to solve known problems, you now need to know how to develop skills for unknown problems. Network, community, or personal learning models are more appropriate, sustainable, and adaptive than the existing hierarchical school models.

The school model measures success in focused areas. In a network model, success depends on creating a map of new territory through a process of flexible exploration. It's the difference between having a single direction versus mastering the art of diffusion. It's the difference between solving a problem according to a formula versus inventing a formula to solve a problem: winning the game versus designing the game.

"Mononucleosis was the biggest blessing, because otherwise I was... dying in that school. Getting sick and having people spend a little time with me, and recognize that maybe I did want to learn something, that I did have an inner life, because I certainly didn't have one at school."
— **George Plotkin**, MD, PhD, engineer, neuroscientist, inventor, from *The Learning Project*

Transformation

This book is for readers who are learning or helping others learn: students, adepts, apprentices, adventurers, therapists, mentors, educators and—may God help them because the institutions that employ them won't—teachers.

Learning is transformation, which means this book's focus is not on how to gain knowledge better, it's about how to gain better knowledge. It's not the quantity of what you learn that generates a positive effect on you and your environment, it's the quality.

6. You can't judge whether something is important to learn until after you understand it.

You can't judge the value of what you've learned while you are undergoing change because your standards are changing. You can't assess the value of what you've learned until its effect is clear. You can only assess its value once you've gained insight from it. Tests that don't measure how your understanding has changed are not tests of learning.

You cannot judge what will do well for you when you are in the process of transformation because your ability to make judgments are changing too. Your view of your problem generally does not include its solution as finding solutions requires the insight you don't have. You must develop a nose for finding insight and the ability to discriminate between things you don't yet fully understand.

You can judge what feels important or right but you'll often have to store things away in order to later extract understanding from them. Successful transformation rests on the accumulation of resources you won't yet know exactly what to do with. Nevertheless, it is essentially

21

important that you develop a skill in distinguishing what will be helpful to you, from what is toxic. This requires lateral thinking, which is thinking outside the box, and systems thinking, which is understanding what's holding things up.

Most teachers who follow traditional curricula justify the material they teach based on things they feel you are not qualified to judge. If you believe this, then you can't pass judgment on their qualifications, the materials, or their methods. In such a situation you can't develop the skills of discernment. If you're suspicious of the qualifications, value, or appropriateness of what you're being taught, then the safest approach is either to insist on enough information to make a judgment, or excuse yourself from further participation in an equivocal process.

> *"When he's in town, [Colonel Lindbergh] will come to the service entrance and I'll let him in, and he'll sit there and look at* The Spirit *for 10 or 15 minutes, until it gets time to open, and then he'll get up and leave. And every time he gets up to walk with me to the door he'll look up at it and say, 'I still can't believe I made it.'"*
> — **Clarance W. See**, test pilot and aircraft mechanic, from *The Learning Project*

7. Measure how well you learn not by what you can remember, but by what you can imagine.

Imagination takes memory and projects it into the future. Memory is useful because we can imagine how to apply it to new situations. Raw, factual memory—to the extent that it exists at all—is a catalog of things that have little effect on you. The process of moving yourself forward, which is always accompanied by some change, relies on imagination.

We often fail to distinguish the routine from the innovative. We fail in this when we don't understand the problem and cannot judge what's necessary to solve it. Sometimes, we think it's just a question of being told the secret. Other times, we might recognize that the secret was unknown and someone had to discover it. And in yet other times, there was no secret at all because it was the wrong problem. These are three different types of obstacles that require different kinds of thinking and radically different kinds of learning.

Some people learn things just because they enjoy doing them repeatedly. I understand learning to dance is rewarding because it engages you with your body, or with new partners, or with partners in new ways. Certain skills reveal deeper puzzles and greater rewards through repetition. Such are the skills of throwing clay or working with wood because these materials have detailed and subtle properties. Practice results in improvement only when done with that aim. What an outsider sees as repetition is not repetitive to the adept, for whom new insights are unfolding.

My college physics teacher was fascinated by a famous calculation whose steps he would write it down in full, repeatedly, like a scribe recopying the same text. The calculation was Richard Feynman's second order, quantum field theoretic calculation of the gyromagnetic moment of the electron, and it is a calculation that stood for many years as the most accurate prediction of any quantity ever measured. The calculation requires twenty pages of algebra and days to condense the details to a single number.

My teacher memorized the calculation to the point that he could reproduce it in its totality in a couple of hours. He taught me how to do this calculation, and it took me months to fully understand what each term in these formulas represented and to understand the whole formula as a physical process. I was stunned when, in my application to a particular graduate school, a professor at that school—his name was Max Dresden—refused to believe I could have reproduced the calculation. It was just a long series of steps and, to this day, I cannot fathom what was so unbelievable about my having repeated it.

I have always wondered why my teacher repeated this calculation over and over, repeating it almost like a psalm. Unlike a musical performance, a mathematical expression cannot be performed with ever greater subtlety, grace, and nuance. I was never sure what he gained from this practice. The best I can surmise is that, like an endlessly spinning Sufi dancer, this brought him a kind of mental transcendence.

"You see, you're asking me how I go about things. I go about things in a way that has nothing to do with what universities teach. It's very different from what universities tell you to do, what teachers tell you to do. You make it up as you go along, and God knows how it comes out; you don't know... Play around. You play around."
— **Jerome Lettvin**, MD, PhD, psychiatrist, engineer, and neuroscientist, from *The Learning Project*

Development

Our emerging understanding of human behavior and development— codified in the early 20th-century following William James, Freud, and others—occurred after public schooling was conceived in Prussia in the 18th and 19th centuries and then instituted in the West. Our understanding of human development is still evolving and is only vaguely appreciated. It has given rise to the holistic models of learning developed by the educators Ferrer, Waldorf, Montessori; schools named

Summerhill, Sudbury, and 8-Shields; and outdoor, leadership, and other humanistic programs.

Modern education recovers old understandings and attempts to inject it into our dislocated, modern culture. The effect of these models on mainstream education has yet to be felt. It still feels like real cultural change must wait for future generations.

> *"Rather than improve 'school,' maybe we should think of what students need to know to grow healthy communities, and work backwards from there. To do that, we have to be willing to leave 'school,' as we know it, behind."*
> — **Terry Heick**, Founder & Director of *TeachThought*, (Heick, 2020)

The secrets of learning have little to do with schooling, except with regard to making the best of limited resources. Deep learning is self-motivated. Any other form of learning is conditioning at best or damaging at worst.

This book digests my experiences and those I've learned from, to consider a balance between stimulation and reward, competence in modern skills, creativity, integrated relationships, and the development of the self.

Schooling has played an insignificant role for me, though this is partly a preference of style. I prefer to make my own mistakes in order to gain a deeper understanding, rather than gain through the filtered experience of others for a more superficial understanding.

It's about developing a subtle perception of what's good for you for your whole life. To accomplish this, you'll need to discriminate between positively and negatively directed resources: those designed to benefit you are gifts; those designed to exploit you are land mines. You'll also need to develop an appreciation of yourself and the scope of your life.

8.   The only learning you need is that which changes your life.

Only the things that will change your life, or the lives of others, are worth taking up space in your mind or imprinting on your character. Things that change your life make you feel different. If you don't feel different as the result of learning something, then it probably wasn't worth the effort.

Change is adaptation and evolution. The skills needed are both the mechanism to manage change and the foresight to choose the right path. This kind of learning happens at several levels. A component of skill exists in your perception, discernment, balance, and dexterity. In addition, there is a skill at communication, presentation, or engagement. Finally, there should be an element of uncertainty, unfamiliarity, or unlimited possibility. To put it another way, change results from the combination of ability and intent. Either can be lacking, but both can be learned.

Change is a moving target you want to follow. When the target stops moving, the system settles to a consuming hierarchy. That is, at that point you stop striving and settle into a mode of consuming or assimilating. Your role changes from being the captain of your ship to a crew on someone else's. Your rewards then change from being personal and transformative, to being monetary, material, and hedonic.

When change ceases and the situation becomes static, the path of learning changes too. In many cases, this was the goal: to gain comfort, security, and stability and to ensure against future risk and change. This plateau could be a secure post in an organization, a retirement and pension, or a comfortable routine. Learning is seriously curtailed once these plateaus are reached, as is tolerance for change.

Many people who plateau find themselves reconsidering the value of what they've achieved. They have navigated a maze and now they have reached the end. If the steps have been conscious and careful and you're not satisfied with what you've achieved, then you might retrace your steps and even carry your gains in another direction. But if your investment has been an exclusive commitment that has narrowed your community and identity, then there will be little opportunity to retrace your steps, redefine yourself, and create a different outcome.

The lure in finishing one's study, accepting a profession, and retiring is that you'll have greater freedom later. This is true to a limited degree, if it's true at all. Once you've reached a point of planned obsolescence there may only be limited opportunities, resources, and companions available to you; not to mention the continuing responsibilities you may have collected along the way, such as protecting your family, health, and assets.

> *"You have to figure it out for yourself. A lot of unhappiness comes from people using someone else's ladder. You need to design your own ladder and climb that one. Otherwise you get to the top of someone else's mountain and you don't really want to be there."*
> — **Esther Dyson**, journalist and entrepreneur, from *The Learning Project*

Equally important is not to expect that ladders of opportunity will always be available to you. Depending on your resources and circumstances, there will come a point where new opportunities are no longer available.

At that point, the opportunities you have are only those that you've built for yourself.

> *"What you're supposed to do is work hard at what you don't really like very much, and then later you get time to play. I never lived my life that way, and I could never imagine doing it. Let me do what I enjoy. Let me do what makes sense for me. Let me do what I feel fulfilled in. That's always been the way I've been."*
> — **Michelle Murrain**, PhD, neuroscientist, consultant, writer, activist, from *The Learning Project*

2 – Attitudes

The Landscape

The arena of learning is everywhere; there is no one right learning path to any particular competence. Even if you have a particular goal, the notion of "the one path" is still ridiculous. Nevertheless, that's the idea implicit in most learning programs, and it's what most people are searching for.

You may object that one right thing does not preclude other right things, and that things are not black and white. This is true, but most of us do think in terms of black and white.

We dichotomize everything. This seems to be wired into us. We're always amplifying the contrast in what we see. This helps us wade through vast numbers of possibilities. We'll admit the world is not black and white but we're constantly creating black and white in what we see. Everywhere you look—in family, community, religion, politics, and the workplaces—the rules of behavior are narrow, the criteria for inclusion are arbitrary, and deviations from the norm are discouraged.

Your learning landscape is the realm of experiences you're allowed. Learning in a tightly structured society, such as Singapore or Japan, will be wholly different from learning to fend for oneself in the bush. In society we follow rules; outside of society we follow opportunity. The difference encompasses what you learn, how you learn, and what you understand learning to be.

9.   See connections everywhere.

Events cascade to create relationships that extend far outward to other situations and events that can be distanced in space and separated in time. These relationships get thin over large distances and long times, but they extend much farther than you would expect.

The interactions that develop between events are going on at once, at every point. No matter where you are or when things have happened, you are involved in creating a legacy for a host of converging and diverging events. You will be unaware of these connections running like unseen rivers beneath the forest canopy of your awareness. Even though you're unaware, you're playing a supporting role in maintaining the channels through which other things occur.

Only a tiny fraction of what's going on demands our attention and fills our plates. You can change your environment—take a vacation, change your job, build a family—and you'll still find yourself working on the same fundamental issues.

You can analyze your experiences microscopically or macroscopically, taking everything literally or being open to every memory and association. All of these possibilities contribute to the "whole you." In this, the world is better described as a hologram rather than a landscape. A hologram, as you may recall, contains all the details of many perspectives so that when this information is extracted the hologram can recreate a three-dimensional image. However, in the case of the world around us, the image is more than visual and is larger than can be expressed in three dimensions.

10. Recognize that everything is learning.

There are structures to things and organizations in things that you are not aware of. Every person is more complex than you, or they, can imagine. You might ask yourself, "What is there here that I can learn?" A better question might be, "What do I want to learn more about, and how much can I take in?"

The accurate definition of information is the inverse of what's probable—the more probable something is the more certain it is, and the more certain it is the less information it can contain.

In the same way, the more you learn, the more possibilities there are, and the greater the uncertainty of things. If what you learn is making things more certain, then what you're learning amounts to less information, not more. The more certain things are, the more shallowly you understand them.

We generally have it backwards when we think understanding means certainty. It is the opposite: greater understanding comes with more information, wider connections, and varied possibilities.

All trails of discovery lead us finally to what we take for granted. But if you question what you take for granted, a whole universe of possibilities opens up to you. This is probably why few people want to question what they take for granted, and why those of us addicted to amazement are endlessly attracted to new learning.

Essential to your learning landscape is who you are; take this as your starting point. There are resources available to you, and paths of varying difficulty to objectives of various value. There are actors you'll meet along the path. We can stereotype them as enablers or disablers, heroes or villains, allies or enemies, guides or misleaders, truth-tellers or dissemblers. It's a role-playing game.

This picture may seem like a fantasy because it's imaginary, but the "real world" is largely imaginary, too. You can move to different worlds of opportunity, and you can change any world you find yourself in. Each person has some authority for their identity, and each situation is stable or changeable to varying degrees.

> *"Scientific views end in awe and mystery, lost at the edge in uncertainty..."*
> — **Richard P. Feynman**, PhD, physicist

11. What is real for other people is only real to them and those around them.

People create their reality, stabilize it, and build themselves into it. People build a membrane around themselves and project on its inner surface a vision of the world they see around them. Look for those people with the largest and most flexible vision of the world. Avoid visions that are narrow and rigid. Avoid narrow paths and circumscribed opportunities. I would say this is true even if you think their vision fits you. If you're learning, then you're growing, and your vision of the world will change.

What "real world" there is out there is the world we have imagined into existence. We are told our options are real, well-defined things, and their navigation is best done by people who are fully informed. Both of these things are untrue. Exploration is a process of discovery, skill is a process of refinement. In some cases, you can skillfully discover—and it's worth trying—but whatever the result, it's determination that gets you there.

In this world you're cast first as a child, then an adult, and finally an elder. You're offered roles of student, teacher, leader, follower, visionary, fool, success, failure, as well as many others. The reality of these roles is told to you by someone who has invested themselves in them, but the reality of these roles is by consent. If freedom is what you value, don't accept any role at all.

> *"I'm just an individual who doesn't feel that I need to have somebody qualify my work in any particular way. I'm working for me."*
> — **David Bowie**, musician

There is a physical landscape, built of atoms and elements, forests and oceans. There is an imaginal landscape that includes our bodies, our knowledge, or our effect on our environment. These are things that are seen through the filter of our knowledge.

There are physical aspects to our imaginal world, but we have tunnel vision and largely rely on what other people tell us. We also have a hand in creating our vision of ourselves and our social image. This, too, depends largely on what other people tell us. Our identity is governed more by magic than by physics. We're easily fooled, but we're always in denial of it. Because we overestimate our understanding, magicians always amaze us.

12. Be a victim.

We often hear of the weaknesses of being a victim, but rarely of the strengths. This is short-sighted. Being a victim is exactly what you should expect to be when you venture into new territory, and especially if you attempt to repair an aspect of yourself. Whether you're a victim of novelty, need, or your ignorance, these sorts of victim roles are essential for knowledge and exploration.

Those who tell us to avoid becoming a victim are telling us to stay in our place, retain our limited power, and follow orders: to remain satisfied with the powers we've earned or been accorded. Instead, allow yourself to be victimized as much as you can afford. Resolve old conflicts, explore new territory, and open to new dreams.

If you want to fully understand another person, then give them all the power and the permission to use it. They will be surprised. You will be amazed at how poorly most people behave when they have complete authority. The only way to really see how people think and feel is to allow them to reveal all parts of themselves. Make sure you can regain control when the experiment is over.

It's not victimhood that's a problem, it's being imprisoned, failing to recognize your mistake, and failing to correct it. Given that any attempt at gaining new power will result in a certain measure of failure, your strategy should be to discover what is to be learned from these failures as quickly as possible, and reapply yourself with greater insight.

In knowledge, you are a blind person tapping your cane to move forward. Every object you strike is a failure, but you would not expect otherwise, and this should not cause you to lose faith or self-esteem. The alternative is to have unreasonable expectations or to do nothing at all. No matter what you think, you are always a victim of your circumstances.

We feel victimized in personal relationships when these relationships are rooted in our needs. Both you and your partner, colleague, or associate are there because you need something, not first because you have something to give. At least that's what prevails among less experienced people. When relationships don't work as expected, it's natural that you'll feel you got less than you bargained for, and probably gave away more than your share.

You may object that this is unfair. So what? It's a necessary dynamic if you're to grow to understand the extent of other people's neediness, and the lengths they'll go in order to meet those needs. And this is almost certainly a lesson you'll need to learn before you're able to see your own neediness and the rationalizations that you're willing to put forward in your defense.

It's a mark of maturity to admit your needs and limitations. It's a mark of maturity when you accept honesty, clarity, and disclosure as the best strategies for establishing trust, rapport, and a co-creative bond. You don't mature suddenly; you work your way there over time. We never quite get there because there is always more to admit, reveal, and understand.

It is not until you've reached this level, the level that follows being a victim and seeing how you're willing to victimize others, that you can approach the real meaning of love. The best counselors and therapists will tell you this. For more details read Kathlyn and Gay Hendricks, or the team of Harville Hendrix and Helen Hunt.

13. It's better to be fooled and know you're fooled.

It's often better to accept a different point of view, be fooled by it and see how you're fooled by it, than it is to defend your point of view, refuse to see a different perspective, and never learn more about it. In this, you'll often find yourself the victim and to have been taken advantage of. Limit your risk but expand your exposure. Accept being the victim of your ignorance: your ignorance is exactly where you want to go. Do not be attached to judgments made within other people's points of view.

Consider a game you play in which your victory is assured. You would quickly bore of it. Consider a game you sometimes win because you do some things wrong and some things right. You endure frustration to learn which strategy wins and do more of it.

Consider a game in which you always lose. Here, becoming a winner requires a complete transformation. That might be something of great value, or of no value, but this position has the most potential.

"I started wrestling my freshman year, and ... I lost every single one of my matches I came upon, and it was a little difficult... What Paul made me realize is that the person who wants it the most is the one that's going to win. The person that's not afraid to go out there and do it."
— **Mike Short**, student, from *The Learning Project*

When learning is the game, the loser who's done their best stands more to gain:

- They accept what they're capable of.

- They experience what does not work.

- They may observe what works.

- After balancing the costs against the rewards they can reapply themselves.

"I have failed more often and in a greater variety of attempts than anyone I know. I also have had some spectacular successes that I would not have experienced if I

had not been willing to risk failing. I'll take that a step further and admit that I've learned far more from my mistakes and failures than from any of my accomplishments."
— **Curtis M. Faith**, commodities trader (Faith, 2007, p. 239).

Culture is built of and by people. It's constantly changing and varies from place to place: different groups have different expectations of each other and views of themselves. Differences between people within a small group can be huge—such as in a family—both in their abilities and their expectations.

Over large distances in age, location, and background—such as between cultures—these different understandings can be unbridgeable. In spite of this, current education would funnel all kids into the same learning process, present them with one truth, and expect them to perform in the same way.

14. Discover what you need to learn.

What do you need to know? Take the holographic perspective: it lies in the whole of you, your family, culture, and environment.

What you need to know is not what offers the single, largest reward, it's knowledge in the area that will accumulate the greatest effect on your life. What is of greatest value must be judged over time, the different choices you make, and the opportunities you encounter. You might call this "the development of your true aptitude." This is not the same as what others see in you. You find it in yourself, and it will almost certainly take a good deal of exploration.

15. Be aware of the attractions of pleasure.

Learning through struggle and loss is a proud and time-honored approach to problem-solving. One can make undeserved suffering redemptive even when incited. If you're determined to prevail, then losses can be seen as learning opportunities and honored as such.

While it may seem clear that the needs for food, sex, love, safety, and the like must be satisfied and satisfied repeatedly, this is not as clear as it would seem. In many cases of chronic need, what one seeks is not sufficiency but the ability to be satisfied, and, if you cannot be satisfied, then all attempts are temporary. It is quite common for these needs to be abused so that they become coping strategies or addictions and, in doing so, they become traps of permanent victimhood and dependence.

The exceptions are games of survival. These are not games of learning, they are unmet needs and you must view them differently. In the game of unmet needs, victory is necessary. If the needs are food, sex, love, or safety then the stakes of the game can be as high as life or death.

It is in the nature of a healthy coping strategy that it eventually wears out, and, when it does, you once again return to the underlying problem. A healthy coping strategy takes some of the pressure off and gives you more time. Failing to recognize this is a double abuse, the first being problem avoidance, and the second being deluded by the disguise of temporary satisfaction. This is the birthplace of addiction.

I experienced the addictive quality of mountaineering. Aside from the fixation of the summit and the intoxication of success, there is a release from the feeling of smallness that pervades normal life. It was this release, that I could not gain in any other way, that worried me as an increasing number of climbing partners died in the mountains. If there is something missing in what you're doing, then doing more of it isn't going to get you what you need. Instead, it may lead you to disaster.

In my case, mountaineering offered myriad benefits for the risks to which I was exposed. I look back on it as a learning addiction. Other addictions are not so beneficial. Being addicted to work or fame can be exhausting. Chemical addictions are not beneficial at all.

> *"Why do people climb? There's got to be a reason... I can't figure it out. It's a lot easier to play tennis or golf, bicycle; a lot less stress, not dangerous, doesn't have the risk, doesn't have the suffering. Climbing's got a lot of suffering, a lot of it..."*
> — **Fred Beckey**, mountaineer and author, from *The Learning Project*

Ultimately, you must follow what your heart tells you, not what your mind tells you. And as long as your mind tells you to continue your coping strategy, you probably will, and you're probably not ready to move toward a healthy solution. But the sooner you can get back on your feet and gather your resources to find a stable, enduring, and self-respecting way of providing for your needs, the sooner you'll appreciate yourself.

For most people this never happens; they struggle under their self-delusions for their entire life. You do have some choice in the matter. You can choose to face the music now rather than never. It's a decision you must take under consideration with your higher self. No one else will even understand the question.

16. Don't believe what you're told.

Just as your body organizes your cells, every culture organizes its people. A large part of what you learn from other people is your role in the culture. This is invariably offered as the truth and mistaken for it, but you can feel its relative nature by virtue of its emotional content—the emotions it stirs in you and in those you're dealing with. This does not make it bad or unnecessary, just relative. Continue to make your own choices.

"Universities are stuck in this mind frame where they give classes according to their departments and their majors, give classes in everything besides what's going to be in life ... they're not going to give you exactly what you need to know: 'This is the key to life. This is what you're going to learn in life!' No. It's not that."
— **MaryAnn MaNais**, student, from *The Learning Project*

It is healthy to question yourself, to question whether you understand your culture and whether your culture attempts to understand itself. Individual self-knowledge and collective self-knowledge grow and change over time. You see them changing everywhere you look. Notice the different scale and speed at which individuals and cultures reflect on themselves. Notice how the two are built out of components of each other.

In general, this is a good thing. Individuals consider for themselves ideas that they pick up from others in their culture, and culture changes to reflect the range and force of the ideas held by the individuals within it. At the same time, any individual or culture-wide idea that depends on other ideas remaining unchanged rests on shaky ground. The landscape of ideas undergoes constant upheaval and any plan that depends on the landscape remaining static is built on a swamp.

"It's very strange how much shit there is. Between the direct view of what's going on and what you might call the academic view. This applies all across the board, it's not only in biology and science and psychiatry, it holds practically everywhere."
— **Jerome Lettvin**, MD, PhD, psychiatrist, engineer, and neuroscientist, from *The Learning Project*

"I have a dream that one day this nation will rise up and live out the true meaning of its creed: 'We hold these truths to be self-evident, that all men are created equal.' "
— **Martin Luther King, Jr.**, minister and civil rights activist

Conflicts in moral, personal, and social attitudes, as well as their constant shift over time, suggests that a sea of ideas would be a better metaphor than the landscape when it comes to our ideas. The unchanging legacy of a pyramid was attractive to a pharaoh—in a culture that changed little—but in our constantly changing world of opportunities, it would be better to build an ark.

The Future

Learning underlies consciousness and evolution. Recognize that acquiring established facts generates reflex actions, not thoughts, and reflexive actions do not change things.

Evolution takes place because new opportunities arise, and the choices we make lead to new ways of interacting with the world. Evolution requires only that choices be made. It's not good or bad, it's adaptive. The multiply-connected nature of events—their holographic nature—acts as a kind of computing machine that selects, over the course of many trials, the ideas that best support the most influential actors. This same multiple connection distributes forces of change through all the connected systems.

Our ability to guide an evolution that's positive for us is possible because we can learn. Through the process of learning, we improve the consequences of our choices even when we have never confronted these choices before. This applies to individuals, collections of people, cultures, and species. The understanding of life and consciousness lies in the understanding of learning at its instantaneous, immediate, and personal level.

17. Everything is art.

Thought is a high-level process; it doesn't just happen, you have to make it happen. It's always a work of art. The question is, then, is your thought good art?

The answer is simple: it's good when it adds something to what existed before, regardless of whether this addition results in more or less structure and stability. "Good" means expansive, enlarged, and illuminating. "Bad" means less active, less creative, and more obscuring. Degraded and repetitive thoughts are "not good art," although they could be steps on the path toward it. The difficulty comes in judging intermediate thoughts, or in making judgments outside the context of the whole.

You cannot judge intermediate thoughts with any certainty and this is where one needs skill in discernment. Intermediate thoughts take you between what exists and something new, but the new cannot be judged based on the old, and a new basis for judgment does not yet exist.

So how to judge? I can only guess that honesty is key, a kind of transcendent honesty. Honesty regarding things you don't yet know and may never know. There has to be some sort of guidance. Maybe it's guidance from the early stages of what is starting to form, or maybe what's starting to form has a connection to a higher structure that already exists, something like Rupert Sheldrake's "morphic field."

In the first case, you might ascribe your sense of direction to intuition, the unconscious assembly of things you already know. In the second case, you might ascribe it to inspiration, the introduction of new insight from sources outside your control. In either case, it's nice to feel some sense of rectitude or encouragement, but sometimes there seems to be none and maybe that is honest too.

Underneath the force of creation is patience and a willingness to let go. Endurance is required and the ability to move past the discomfort of change. This is no small matter: the discomfort can range from disquiet to suicidal. It can make you unsure or it can tear you apart. Whether you feel it's true or not, it's healthy to believe that you are responsible for the processes that affect you and that you could exert control.

> *"Anything that takes time to create. Anything that takes time to build. Anything that takes time to do anything would be art... The artist is the art when it's creating art. It's the art and it's creating art... Thinking with your brain is art."*
> —**Kiran Fox Stoller**, five years old, from George Quasha's *Art Is* video series.

> *"Where creative effort is involved, there are no trivial circumstances."*
> — **Frank Lloyd Wright**, architect

18. Work to find your roots.

The deeper your roots, the more change you'll navigate with less damage to yourself and others. Be honest. As you enter the realm of new ideas you know nothing. Honesty is all you've got.

Your roots are what constitute your identity. This consists mostly of your attitudes, aptitudes, inclinations, and reactions. Recognize how much of this you're unaware of or exercise minimal control over. Work to become aware of more of it.

These attitudes, aptitudes, inclinations, and reactions do have a life of their own, but if you can separate yourself from them to some degree, then you can exercise a degree of control, and you can be a conduit of guidance. In many cases you won't know what to say or do that will guide your emotions and inclinations, but if you create a separate space in your mind for reflection, then you can become a channel for insight and inspiration.

> *"There is always an enormous temptation in all of life to diddle around making itsy-bitsy friends and meals and journeys for itsy-bitsy years on end. It is so self-conscious, so apparently moral, simply to step aside from the gaps where the creeks and winds pour down, saying, I never merited this grace, quite rightly, and then to sulk along the rest of your days on the edge of rage.*
>
> *"I won't have it. The world is wilder than that in all directions, more dangerous and bitter, more extravagant and bright. We are making hay when we should be making whoopee; we are raising tomatoes when we should be raising Cain, or Lazarus."*
> — **Annie Dillard**, from *Pilgrim at Tinker Creek*

19. Unclutter your mind.

A clear mind is supposed to be the goal; make it your starting point. Forget time as something that is measured and linear; focus on time as something open-ended: time as ritual. Just watch the clutter that washes over you like debris over a rain-washed roof. Review your clutter with detachment; begin with an uncluttered mind.

Being uncluttered does not mean being empty or without objects or objectives. You can be constantly seeking, narrowly focused, engaged, and still be uncluttered. One learns to rise above the clutter, to find silence amid the noise, to sense emptiness even when you're surrounded by things. It is a useful exercise to walk through a city and see only the auras around the people. An auras is easy to see if you ignore everything except what is emanating from a person. By "aura" I mean as a person's presence, not necessarily a physical light.

> *"If a cluttered desk is a sign of a cluttered mind, of what, then, is an empty desk a sign?"*
> — **Albert Einstein**, PhD, physicist

We're usually taught that experience equals knowledge, and having ability means knowing a lot of things. But understanding things does not mean you know a lot of facts. Understanding means you know why things develop and how they change.

For example, the most important thing in business is understanding people and this is not a matter of facts but rather a sensitivity to emotion. Emotional intelligence is more important than intellectual intelligence in almost all things pertaining to personal growth.

Two people whom I considered wise were Arlington Richardson and Legio. Arlington was a fisherman and whaler in the Caribbean, and Legio was an elder of a tribe in the Darien Jungle of Panama. Neither went to school and neither learned to read or write. In their respective cultures, this was not a problem. What they knew was written in the landscape, which they knew how to read better than others.

I was 16 when I lived next to Alda and Arlington Richardson in the Caribbean. I didn't understand what Arlington knew, and I didn't ask the right questions. I was simply affected by his humble presence and his reputation as a person who could foretell the future.

I was 29 when I spent a month living next to Legio on a thatch-roofed platform in the jungle. Legio wore a red loincloth, went barefoot, and wielded a sharp axe. He let me watch him build a dugout canoe out of a cashew tree. It took a couple of weeks and I just watched. I think he felt I added a positive energy. I got paid for writing an about it, and I sent him half the money (Stoller, 1987).

20. Change direction rather than giving up.

The obvious reason not to give up is that you don't need to. Don't abandon the experience you've gained. There may be good reasons to reconsider your goal or your direction, but reconsidering is not giving up. Even if you recognize that where you want to go is very different from the direction you've been going, take all that you can from the experiences you've had. If you do cease in your efforts, do it understanding all you've learned, and that you have learned all you need from this endeavor.

Whatever you do, you develop a certain momentum in doing it. Momentum is a form of energy, just like learning or knowledge.

> Momentum will move you forward even if you've run out of things to do.

Being a forward thinker is having knowledge without anywhere to apply it. You have a map to a territory you have not yet reached. You have resources but no one to trade with. Successful people are recognized after they have succeeded, but their success developed well before they were recognized, in times when they don't appear to be successful at all.

Yvon Chouinard learned to be a mountain-climbing dirt-bag from our climbing partner Fred Beckey, sleeping in the rain for lack of shelter and going days with scant food. He worked for himself as a blacksmith beating steel into pitons because no one else was making them, and later marketed outdoor clothing through a company he named after the world's most intimidating mountains: Patagonia. Chouinard is now chagrined to find himself a billionaire. It wasn't money that motivated him.

Steven King, one of the world's most successful horror and sci-fi writers, developed his craft without support, success, or independent resources. He didn't conduct himself well early in his career, and he was not skilled at using his resources, but he hung on. His skill lay in his craft, his continuous output, and his bet that he would eventually succeed (King, 2000).

After spending more than a decade in physics, I went into business because I wanted to learn about business people, issues, and opportunities. I applied what I learned in physics to my projects in business with some success. I accomplished some things that others had not, and failed—for reasons I now better understand—where others succeeded, such as making a profit!

After writing software for two decades, I became a therapist. By this point, I'd accumulated knowledge that specialists don't have. I continue to work alone, exploring breakthroughs that come from combining fields.

I marvel at results few others encounter or are interested to learn. Building a language that combines specialties, results in no single specialist being able to understand the problems I work on. I am combining psychology and mathematics, hypnosis and brain science, ecology and culture. I make it up as I go along.

I see opportunities to take what I've learned in science back into business. I have tools that I've either learned from other fields or developed myself that take me into unexplored territories, such as offering counseling to physicists, spirituality to business people, and physics to therapy clients.

New ideas about old problems meet with confusion and resistance. This presents fascinating questions about what kinds of progress are possible. It is ironic that the more inclusive my understanding, the more I am excluded from the worldview of specialists. And, almost by definition, if you fall outside a specialist's worldview, then your ideas are uninteresting to them.

> *"How did I become passionate? How did I become an activist? It was one step at a time. I grew up a very shy person. I wasn't a leader. If I can be a leader, then anybody can be a leader. Some leaders are born, and I was not a born social person. I had to learn it all."*
> — **Phyllis Schlafly**, JD, politician and social activist, from *The Learning Project*

With the advent of information processing and enhanced access to information, we—as individuals, cultures, and economies—have reconsidered the role of thinking. What used to be the rarified domain of philosophy, theology, and metaphysics is increasingly discussed on the street: consciousness, ecology, and globalism.

If you take a broad view—judging by how vaguely people think about these things—we have not come very far. People go about their daily lives indifferent to these issues, without paying much attention to the difference between their internal and their external state of affairs.

I was afforded this startling insight as a result of living in an economically undeveloped Émbera culture in the Panamanian jungle. The people I lived with were more aware of themselves and their environment than people from my own culture.

The Émbera live by their wits as they have no outside services and their environment is dominated by nature. Living in small, isolated groups their minds are the only force ensuring their future and safety. They have no formal education and their material possessions amount to little more than a few pots, clothes, and tools, yet they are more aware of what is happening around them than most of us. Their minds are sharper than ours.

It's been less than one hundred years since we started building information machines and this has had a tremendous effect on how we view ourselves. Our unique place in the world is no longer so unique. Our minds have put us at the top of the food chain, but—in the context of ever larger, complex, and smarter systems—our individual survival is not of paramount importance.

> *"The world has arrived at an age of cheap complex devices of great reliability; and something is bound to come of it."*
> — **Vannevar Bush**, PhD, engineer, and administrator

"Computers are useless. They can only give you answers."
— **Pablo Picasso**, artist

21. Don't let your ideas grow too fast.

It's easy to have ideas that are too big to understand, manage, or pursue. There is an art to creating a small, workable idea from a large and important one. It's more important to ask the right questions than to chase what you think are the right answers because your questions determine how you see things.

In the normal course of inquiry, the search for answers tends to get bigger while the search for questions gets smaller. Looking for answers is the harvesting stage; examining the questions is the planting stage.

Take small steps and become adept at storing both finished and unfinished projects. Don't give up on unanswerable questions or unfinishable projects. Wait for the key to their next step, or for their best application.

With easy access to information comes a lot of distracting, incorrect, and useless information. If you're just starting to learn about a topic, it's important not to go too deep. Maintain perspective and build connections to other ideas. The danger is that you'll be overwhelmed, lost, or stop exploring altogether.

Set goals you can accomplish and a pace you can maintain. If you do become overwhelmed, be aware of it. Better management will get you further.

I like big problems. I savor them, revisit them, and apply whatever new thoughts I find to them. Some of the big problems that retain my interest are the meaning of reality, the essence of mind, and the forces of creation. There is so much to read regarding each of these questions—so many opinions—and every approach leads into forests of complexity, difficulty, confusing ideas, and new terminology.

Specialists maintain their own schools of thought which, when I finally understand what they're saying, often disappoint me. Many specialties in physics are out of date, accepted on faith, and have lost the important questions. In psychology and medical technology, I find claims that amount to hucksterism or fraud. We live in a marketplace where lots of money chases undeveloped ideas, most of which are sterile or wrong.

Yet, new insights from disparate fields help to illuminate important questions. Ideas I had long ago, which I never expected would go anywhere—which I had no idea how to apply and were discouraged at the time—have broadened, deepened, and anchored themselves as real possibilities. Studying auction markets affords insights into quantum mechanics. Quantum mechanics offers insight into chaos and creation. Questions of chaos and creation have created new ways to ask questions of the mind.

> *"I'm frustrated by doing things slowly... I just don't have the patience for it, although I appreciate it when it's done well... Learning how to type allowed me to create stories quickly. Without that it would have been too slow and I would have been frustrated: I would have been pulling teeth the entire time."*
> — **Matt Forbeck**, author, from *The Learning Project*

Our education systems are going through a radical change in moving from the industrial to the information age. Previously, we trained people to act and think like machines. Now, machines are smart enough to take care of themselves. We need to stop training people to behave like machines, and to stop wasting students' time. Most of the paradigms of current education will be discarded.

Yesterday's educational philosophy will be undone by machines that can do everything we were taught. Our lackadaisical schools—which currently take thirteen years to teach three years of material—will be abandoned, and with them will go the supporting administrators, teachers, and school boards.

This revolution won't affect everyone equally. Gradually, a separation will grow between those who design things and those who build them. We've seen this in all our complex systems: not everyone needs to know what's going on, as individuals tend only to be effective within a limited domain. Over time, the structure of the economy comes to reflect the structure of its thinking.

22. Accept yourself as a failure.

Always accept yourself, and accept yourself especially when you feel you've failed. You never know when you're going to fail, and this is more true the more creative, adventurous, and forward-thinking you are. It is imperative that you support yourself through troubled times.

Proactively accept your failure. Do this without inviting or attracting failure. It's not that you want to excuse yourself for having failed, it's rather that you want to never indict yourself for it, in the first place.

Failure is a consequence of novelty, change, and adaptation. You will encounter failure because of your growth or changing environment. Grow and participate in the changing environment. Be sure that your self-worth does not suffer from what is presented as failure.

Ignorance is a vaccine: be too dumb to believe the impossible. If you can prevail in spite of your ignorance, which all innovators must do, then you will prosper. If you are wise and well-prepared, you'll recognize the ignorance in innovation. Ignorance is the well-spring of illumination, the background for any new picture. Insight meets ignorance in the way a punch-line resolves a comic set-up: it is enlivening.

> *"The exciting part was coming up with new ideas... You have an idea and in your mind it's beautiful, and you get it on paper, and from paper you go to the actual machining, and the building, and then right there, like they say, you're back to the drawing board! That is exciting."*
> — **Donald Dubois**, machinist and inventor, from *The Learning Project*

Fear of failure leads to inaction. Avoiding failure because of inaction is worse than doing the wrong thing. Doing the wrong thing leads to redirection, while doing nothing leads nowhere. More than that, doing nothing breeds indifference, disengagement, and lack of responsibility. If you do not feel some level of responsibility, then you will never invest yourself, and with no investment there will be no return.

> *"I recognized things that needed to happen and I did 'em. The biggest thing—even to this day—is: 'Failure to act is unacceptable.' Don't sit there and do nothing, at least do something. Even Mallard, the kid that was good at computers, would do something. It was so completely off-the-wall that it had no bearing on what we were doing, but at the very least he was doing something. I taught him that*

so I could feel better about having a loose cannon in the ER."
— **Dave Williamson**, US Army medic, from *The Learning Project*

23. Your situation will develop along the lines of your thinking.

Recognize that thinking is not information processing; thoughts are not data. Understand that wherever you encounter large quantities of information, whether it be on a test, in a class, or in a problem, this is not a human domain. If you're trying to remember more data, then you will fail. Just as happened to the mythical John Henry working on the railroads, the machines will overtake you.

What is it that you can do that is more important than data? Refine what it is that you think about thinking, and if you look at this clumsy sentence you'll see that this starts by rebuilding your words, sentences, and the interlacing of your ideas.

Thinking is the process of making a story from words, a journey from snapshots, meaning from facts. The notion of time as even-paced and unassailable is not true. You lose time by letting it go past, and you gain time by filling it with thoughts and actions. It is the story you make that is true; time is just the duration of its telling.

"I feel like a lot of people get stuck in their life, do you know what I mean? They buy into something that they want without really understanding what it is. They don't even think about it. You're giving up stuff that may be a good thing in your life because you're so focused on a goal. They

want to get married, they want to have kids, they want to move to the suburbs. And they get there and it's like, 'Holy shit! I've been doing the same thing for the last 15 years, and I'm really not happy.' "
— **Alice Placert**, editor, from *The Learning Project*

"To improve is to change; to be perfect is to change often."
— **Winston Churchill**, politician

"If you do not change direction, you may end up where you are heading."
— **Lao Tzu**, philosopher

"Only the wisest and the stupidest of men never change."
— **Confucius**, philosopher

Understand the difference between computers and you, between artificial intelligence and your intelligence. An increasing amount of intelligence is being removed from people and put into machines. You may have thought you were getting smarter and your authority was getting larger, but the evidence is to the contrary.

In the information economy of the future you are less important, and, as a consequence, you will need to justify yourself. If you cannot demonstrate you can do better than the machines, you will find yourself working for them. Most people will find professions building, guiding, controlling, designing, repairing, and reclaiming machines, and training more people to do the same.

Today's machines are classical objects; they process classical information. That means they follow specific paths in an attempt to optimally solve specific problems. In the past, they were sequential in their operation, but newer technology allows them to operate through feedback and improve themselves. They are still oriented toward a known goal and cannot yet evolve themselves. However, that is a somewhat vague distinction as evolution happens at many levels. The difference between evolution and improvement is one of context.

These are the things that you can do that machines cannot do, and likely will not do for a long time coming:

- Think and act creatively.

- Be emotional, chaotic, and expansive.

- Manage highly complex systems, where "complex" means many different parts and not just many of the same kinds of parts.

- Recognize different ways of thinking—structurally, randomly, and organically—and apply these styles of thinking to the situations, problems, and people around you.

- Invent a new solution, start a company, build a community.

- Infer or deduce the existence of patterns and trends that have not yet become clear.

- Build toys, models, games, inventions. Things that break easily and from which new ideas emerge.

- Be wary of the things you're good at. Avoid your automation lest you become superfluous.

- Find something you like that you're bad at. Fail at it repeatedly, but not repetitively.

- Invest in yourself. Manage your assets. Maintain your resources.

24. Engage practice; avoid repetition.

Skills require practice to perfect, but what looks like repetition to someone who is not involved is actually a process of change. There is an appropriate level of perfection that makes the result clear, reliable, and valuable. Perfection beyond this is superfluous, it leaves no room for serendipity.

Consider how much time it takes to achieve one percent more perfection, and weigh this against what could be gained by adding, doing, or thinking something new. Things that appear repetitive from the outside can—when viewed from the inside—be unfolding and lead to new understanding.

Things that appear diverse and unrelated from the outside can actually be a practice of focusing the mind of the explorer. Gather enough diversity and you'll find many things come back to relevance, and come back into focus.

I studied classical guitar through my teenage years. With my first teacher, I learned pieces by heart, but never understood them. With my second teacher, I practiced scales like jumping rope, allowing me to slow down and perfect the details. With my last teacher, I spent months playing a single note to master control and understand the shape of sound. It was the last teacher that opened the depth of music and sound. Once I'd reached the level of the note, I could build anything.

If you do play an instrument, practice scales. They are a walking meditation that improves your pace, balance, and control. But go beyond that: put beauty into scales. Play them with lyricism and emotion. Beauty is what you put into something, it is not in the structure. Beauty is something that you add, and if you can add beauty to a scale, then you can add beauty to anything.

"I was interested in facts and I absorbed them kind of like a sponge. As I got older I got interested in why things happened... I became less interested in facts and more interested in the reasons behind things... I got into thinking about morality... I got interested in the idea that complicated systems arise from simple forces."
— **Andrew Reese Crowe**, student, from *The Learning Project*

"We are what we repeatedly do. Excellence, then, is not an act, but a habit."
— **Aristotle**, philosopher

25. Avoid awards and celebrity.

People love spectacles and stories, and the award of prizes makes more consumers. Prizes play on peoples' emotions, and focused emotions make for more manageable people. Prizes don't make things better, they make things quieter. Prizes are stultifying.

Celebrity is rarely rewarding. Most celebrities manage it as a resource and keep it away from home as much as they can. Fame is average by its nature. There is a reason why our most iconic figures lived solitary and unrecognized lives: it suited their work. That's not to say that isolation is best, but it allows you to make your own decisions. Do what's good for you. Recognize assets are only as good as the use to which they're put.

Can you imagine anyone who did something great, doing it for a prize? In some cases, prizewinners gain fame and money, but the compensation isn't fair, given how many others work just as hard. Do prizes make for better work? Why are prizes awarded? You are awarded a prize for doing what someone else values. The more they value it, the more they'll want you to keep doing it.

> *"Nobel Prizes are… an absurd and anachronistic way of recognizing scientists for their work. Instead of honoring science, they distort its nature, rewrite its history, and overlook many of its important contributors."*
> — **Ed Yong**, journalist, from "The absurdity of the Nobel Prizes in science" (Yong, 2017)

> *"Fame itself… doesn't really afford you anything more than a good seat in a restaurant."*
> — **David Bowie**, musician

26. Develop your subtle senses.

Your subtle senses are the senses you do not know you have. They are the skills that a machine would not "think" to optimize, skills that we don't understand. Your subtle senses are things we cannot build into machines or know how to improve. Improve those.

Do this by giving yourself time and space; by allowing yourself to be confused and letting ideas and sensations form. By combining thoughtfulness and thoughtlessness you allow novelty to emerge from the field of well-formed thoughts. The subtlety lies in the in-between spaces, the connections between the careful and the careless. You can foster this through contemplation, daydreaming, meditation, whimsy, exercise, exuberance… anything that might rearrange thought and behavior.

Surround yourself with creative people. They don't have to be good people as long as you don't let them hurt you. Do crazy things, feel deeply, and think expansively. Then, when there's some peace, watch the subtle strands that pull things together.

> *"In those days the Factory was like a medieval court of lunatics. You pledged allegiance to the king—King Warhol. Yet there was oddly no hierarchy. Warhol was also one of us. He accepted the responsibility. He accepted the insanity."*
> — **Mary Woronov**, actress, author, and artist (Trebay, 2018)

Some people see things that others say aren't there. Some claim these things are real, which fascinates me. Personally, I don't think it matters. This is just your mind working and to fuss about the line between reality and imagination can kill the process. Many native shamans will tell you of the characters they meet and converse with in other worlds. These are strange and compelling stories, but what really matters is what these shamans can teach you.

> *"You have to forget about what other people say, when you're supposed to die, or when you're supposed to be loving. You have to forget about all these things. You have to go on and be crazy. Craziness is like heaven."*
> — **Jimi Hendrix**, musician

> *"The most interesting phenomena are, of course, in the new places, the places where the rules do not work—not the places where they do work! That is the way in which we discover new rules."*
> — **Richard P. Feynman**, PhD, physicist

One of the many things that distinguish evolved beings from machines is the number of old parts we continue to use and support. Where a machine is designed and built for a purpose and toward some end, evolved organisms are a collection of unused, reused, and overused parts. Some changes support new functions, like a spine for walking and a pre-frontal cortex for thinking, and others support new functions, like thumbs for tooling and hairlessness for... for what?

Consider emotion, largely relegated to irrelevance by modern society. Western society has acted as if emotions were of no importance, but it's now recognized that emotions were running the show all along. They are the fundamental motivators of community, empathy, exploration, and antagonism.

And what about imagination? To what extent do we use our imagination in a refined and effective way? Can you imagine skills that you might have and could put to use if you could develop them? But you haven't, and maybe no one has, so you don't know how to do it.

> *"For the next twelve hours Walter Pitts and I were walking in a world in which every single thing became completely clear. The clarity was the likes of which you don't experience ordinarily."*
> — **Jerome Lettvin**, MD, PhD, psychiatrist, engineer, and neuroscientist , from *The Learning Project*

A few people extend themselves to extremes. Most only venture to extremes by accident, but a few do it intentionally. We're fascinated by the stories brought back to us by explorers. We want to know what lies beyond the familiar.

"Everything that I've done has been a journey of exploration, of outer and inner exploration, without any focus or commitment, which I would like to have, but maybe I'm just not ready for it."
— **Jaz Lin**, traveler, from *The Learning Project*

27. Get a lot of sleep, more than you think you need.

Sleep is when we evolve and our minds reform. During sleep, your body rebuilds, recovers, and maintains. Your mind consolidates memories and your emotional character incorporates new experiences. During sleep, you grow in all directions. Without sleep, you quickly lose skill, knowledge, memory, sanity, ability, and health.

Sleep is the best investment you can make in your future. By under-sleeping you can get more done in the short term, but you suffer losses you cannot recoup. Because we're not witness to what happens during sleep, we fail to appreciate it.

We devalue sleep for people of all ages, except infants whose sleep we encourage because they bother us. We'll talk about our lack of sleep, but rarely make any lifestyle change that will correct it. I know this because I'm a sleep therapist.

Once kids are old enough, we put them to work. Teenagers are famously sleep-deprived, and their health and welfare suffer for it. With more time asleep and less time in school teenagers' distress goes down, their grades go up, and their accident rate goes down. This is well-documented (Walker, 2018) yet the early and long school days dictated by our education requirements continue to abuse them. Why?

Four things our culture does to threaten our longevity are increase our stress, feed us toxins, encourage our sloth, and deprive us of sleep.

Chronically sleep-deprived people shave years off their lives. Over sixty percent of teenagers are sleep-deprived and suffer emotional problems and learning deficits because of it. This is a huge blind-spot in our culture.

Once you have learned how to do your job, our system will work you to death. This reflects the unimportance of health, insight, and self-reflection in our industrial age. Mechanization is like the asteroid that wiped out the dinosaurs, only this asteroid focuses on humanity.

Just as animals lower on the food chain once emerged as the new apex species, today's ecological disasters will remove us too. We think we're so smart, but what does that mean? Something more balanced, robust, and adaptable will replace us. It need not be more intelligent, just more efficient.

If, like most people, you're not getting enough sleep, then examine your environment and reconsider who your friends are. If you're a young person, then a lack of sufficient sleep will decrease your future potential for anything. Athletes find their performance enhanced if they couple serious practice with sleeping up to ten hours a day. If you think you have to overextend yourself, then stop thinking. Listen to your body; it knows more than you do.

3 – Actors

Introduction

The preceding discussion may have seemed abstract, or impractical, but it is necessary before we can define the actors in our drama. Our images create the context that gives actors meaning in our lives. We invent these images.

Modern, Western cultures hold the notion that children are ignorant and adults are insightful. This depends crucially on this culture's investment in knowledge as facts. It has not always been true and it is not shared by all other cultures. In traditional cultures, the distinction between those who teach and those who learn is not so clear as it is in ours, so it's worth examining what we think we need and what's on offer.

28. Change is harder than you think.

Three changes that could better your life are: changing yourself in a way you know, effecting a change in yourself of which you're not currently aware of or know how to achieve, and changing other people, or another person, in ways that might benefit you.

The changes that you know you can make might get you what you want but probably won't. If you knew how to make these changes, then you would have been exploring them all along. And if you had been, then most likely you would have adopted them. And if you haven't been exploring these ideas, implementing and testing versions of them, then there's something you don't know.

A change that you don't know how to make can either be something you're unfamiliar with or something you don't want. In either case, there are going to be unknown obstacles ahead of you that will require more effort.

The last kind of change, the change you want in other people, is an illusion. It's either wrong because you're seeing it from your point of view—and no one else is going to change unless they see what you see from their point of view—or it's impossible because lasting change only happens when it is put into effect by those responsible for it. If other people have not been exploring this change, then it's probably impractical, unwise, unsafe, or impossible.

In my experience, changes needed, that I don't know how to make, are a combination of what I don't know and don't want to know. Approaching this kind of change has required me to make clear what I don't want and find something I do want within the scope of what I don't know. That way, I can move forward into the confusing work of learning something new. Hopefully, I will find reward and some guidance that I can trust.

Don't overlook or dismiss what you don't want. Don't force yourself to do what feels wrong as that is inevitably the wrong thing to do. Learning more opens new options. Then, when it's time to act, do what feels right.

Teachers

29. Look far beyond what's offered to you.

Be careful what you ask for. Expressing your feelings and asking unapproved questions can be dangerous to your reputation and your health because, before you know it, you'll find yourself exploring the unknown. You'll find no one has answers to the important questions. It is often the case that others are scared to ask these questions. Your asking these questions will cause others dis-ease that they will want to stop.

When you find yourself in the area of a "great unknown," you need to grow up quickly. In the territory of what is important, there is a great deal of confusion. People do not act or think when threatened as they do when they feel safe. In these areas, people are confused at all levels: intellectually, morally, and emotionally. Their personalities become unstable and their behavior will surprise you.

> *"I had a strange feeling, it was around evening, I was this stupid gringa that was going to get lost in the jungle. So I walked and I found lots of people in the river washing. The men use the loincloths and the women use a wrap. They didn't run away but many of them turned away when I came.*
>
> *"A guy came up to where I was walking. He was all painted black on his arms and his face. He asked me in Spanish... 'And what do you want?' I said I don't want much of you but I would ask if I could maybe stay with you and learn something from you. The first question then was 'Are you a missionary?' I said 'No!' Then he said, 'OK, come on.' "*
> — **Gudrun Sperrer**, wildlife conservator and animal rescuer, from *The Learning Project*

It is shockingly easy to find yourself on the frontier of knowledge. The reasons you are denied certain ideas and experiences might be to protect you. This is all the more so when you cannot get a straight answer. These areas instill fear.

I experienced this myself when I became interested in mountain climbing while living in the New York suburbs. I was fourteen, and no one knew what I was talking about. No one had the slightest interest. Camping was considered odd and "active wear" was not yet fashionable. People wore loafers, not running shoes; sneakers were for gym class.

Fascinated by the idea—and having no idea what to expect—a friend and I packed a few day's worth of food, stuck out our thumbs, went to the mountains. Finding myself at the base of a 300-foot, near-vertical cliff, a rope tied around my waist which I didn't know what to do with, I started climbing, trailing the rope behind me. I had no idea what I was doing and I nearly killed myself. I was lucky. I made it to the top and helped my equally dazed friend come up behind me. I'd walked off the edge of the world and into the blank area of the map.

When I came back, no one could relate to what I'd done. Such behavior made no sense and simply couldn't exist. Feeling like a pig among sheep, I continued my explorations with no idea of what would come of it. It's taken me fifty years to begin to understand all the forces that were at play.

30. When you learn something by yourself, you learn it deeply.

Kids are disappointed when adults don't appreciate what they've accomplished. Others generally cannot appreciate what you've done. They didn't have the experience and they didn't share your frame of mind. Most people are unfamiliar with the process of learning by discovery, as it is not the usual process. The rewards you gain will take time to digest. Many of the things I've learned I am still digesting, and will continue to digest for a long time.

When teaching returns to being an extension of practice, teachers will return to the realm of practitioners. In that realm, students will no longer be labeled by institutional measures of intelligence but by their accomplishments. This can apply to students of anything, at any age.

> **Lincoln Stoller**: *"If you can imagine other people in the space where you were, a few years ago, people without the clarity that you have now, what could you tell them that would help them get the kind of clarity for themselves that you have now?"*
>
> **William Ashburton**: *"I'd say, 'It comes from yourself,' but I really can't tell them. I wouldn't want to tell them. I just want them to learn on their own."*
> — from *The Learning Project*

As our culture becomes automated, human skills become unique and specialized. There is still plenty of room on the bottom for mechanics, managers, programmers, and agents, but there is a greater need for elders, intuitives, and visionaries. These skills are not easily taught or scored, and people with these skills are increasingly recognized by their experience.

Those who taught you will be less important than what you know. How you demonstrate what you know will be less circumscribed and more a matter of your ability to present yourself. How you present yourself has always been crucial to how you're received, in spite of the pretense that your value lies in your certification.

Students

Teachers, coaches, advisors, and administrators all have a job to do, and that job depends on you playing your role. In most cases, they feel overworked and struggle for advancement. Helping you to advance beyond what they expect of you is not on their radar. And what they expect of you, in most cases, is not much.

Teachers say they want you to be perfect, the standard toward which you are directed. Perfection is an artificial construct; don't be fooled. Employers are more reasonable. What managers want is to be taken seriously; for their value to be confirmed. Make their lives easier and they'll make your life easier, too.

What my teachers wanted was more than I was interested in providing. I did not take them seriously, and I was not going to follow their directions. I had other ideas. School angered, frustrated, and annoyed me, but I thought I had to put up with it. I did not yet understand that institutions are arbitrary and most people don't think.

In elementary school, I was considered retarded. In middle school, I was seen as a trouble maker. In high school, I engineered a plan to graduate early in order to go to college, which I did. College was not much better, but the opportunities were different and more numerous. The key, as I later discovered, was in learning how to create opportunities.

If you challenge your teacher, manager, or boss, or criticize them for failing your expectations, don't expect to feel welcome. Inequality is built into the student-teacher, employer-employee relationship and inequity results.

The only time I was treated equally was when I played an equal role, which happened when I was given responsibility and authority. In those cases, you are an assistant, apprentice, or team member. You still know less, but the way you're treated is entirely different.

31. Manage your own identity.

Be aware of the role in which you're cast. You cannot play a role you do not agree to play. You bear some responsibility for how you're treated. Learn to manage your emotions so that other people do not. Stand up for yourself; have self-respect, which you should maintain always. Never accept humiliation, and if you feel humiliated for your own reasons, repair it.

Be proud of your efforts when you succeed or fail. Success comes with good luck, skill, strategy, or advice, and failure may result from the lack of any one of these. Other people need these, too, and you would do well to share them. Recognize that when support is conditional, gains and rewards can be as coercive as losses and punishments.

Many programs judge in order to reward the winners and dismiss the losers. Authentic privilege comes with responsibility, not authority. Consider how your program treats other people. It is in the nature of dichotomy that there is always a reflection of the negative in the vision of the positive, and vice versa: heroes have flaws and villains have attractions. Reject both or accept both and you'll be in a more balanced position.

"History was replaced by pseudo-history, by a calendar of rhythmically recurring anniversaries, congresses, celebrations, and mass gymnastic events; by the kind of artificial activity that is... a one-dimensional, transparent, predictable self-manifestation (and self-celebration) of a single, central agent of truth and power... life became nonsense."
— **Václev Havel**, poet and politician, from *Stories and Totalitarianism* (Havel, 1988).

A change in thinking is afoot to recognize emotion, not reason, as underling our most important decisions. In the realm of emotion, children are more insightful than adults. It may help you to reconnect with your childhood in order to better appreciate that people who repress their emotions are dysfunctional.

> *"Grown-ups never understand anything by themselves, and it is tiresome for children to be always and forever explaining things to them."*
> — **Antoine de Saint-Exupéry**, from *The Little Prince*

As a therapist, I can say with some authority that most people are emotionally dysfunctional. There is a reason for this. Our emotions tell us what we feel is true, and most of what we're called to do does not feel true to our nature.

Socialization—which constitutes roughly eighty percent of K-12 schooling in terms of time spent—is designed to convince us to want to do what we're required to do: work regular hours in the roles for which we are trained, and to respect the rules of our changing jurisdictions. Because people cannot resolve the emotional conflicts these imperatives raise—and it is not wanted that people should resolve these for themselves—emotional repression is the underlying lesson.

Strong emotions make repressed people feel uncomfortable. Enthusiasm, jubilance, frustration, anger, sadness, intransigence, epiphany, affection, passion, and belligerence have their place, which is not in the workplace and not in public. Many forms of emotional expression are not tolerated ever, which is why people explode in private.

People consider repression normal. They feel it's okay to explode at friends and family, as long as it's done in private. Anger and violence become the norm, and the norm becomes accepted. In private, no one else can hear you scream. For many, this is how they've been brought up; it's all they know.

32. Explosive emotions are not okay.

You can feel emotions as they build; you know when things become uncomfortable. Emotional aggression is used to make or win a point: raising one's voice, making a gesture, or uttering a threat. Adults are practiced at making these threats. Authorities deliver threats in a tempered and placating tone of voice with undertones of emotional violence.

Just as explosions of emotions are not okay, the threatening to let things get out of hand is also not okay. When someone claims that you must do something or else something bad will happen, recognize this as a threat of violence even if that violence is academic or to be suffered by someone else.

"So I stabbed her... with a pencil. That was bad. I'd never done anything like that before. I just got so mad so quickly that I thought it was okay (laughs... sighs), but it wasn't. My Dad said I was lucky she didn't press charges. What could she have pressed charges for? I don't think it would have killed her. It was right here... Oh, what a life..."
— **William Ashburton**, student, from *The Learning Project*

Warned or threatened consequences may come to pass. If you honestly believe in what you're doing, then address these threats before they become a reality. The next time you're metaphorically told to, "eat your vegetables because there are homeless people who don't have enough food," put down your fork and make it clear that you will not be coerced by someone else's agenda; you do not accept their story.

> *"My entire life I had an emotionally abusive father, physically abusive to my brothers, so I had a very low sense of self-worth, so I always felt like I never fit in anywhere, like the outsider... I was always trying to please everybody so they would like me... When I was 24 I started to do self harm. Everything seemed repetitive, it was the same every day. I felt it was never going to change... it just felt so pointless. This was one of the reasons I became suicidal."*
> — **Lotus Bringing**, fashion model, *from The Learning Project*

Agents

A lot of your learning will come from learning agents. Some may be teachers, but usually not explicitly. They are more the kind of people who are going to "teach you a thing or two," which is to say they have engaged with you for some gain of their own. You can't fault them, as they made no promises otherwise. They're important because they model authentic behavior, situations where there's skin in the game, not didactic learning that's circumscribed and declawed.

For me, many of the people who've acted as agents of learning have presented themselves as teachers. On the whole, they were such bad teachers I hesitate to credit them with any mastery. Being able to learn from lousy teachers is tremendously important as they are often the best teachers of the worst lessons. Appreciate them for the negative role models that they are.

33. You cannot fully learn from the mistakes of others.

We're often advised to learn from the mistakes of others. This is not really possible. You can consider the errors other people make, and you can surmise how you might avoid them yourself, but—when you find yourself in a similar situation—your choices will not be so clear.

Most serious mistakes are a combination of errors. One correction may avoid calamity, but that does not make your other choices right. You may study how to get out of a predicament, or you may study how to avoid getting into one. In the real world, predicaments sneak up on you. Getting out of them can often be done with greater skill than that exhibited by the ones who survived. There is always more to the story than the survivors tell.

You can learn caution by watching the mistakes of others, but you cannot plumb the depths of the experience unless you're there yourself. You are often drawn into these situations by what appears as an opportunity, and if you "learn" to avoid these situations you will also have learned to deny yourself these opportunities. Maybe that's good, maybe you should avoid them. At the same time, those are often the situations where important things happen.

When I began mountaineering, my favorite reading was the annual publication, *Accidents in North American Mountaineering*. Exciting stories in which you knew something dreadful was going to happen. I always puzzled at why people didn't see it coming. It feels very different when you're the one making the decisions.

I memorized the stories of others who had gotten lost, frozen, and caught in avalanches and it made me suitably nervous. Nevertheless, I still got lost, frozen, and caught in avalanches, but I survived. Little mistakes with big potential happen all the time in mountaineering, that's why it's a rush. Practice never makes perfect.

"Good judgment comes from experience. Experience comes from bad judgment."
— **Mark Twain**, writer

When I started flying soar planes I would read the monthly accident reports and found an even greater discrepancy between my real-time situations and their forensic advice. These reports taught more about avoidable accidents than how to avoid accidents. I spite of the righteous judgments of the authors, one was left with the impression that there was a lot more to the story.

My accident record—which was bad but could have been much worse—was my effort to better understand the boundary of safety. Because I could not hold to this boundary—always feeling like a blind man crossing a highway with a white cane—I stopped flying.

Why don't they publish accident reports in a wider variety of fields? There are plenty of mistakes to be made and avoided in all sorts of endeavors, and some of them have serious consequences. Where is *Accidents in North American Pedestrian Traffic*, or *Accidents in North American Student Education*?

Lincoln Stoller: *"What would you say about failure?"*

Jerry Lettvin: *"Such as? If something doesn't work, it doesn't work."*

Maggie Lettvin: *"You know what he taught me? He taught me that that's how you find the right route, by doing one failure after another until you find there's only one* *route left. He used to let his students make one mistake after another, even through he knew that what they were doing was going to lead to failure. He said, 'That's the way they learn.' Long and tedious."*

Jerry Lettvin: *"Well, it isn't tedious. It's really an adventure most of the time."*
— from *The Learning Project*

There is a certain deception in thinking that you can, or that you have, learned from the mistakes of others. You can learn to avoid the situations of others, but, once things get rolling, no two situations are exactly the same. This is all the more true where emotional control or reflex actions are involved. These are essential skills, and they are exactly the kind of skills that you can only develop by experiencing these situations.

Skills are learned by making mistakes, and you cannot learn them by avoiding the errors that other people made. By all means, learn all you can about the mistakes that other people made. Know too, that if you're going to learn what they learned, then you'll have to follow in their footsteps.

34. Be aware of what virtual worlds teach.

All computer games share the quality that you play within the rules. Some computer games—such as the world-building game *Minecraft*—provide a toolkit in which gamers create new games. In these cases, the toolkit defines the bounds of the possible.

There are two sides that have formed opinions regarding what computer games teach: one extols the skills developed, the other decries the attitudes endorsed. It's simple to integrate both perspectives by focusing on the attention that's required.

Today's computer games respond in a repetitive manner. Games don't metamorphosize into something new in mid-play; they do not change how they respond according to the character of the player. Their trajectory is pre-programmed. The scope and range of a computer's response can be large enough to fool you into believing the game is exercising "free will," but it isn't.

A player learns in accordance with their reward. As computer characters become more nuanced and unpredictable they more deeply test a player's thoughts. We will come to a point where computer characters have distinct human personalities, at which point they will teach human behavior. What will they endorse?

The most prevalent computer game strategies involve logical connections, pattern recognition, manual dexterity, and response. These are valuable skills, but they are not social forms. As a result, the skills one obtains are at the cost of those skills they don't require: human connections, human patterns, social dexterity, and human responses.

If you want to know what skills children learn through their immersion in virtual worlds, look at the game mechanisms. If you're concerned with the values games are teaching, then learn to play them and you will find out.

Remember that a gamer's attitude is largely determined by, and exists only within, the virtual world. Serious gamers do not impose their values on the game, and do not take the game's values into the world. They may bring back game-developed skills and attention patterns, but likely not the story or the human element, which is usually exaggerated, contrived, and laughably thin, at best.

"When 3,034 Singaporean children and adolescents were followed for two years, those who became extreme gamers showed increases in anxiety, depression, and social phobia, and a drop in grades. But if they stopped their gaming habit, all these problems decreased."
— **Daniel Goleman**, PhD, psychologist and journalist, from *Focus, The Hidden Driver of Excellence* (Goleman, 2013)

Mentors

In most teaching situations—at least as things are taught in schools—the student never gains competence, because they're constantly shuttled between subjects. In compulsory schooling, students never gain autonomy while they remain within the system. You might think this would end when a student specializes, as in trade or graduate school but it doesn't. To gain competence requires apprenticeship.

Before compulsory education, you learned your trade through practice and apprenticeship. An apprentice is a junior partner, which is entirely different from being a student. In an apprentice relationship, all parties have tasks to accomplish. They share a common goal. The senior partner does not exclusively teach the junior partner, though their guidance will be needed. Moreover, the senior partner is more a leader than a teacher, leading the junior partner to competence and autonomy as soon as possible.

A mentor guides and informs an apprentice or mentee. They are not a teacher, tutor, guidance counselor, administrator, or boss. A mentor's mandate is to help you become competent and responsible as quickly as possible, and the more competent and more responsible, the better.

A mentor does not grade or punish you, though they may benefit from your success and suffer from your failure. They might share the benefits and risks of your work, or not. You might work or play alongside a mentor, or you may simply share their enthusiasm.

> *"I can't be an advisor. I can't give advice to anybody. I don't feel the right to advise."*
> — **Claude Shannon**, PhD, mathematician, engineer, and inventor

The personal traits that a mentor looks for in a mentee are responsibility and commitment. The mentor may gain in the relationship, but often their gain is emotional and not material. A good mentor learns from those they work with and, often, mentors everyone around them, although they are not recognized for it.

> *"My advisor was Roy Ritzmann, who's still at Case Western, and he was a great guy. He was a really good advisor who was encouraging and he gave me enough rope —luckily I didn't hang myself. His style was interesting because he assumed that I could do the work. He made the assumption that I would learn to do what I needed to do, one way or another. He provided enough structure and support to get there, but no constraints... That was a really good experience, and he was a really good scientist."*
> — **Michelle Murrain**, PhD, neuroscientist, consultant, writer, activist, from *The Learning Project*

35. Begin what interests you, then look for mentors.

A mentor-mentee relationship rests on intrinsic motivation, equal respect, and shared responsibility. You must find the motivation in yourself and begin your efforts without depending on anyone. You must recognize and respect those from whom you can learn, and you must be in a position where you are responsible for your success or failure. Once this has been established, many people may be willing to help you. If you don't need help right now, then advance to the next level.

"Look for mentors; it's a very simple learning process. Look for the mentors. Channel, find purpose, and look for your destiny. Search for the moment when opportunity will knock on your door. Try to find your place in the world, and make your mark in that world either through accomplishments or through your voice. This gives things value. This is value."
— **The Phantom Street Artist**, graffiti artist, from *The Learning Project*

There is an old expression that says, "When the student is ready, the teacher will appear." This implies that serious teachers await serious students. To read into the expression anything beyond that confers on teachers a kind of omniscience they don't have. The expression reflects the short-sighted dualism bred in academic halls or, perhaps, Buddhist monasteries. Students don't look for mentors in these institutions, and teachers don't recognize their own irrelevance.

It is my opinion that the student is only "ready" when they are ready to no longer be a student. Until you reach that point, you're not taking full responsibility and you're looking for someone to hold your hand. In that capacity, you get teachers, not mentors.

36. Be outgoing, confident, and declarative.

Don't expect to be recognized, announce yourself. The teacher will not come to you when you are ready, nor will your friends, guides, mentors, or family. You must announce your presence, describe your vision, and state your needs.

If you feel yourself to be smart, promising, honest, curious, serious, and sincere, then you will find yourself alone much of the time. I don't know if these characteristics are lacking in others from the start, or squeezed out of them as they're growing up, but I've found few people will proclaim, insist, and advance these aspects of themselves.

By being who you're proud to be and stating to others what you value in yourself, you will draw to you those people and energies that resonate with you. You may also draw people who will take advantage of you, so make sure that vulnerability, foolishness, vampirism, and negativity are not characteristics that you nurture.

Most people hide their true feelings from others and from themselves. Most people have difficulty making deep and lasting connections. By making such connections with yourself you can follow a constant track through your life. These are issues of truth, honesty, clarity, commitment, and emotion. By working these virtues, benefits will follow.

Around the age of twelve I came to the conclusion I was surrounded by idiots. I could not really believe this, but it seemed that everyone acted that way. Everyone seemed to be in a kind of dull haze, never connecting intellectually or expressing real emotion.

Certainly, my parents seemed like idiots, and so did all the other adults in my life. I felt like a fish in water looking to breath something else, but I didn't know what else there was to breath. The water in which I was immersed was the liquid of half-consciousness, in which was dissolved a disinterest in and disrespect for just about everything. In short, I was starting to see the adult world.

What I needed was a wise person. I think this is what grandparents are for, but I was a late child and my ancient grandparents played no role. Perhaps children have the instinct to look for grandparents, like plants that move toward light. I started to look for wise people.

At first, I asked for tutors. I got high school teachers who did tutoring on the side. They were of no use. I took up hobbies hoping to find serious people in model building, bicycle racing, stagecraft, guitar playing, map making, competitive diving, chess, literature, archery, and other pursuits. It was a good idea, but I could not find people I took seriously, or who took me seriously.

I found some adults who took themselves seriously, but they lacked vision: the music teacher played notes, the gym teacher counted points, and the math teacher calculated numbers. Everything seemed to be done by wrote. No one was inspired to understand what they were doing. I kept looking.

I looked for names in a list of emeritus physics professors at the best university within driving distance. I had no connections and no introduction—I was not even a senior in high school—but I found Eugene Wigner, and I called to see if I could visit him.

Wigner was the first person who really inspired me. He was so excited to hear from me that he couldn't get his words straight. He fell over himself in encouraging me to visit, offered to pick me up from the train station, and said he would give me whatever time I needed. I had no idea of what he had to offer, but he made me feel valuable and welcome.

I think I was seventeen, and I drove myself to Princeton to spend the afternoon with him. We talked about all the things that interested us, and the things I wanted to learn about. There were no interruptions. I don't remember much, but he was strongly encouraging and emphatic that I continue to ask fundamental questions.

I had planed to return home that afternoon, but he told me to come back the next day. Since I had no where to stay, I slept in the bushes and spent the next afternoon with him, as well.

While I had no idea at the time, I was later to learn that Wigner won the 1963 Noble Prize for inventing quantum chemistry. He, Leo Szilard, and Albert Einstein wrote the letter to Franklin D. Roosevelt that started the Manhattan Project and developed the first atomic bombs. His "famous brother-in-law" Paul Dirac—as Wigner referred to him—discovered anti-matter. And his student, John Bardeen, was the only person to win two Noble Prizes in physics.

I don't know what Eugene Wigner did for me, but he did something. Ever since then, I've been an advocate of looking for guidance from the best people you can find. I thought I could encourage other people to do the same, and I started a website for this purpose, but no one has responded. It seems that being outgoing, confident, and declarative are personality characteristics that are generally discouraged.

> *"Where in the Schrödinger equation do you put the joy of being alive?"*
> — **Eugene P. Wigner**, PhD, physicist

Explorers

Any explorer will be quick to tell you that they still have a lot to learn. Explorers are learners. You would not think of calling an explorer a student, even though they might be. There is something quite different in their objective. A student is a person whose past and future are constrained. An explorer is leaving their past behind, while their future is unbounded.

Students do a lot of exploring in the course of their studies, but it is in the nature of teaching that these explorations are circumscribed and their direction preconceived. The outcomes are both known and graded. This kind of exploration is game-like, and in this game, the real adversary is not the other players but the design that constrains the players. Win against your opponents and the game goes on to be played again. Win against the designer and the game is yours, you decide what happens next, and that could be anything.

> *"Perfection is achieved, not when there is nothing more to add, but when there is nothing left to take away."*
> — **Antoine de Saint-Exupéry**, from *Airman's Odyssey*

37. If schooling is learning how to behave, then exploration is otherwise.

What do you want to achieve? If it's to meet expectations—and that could be expectations in the performance of anything— then you can be taught. If it's to discover new understanding, then you cannot be taught, at least not in the sense of being given a program.

There are many ways forward in any situation: some are better, many are poor, and most are entirely wrong. Learning to explore is not about knowing the right answer, it's about recognizing the wrong ones.

"I didn't have any ambitions at all. The only thing I was interested in was curiosities. I wasn't particularly interested in what you might call standard physics, standard neurology, or standard physiology. I looked for the corners that were unoccupied and which, for some reason or another, had escaped attention. That's not a way in which you go about doing things, but I was fortunate enough to have had a father who was an anarchist who pointed out to me that the interesting things always lay outside the beaten path. You look for them, and when you find them you play with them."
— **Jerome Lettvin**, MD, PhD, psychiatrist, engineer, and neuroscientist , from *The Learning Project*

"People come to me and say, 'I don't have any goals!' And I say, 'Uhh, I've never had any goals either!' If I had goals they would have acted like blinders and I wouldn't have noticed what was going on. I just notice what's happening around me and if it interests me I go after it, and if doesn't I walk on past."
— **Nancy White**, PhD, neuro-psychotherapist, from *The Learning Project*

There is an expression that says, "When you meet the Buddha in the road, kill him." This abstruse expression means that when you know that you are on the right path you are not subject to anyone's authority. Once you know what is true, your truth is the authority. This reflects the importance of taking responsibility and recognizes that no one can teach you mastery. You may be a partner or apprentice, you may consider the advice of others, but you must be your own teacher in the end.

> *"The drive for exploration, in its many forms, may be the single most important personal factor predicting creative achievement... An intense desire and motivation to seek new information... forms the very core of his or her personality."*
> — **Scott Barry Kaufman** and **Carolyn Gregoire** (2016), from *Wired to Create, Unraveling the Mysteries of the Creative Mind*

38. You are on the road to mastery when you learn from everything.

I try to learn from every person and situation. Everything that taxes or rewards me, anyone who enlightens or annoys me. Even frustration is a lesson in frustration. The harder the lesson, or the harder to recognize the situation as a lesson, the deeper a lesson it is.

There are the big lessons like death and heartbreak—which resonate deeply—and the small lessons such as forgetting your keys and confusing your schedule—which don't. There are little things that weren't supposed to happen and seem incidental. There are the recognized lessons of school, work, practice, and responsibility.

> *"When I was a youngster I was very interested in natural history. I used to walk in the woods and the streams and catch butterflies, and watch birds and look at the stars, and so on. All the universe was fascinating to me..."*
> — **Charles H. Townes**, PhD, physicist, inventor of the laser, from *The Learning Project*

There is always a second level to any lesson that involves your coming to understand why you're doing something, or why you care. There is the meta-understanding of whether anyone really knows what they're talking about, in spite of what is or isn't correct.

I remember walking down the street one morning when I was seven, contemplating the word "milk." I repeated it over and over, exploring the gaging "L" sound that reminded me of what it felt like when the back of my throat was covered in milk.

Psychologists call this speech pattern echolalia, but I have not read a single psychologist who understood what was going on in my head at the time. It was obvious to me why I was doing this, even at the age of seven, yet you'll never learn it in psychology. A surprisingly large number of learned people know surprisingly little.

Not only is there no right answer, there is no answer. That is because, in reality, there is no question. All questions are a figment of our imaginations, and there are multiple answers to any question. Locate as many answers as possible subject only to the usefulness of the result. In this, you are always a success and a failure. No one teacher could serve all these purposes. That's how it should be.

> "So I decided, well, I'm young and full of energy, so I'm going into the logging business... I learned a lot of lessons through that. It was a really good experience. I never would have seen that. I could have been buying an education when I was 50, but I was doing it in my 20's. It taught me a lot about people. I got to say, that was a good time."
> — **Tom Kellogg**, landscaper, logger, excavator, and heavy equipment operator, *from The Learning Project*

People

There are people in your orbit that have no label and who could play any role. They may have a role or may play a role by circumstance or invitation. Your preconception, which you will communicate to them with subtle cues, will put a spin on future interactions with them. These cues are usually subliminal, meaning they are both unintentional and they are broadcast and received without conscious intention.

39. Choose your friends judiciously.

You are affected by those around you. Most of us gravitate toward others who support our weaknesses and sustain our needs. There is a big risk of becoming dependent on others for what you cannot provide, or do not want to learn to provide for yourself.

The effect of your friendships is too important to be left to chance or circumstance. Take an active role. Take a stance in representing yourself. Don't be afraid to be yourself and to express yourself even when that violates social protocol. You only begin being yourself when you begin mothering yourself. That means looking after yourself and kicking your own butt.

Those who provide us what we don't need now—but may need later—can lead us forward. They're usually not teachers or family. They have other obligations and personal motives. They may be friends or mentors.

Learn to recognize the people in your life at as deep a level as you can. Look beyond circumstance and presentation. It's okay to offend or rebuff a prospective friend or mentor in order to express your honest opinion because the connection that you're looking for goes beyond what you say or inexpertly demonstrate. Deep connections are built holistically, on personal histories—even aspects of your own history—that you are hardly aware of. The first and most important key is paying attention; to be perceptive.

> *"Always try to associate with people from whom you can learn something. All the knowledge that you want is in the world, and all you have to do is go and seek it."*
> — **Marcus Garvey**, civil rights activist

I was bustling through the crowded Lexington Avenue subway in New York City with my 7-year-old son when I brushed past a stranger who turned and said to me, "You have a beautiful son." I squeezed my son's shoulders, glanced back, gave the stranger a blink and a nod, and continued forward.

Undeterred, they called back, "You have to acknowledge a blessing or it won't stick to you!" So I stopped, turned against the crush of the crowd, and I shouted back, "Thanks for your blessing! We will always remember it!"

> *"He grew smarter and more creative because he chose to surround himself, almost exclusively, with people whose smarts and creativity he admired. More than most of us, he was deliberate in his friendships, only choosing friends who drew out his best... (Ask) yourself not just who your friends are but what you do together. Think more deliberately about the substance of your time with them, and if you find it lacking, change it."*
> — **Jimmy Soni** and **Rob Goodman** (2017), writing about Claude Shannon in, "10,000 hours with Claude Shannon: How a genius thinks, works and lives."

40. Take note of subtle signals.

Be aware of the signals you're broadcasting and note the signals you receive. Each of us broadcast and receive many levels of signals simultaneously. They are broadcast from different systems, intentionally but not consciously, conveying different, often conflicting messages. We are equally complicated in the messages we receive imprecisely, interpret incorrectly, and unconsciously.

It's difficult to become conscious of what's unconscious, as the unconscious operates by itself, but it's easy to become conscious of what's subconscious. All you need to do is become more aware; to raise from the subconscious the feelings you previously were not conscious of.

It's been said that ninety-five percent of our communication is nonverbal, meaning tone of voice, body language, facial expression, and small and rapid movements of which we're unaware. You can learn to see these and to control your broadcast of them.

Insight comes with careful observation, which means sensitivity. It comes most richly through our limbic system which, like some kind of radio antenna, picks up signals below sight and hearing and translates them into feelings.

Learning subtle perception takes time, but it does not require a teacher. It only requires being present and connecting with new perceptions, thoughts, and feelings. It is a contemplative practice.

As with your other senses, much of perception takes place in your brain; your conceptual abilities improve with your perceptual abilities. Be careful about the signals you're broadcasting; note the signals you're receiving.

41. We don't recognize the most important messages.

Our goal-oriented culture sees life as a series of accomplishments, rather than a cycle of phases. We create conclusions in order to get our reward. We view graduation, marriage, employment, friendship, and promotion as ends rather than means. If we're dissatisfied, we often discard them.

In our ceremonies, we take credit; in our rejections, we evade responsibility. In both, we fail to get the message that these are ongoing processes, not crops to be harvested. Graduation, marriage, promotion, and so forth are continuing relationships.

We don't recognize as messages, signs we don't understand. Some of these are blazes on trails we don't know we're following. The phrase, "Don't shoot the messenger," never gets stale because we never stop doing it. We shoot them because we don't recognize them, and we insist on protecting ourselves.

You can't recognize a message you don't understand, and the greater the message, the more difficult it will be to understand. The best way to ensure you get the most important messages is to accept all messages, at least to the point where you can identify them.

Some messages are bad for you, but you need to know them well enough to be safe in your rejection of them. Taste toxic messages but don't ingest them. What you do with such messages is another question but at least you have received them. Then, you can make use or dispose of them.

Receiving messages is a skill. Understanding them is an art rooted in knowing yourself. Your roots not only protect and stabilize you, but they are the source of your understanding.

42. Be aware of body language.

Subtle perception is different from subtle action. I'm amazed by all the meanings I can read in posture, gesture, and common movements: how a person scans the street, opens a door, or steps off the curb. These simple actions convey volumes about a person's awareness, intention, and attitude.

We refer to the "vibes" of an engagement; you can see them in action if you watch with awareness. When a conversation starts, I feel like I've fallen into a complicated machine. I cannot see inside another's skin—though I may have other superpower senses that can—but what I am aware of is more than I can put together.

People's cues are like a puzzle. It often takes me days to put the pieces together. This is an essential skill for a therapist, coach, or counselor. I find that the more carefully I listen to people, the more of themselves they reveal to me, though they often do so unconsciously. People start to unfold when you give them space and attention.

One can draw out other people's positive nature but, quite often, I draw out the negative. This is something I'm interested in, so it's partially my own doing. I'm more interested in what's under the surface than what floats above it. This is where you go to make changes. Things are rarely what they seem and judgments are relative.

43. Attend to the eyes.

We use our eyes as signals to a degree far beyond what we're aware of, in spite of all the time we spend looking at each other. We're sensitive to all aspects of another person's eyes, and I suspect we communicate in unrecognized ways using our facial muscles, corneas, and irises.

Our language is full of references to seeing, sight, and insight as nearly half of our brain is involved with visual processing. We talk about how people see us, look to us, into us, and through us, these being a few examples of expressions for which words are inadequate.

It has become my habit to think to myself the thoughts I want to communicate to my clients when I am looking at them. In fact, I'll think these thoughts to them even when I'm not looking at them, but I pay special attention to my thoughts when I am. It's not that I expect I'm telepathic, though I might be, but rather that I expect I'll use unconscious means to convey my ideas.

There are ideas I don't want to put into words or state directly due to their sensitive, disruptive, or easily misunderstood nature, but I nevertheless want to communicate to them. I cannot claim my ideas make the jump into another person's consciousness immediately, but I feel I weave these unstated ideas into the nuance of the conversation. Think with your eyes.

> *"My father's deep self-doubt prevented him from understanding love. He never gave emotional support to his family, but he was not rotten. In that very brief moment when he would first see me, in that authentic moment before he started to think, his eyes would light up and he would exclaim, 'Hi, Linco!' And then it was gone."*
> — **Lincoln Stoller**, PhD, CHt, therapist and author, from *The Learning Project*

44. Find your rhythm and watch for the rhythm of others.

You have rhythms layered on top of each other that you don't see. Just as choppy ocean waves are made up of different size waves added on top of each other, you have different rhythmic patterns in your thoughts, actions, and behaviors that are happening simultaneously.

There are rhythms in focus on events, in your patterns of thought, and in your ability to hear. You have different rhythms for different thoughts and perceptions. Your focus and your awareness shrink and expand depending on the topic and the time of day.

The same holds true for other people too. Like the moving train phenomena—where you can't tell whether it's your train or another train that's moving—synchronizing with another person's rhythms requires rhythmic awareness in both people. Naturally, not everyone has it, or not everyone is equally aware, so it's no wonder that we settle for a fairly low level of mutual understanding.

This is why we look for consonance with others, and we feel the best when we find it. This is why monkeys groom each other, and we do too. We like to create large waves of safety, pleasure, and contentment. We are attracted to others who have the same patterns who—we hope—will contribute to and enlarge our shared, positive experience.

Think of these rhythms in combination and not simply as separate frequencies. Think of them as the music of our experience, that has a melody, harmony, rhythm, and tone. Contrast all the rhythms required for a charming presentation with the lack of rhythms in a stolid monotone.

Good relationships are not just one person affirming another, they are symphonic, musical experiences. Our verbal affirmations are almost after-the-fact. Positive experiences have a frequency to them, a groove we want to maintain. That's what we're looking for in relationships: melodies that persist.

Think about how you attend to positive things, how your attention returns to the positive point of view. You will not remain constantly positive, you will relax to consider other situations, feelings, and possibilities. But if you feel authentically drawn to something, then you will resonate with it—and it will come back to you. It will color your experience, and you will work to retain it. Our social conversations are just this: reenactments of positive hypnotic inductions to an enthralled audience.

That is your positive rhythm, and rhythms of this kind enrich and sustain you. You may not even know you're looking for them and creating them, but you like them when you find them!

The more you are aware of these rhythms and play a role in amplifying them and rewarding them in others, the better you'll be at attracting and creating them. This is what we mean when we say that we're "looking for our tribe." Our "tribe" is whomever we resonate with.

> *"From very early on I always knew I wanted to do film, and then it was just a question of how to pursue that. I toyed with the idea of leaving school for a while... It's not like I had any terrible, terrible experiences at (high school), I just knew what I wanted to be doing and that wasn't it..."*
> — **Oliver Pierce**, student, from *The Learning Project*

45. Invite others to be present and equal.

A consequence of our natural self-centeredness is to see our situation as special and to infer that we're special too. We draw a circle around ourselves and decide who to allow within it, and who to keep outside. We naturally divide things, people, and situations into what can come in and what should stay out. We are more sensitive to inequality, than equality.

We are tuned to see things as different, not as the same. We expect differences and are quick to judge them. We have deep-seated fears of being unable to distinguish people, places, and things. It takes an act of will for us to see past superficial differences and experiences in order to recognize similarities that lie below the surface.

Inequality highlights what you don't know, which is useful. Inequality generates fear and we may associate danger with the unknown. These are good inclinations if you have no other basis for judgment—like most of our non-primate ancestors—but with the bigger brains we carry, fearing what we don't know hinders progress. Given the tasks we now face in the world, it's not clear that we're up to the task.

If there is one thing that represents wisdom, it's being able to see new possibilities without being afraid of them. On the naïve and inexperienced side lies curiosity. On the injured and reactive side lies fear.

Staying centered means approaching things head-on and with eyes open. It means accepting things in the widest sense even when you know they might not fit, and putting your best foot forward to invite what you want to occur. In other words, it means broadcasting to others on a positive frequency.

To invite others to be present and equal means fully revealing what appears to you and describing things as you see them. Being present and equal does not mean being vulnerable. Offering presence and equality does not confer special powers to others.

Offering presence and equality is to offer the greatest resonance within you. If you are not looking to create positive resonance, then you're either denying others a way to connect with you, or you're preventing yourself from connecting with others.

I grew up in an affluent, New York City suburb that had no poor or homeless people. Everyone was either rich or adequately cared for. My older brother lived in an abandoned cheese factory in Manhattan, in an area later demolished to make the World Trade Center. He lived on the first floor and his friends lived on the floors above him.

Homeless people lived on the street. People crowded around the warmth of fires set in barrels in an empty lot. My brother befriended a man named Sam and offered him the stairwell to sleep in. Sam lived in a pile of newspapers on a landing. He was a quiet, gentle-faced man. I was 10-years old, I don't remember anything Sam said, but he sat with us sometimes.

It was my first time sharing space with a person who had no home or family. Life is short on the street, and Sam only lasted a year. For me, knowing Sam was heart-opening.

"It's very important to follow your instincts and whatever feels right, because everyone has their own path. Take the experiences as they come, and the people. Remember that every person that walks by is full of stories! Don't look down on anybody for what you see them initially to be, because everybody has something really special and golden inside."
— **Jaz Lin**, traveler, from *The Learning Project*

97

46. Your relationship with yourself is shaped by your parents.

Your parents are the people you look to for parenting, who may or may not be your birth parents. They could be any of the people who raised you and played this role. Their success or failure can only be measured against what you needed. These needs were not optional.

As a child, both mothering and fathering define you for life. Don't confuse the people who played the roles of mother and father with the roles that you needed them to play. Only you can understand what and who are the parents you needed and—in the final analysis—only you can provide them for yourself.

> *"I'm not going to say that I grew up in a troubled home, but my Mom pretty much considered me a lost cause. She put all her time and effort and money into my sister—my parents were divorced—and just considered me to be this great, giant, enormous screw-up. Even when I did something right I was still a screw-up."*
> — **Dave Williamson**, US Army Medic, from *The Learning Project*

Change from relying on your physical parents to relying on your inner parents. The physical ones will never fully understand you even if they want to, and they usually don't want to. The sooner you forgive them for their errors, the better for the both of you.

> *"They found out I was pregnant and they came into this mental hospital and said to me, 'If you don't have an abortion, we're never going to speak to you again.' And I was, like, 'Really? Fine! I'm not having an abortion.*

Goodbye.' It was very difficult because even though it's a very twisted and bad relationship, it's still your parents, and so it was tough."
— **Alice Placert**, editor, from *The Learning Project*

47. You will spend your life searching for your parents.

You will dream about your parents throughout your life. They will likely be the last people you'll think about at the end of your life. This searching, by its nature, will take you beyond your reach: the parents you are looking for never existed.

Your inner parents only exist inside you or, if you prefer, in spirit. They were born in a time before your time, grew as part of your character before you were fully aware, and are connected to you by culture, family, ancestry, genetics, and more. They were connected to the inner parents of the people who raised them.

Your inner parents are likely to be similar to your parents' inner parents, and less likely to be your parents, themselves. That is, you probably need the same things your parents needed, and there's a good chance that none of you got it. The identity of your inner parents is ancestral and grows larger and deeper as you gain greater awareness of, and connection with, yourself and your lineage.

All of our personal problems can be thought of as family problems, and all our personal work can be thought of as family work. Recognize this work as complex, fundamental, and eternal. You broadcast your ancestral issues to those around you, and pass it to your descendants. Approach it gently. It's work that's never be finished.

Jaz Lin: *"I never, never ever, ever talk back to my parents, because that's totally unacceptable. It's unacceptable in our* *culture because you are supposed to respect your elders. For example, if my Dad and my Mom are, like, yelling at us and lecturing us, and if we speak back in some way, then they will get just even more angry, and do something horrible to make us not talk next time.*

"My sister now talks more than I do, she talks back more, and they have more of a dialog, and I've been starting to do it, but still not as much as she can. I just stuff it all in. Like they'll be, like, 'Da da da da!' And I'll be, like, 'Guhhh.'"

Lincoln Stoller: *"Even now?"*

Jaz Lin: *"Yeah still. Even now. I'm learning to express more, but I still can't really talk back, no."*
— from *The Learning Project*

4 – Context

Why bother to learn anything? There's got to be a reason. There's always a goal. The only person who lacks a reason to learn is a person with no future or past. There may be many such people.

If you lack an enthusiastic attitude, your desire to learn will be dull. If your future is limited your will to learn will be weak: take what's given and do what's required. People with a will to learn are agents of change; they change themselves and what's around them.

There's a difference between stability and stasis, but we fail to distinguish them. Stability provides a basis for growth and supports learning; stasis keeps things the way they are and impedes change.

There's a difference between change and difference, but we don't distinguish between them, either. Social, cultural, and political processes have momentum that keep them moving in time, but does not generate change. Evolution is not revolution. Progress simply means moving forward, and it can be repetitive and static in its form.

This combination of momentum and stasis support our efforts to endorse a simple history, one that supports what we project to be the next steps in the kind of change we want. We are always committing the error of accepting the past as a basis for projecting the future. We don't question our presumptions.

The most common objection to new ideas is that they will disrupt the story of the past and upset projections of the future. Seen in this context, education is not so much designed to create change as it is to continue present patterns into the future.

My mother lost her mind in the last years of her life, so I am acquainted with what it means not think or learn. Unless you are demented, this book will help you think and learn.

Purpose

48. The degree to which something is important determines the value of your effort.

We're deceived when we're told that we should develop what others judge to be our greatest skill. What others recognize determines how others value you. What you recognize in yourself determines the value you'll find in doing anything. The extent to which you appreciate yourself determines whether you'll profit from your efforts.

I remember hearing about an art school student, a friend of my housemate in Texas, who decided all her works would look like hearts. Her efforts were considered laughable, and she left the art program.

The Japanese artist Yayoi Kusama is "The Queen of Polka Dots." All of her work is based on polka dots. She, too, was not given much credit, at first. Her compulsively repetitive polka dot works are now described as showing attributes "of feminism, minimalism, surrealism, Art Brut, pop art, and abstract expressionism... infused with autobiographical, psychological, and sexual content." In 2017 a six-story museum was built to hold her works exclusively. She is acknowledged as one of Japan's most important, living artists.

49. Death is an ally.

Death is the only teacher who will stay with you until the end. Not to be morbid, but someday you will see your death in front of you, and when that time comes all your life, all you ever meant, and all the value you'll ever have will be out behind you.

If you look forward at that point and yearn for more life, you may see death as a great horror, stripping everything from you. But if you look backward, you'll see that death is the line drawn beneath the last line of the story of your life; the final line in your life's work, your masterpiece.

Death is not turning out the light; the light is going out of its own accord. What we see as death is simply the ringing of the bell signaling that it's over. You've been sitting on the message all your life, and this message has been trying to speak to you all the time. Don't blame the messenger; it bears you no malice.

"Death is, of course, the paradigm of all change. People are dying all around us, but we don't see it happening; we don't want to see it, and for the most part we manage to keep it hidden... American society is fundamentally committed to not seeing death. And yet, as I discovered while living in India, where dying and death are everywhere in full view, there is a sense of relief that comes from the direct encounter with a universal truth, no matter how unpleasant that truth might be."
— **C. W. Huntington, Jr.**, PhD, from *Seeing Things As They Are*

Speaking from my own experience, situations in which your immediate choices determine whether you live or die bring you face to face with what's important. I believe the reason teenagers engage in high-risk and often foolish activities is in their search for that feeling; the feeling of what's important.

Facing death is the very best way to understand love, meaning, and value. These emotions will present themselves in a pure form, without recourse to words or memories. They'll emerge from somewhere inside of you, a place you may never have been before. Death and love are partners, not in the business sense but in the romantic sense.

> *"Remembering that I'll be dead soon is the most important tool I've ever encountered to help me make the big choices in life. Because almost everything—all external expectations, all pride, all fear of embarrassment or failure—these things just fall away in the face of death, leaving only what is truly important."*
> — **Steve Jobs**, entrepreneur, founder of Apple Computer, NeXt, and Pixar Animation Studios

Meaning

Four reasons to learn are to:

- learn a skill,
- understand how things work,
- gain insight into yourself,
- learn something you can't yet conceive of.

These are not distinct, they can overlap. Any learning path can take you through all territories, but one usually becomes your primary territory. These are four perspectives on what learning means to you. By separating them you might see the need to attend to a goal you might otherwise overlook.

Most education programs focus on skill-building. Skills are the easiest targets to teach, demonstrate, evaluate, and reward. A teacher who does not practice the craft rarely inspires one to learn. Without a demonstration of mastery in doing what is taught, which comes out of deep enthusiasm, there is little inspiration. You can always teach yourself the facts.

50. Becoming inspired will change your life.

Once you're inspired, events can delay your learning but rarely stop you. What is often identified as an innate skill is an enthusiasm. Certain races, cultures, and religions are credited with certain abilities when they're simply more enthusiastic. The heart of the subject draws a person forward, not the reward. What you have a passion for is your future.

A person changes when something significant happens, and the significant good things usually have something to do with love. A person who is inspired is in love with their work. The word "work" is not appropriate because pursuing what you love is not work, it's a part of who you are: you do not work at it. If you didn't do it, you would not feel whole.

You are not being taught when you're learning from someone who is in love with their work. The subject itself is almost incidental. There is something more than skill or craft, and your relationship is more than that of a student. It's hard to describe if you have not felt it, but if you want to learn, this is what you're looking for.

Training and mentoring are different, yet we confuse the two when we use the word "teacher." A trainer habituates behavior as in the training of animals. Today's teaching profession emerged from a time when behaviorists ruled psychology, and they viewed people as creatures of habit to be trained through repetition, reward, and punishment. Teachers were conceived as trainers, and now we don't even recognize it.

A mentor is a guide or a leader, not a trainer. Typically, those who are recognized as mentors are not interested in teaching; they're not there to feed you the details or demonstrate the steps. Their role is to inspire you so that you have the energy, sense of purpose, and enthusiasm to explore and discover. That's what they provide, not learning but energy, purpose, and enthusiasm.

A mentor "teaches" you inspiration, but how is inspiration taught? Inspiration is not a thing, a subject, or a practice. Inspiration has no product and accepts no grade. Inspiration has value, but it can't be bought.

> *"I was at once confused and amazed by Theodore. First, since he was obviously a scientist of considerable repute... In fact he was the only person I had met until now who seemed to share my enthusiasm for zoology. Secondly,... he treated me and talked to me exactly as though I were his own age... but also as though I were as knowledgeable as he."*
> — **Gerald Durrell**, reflecting on Dr. Theodore Stephanides at the time when Gerald was 11, from *My Family and Other Animals* (Durrell, 1977).

Your efforts are easier when you're inspired because everything inspirational guides you. There may be practical rewards, but the personal reward gives more energy back than what you put into it. Inspired people can draw on tremendous resources.

One of my mentors, Eugene Wigner, inspired me by sharing his sincere feelings. Another, Charlie Townes, inspired by sharing his delight. A third, Fred Beckey, shared his passion. And a fourth, Jerry Lettvin, inspired by annoyance. He was famous for greeting his students by saying, "How can I most piss you off, today?" None of them displayed the slightest arrogance and, without exception, each was recognized as one of the greatest practitioners of their crafts.

> *"My high school English teacher... was a 'bachelor'... He had all of the conflict of a person who hasn't fully realized, hasn't allowed his inner self, hasn't allowed the sexuality to come out, and a lot of that came in to the intensity of his teaching. We fought like cats and dogs, and he opened all of literature. It was just incredible..."*
> — **Tom Hurwitz**, filmmaker, from *The Learning Project*

51. Find inspired people.

You will find an audience with an enthusiastic person if you can share their enthusiasm. You have to understand; what they do must have meaning for you. It doesn't have to be a huge thing, it can simply be something you take a personal interest in, something you're curious about.

More enthusiasm is better, but a little enthusiasm is enough to get started. And if you have enthusiasm, you can approach anyone, at any level, simply to share in what they enjoy. You're not approaching them as a student, and there's nothing you should want from them.

> *"When somebody is passionate about something, they create their own reality. Your positive thoughts about whatever you do brings the opportunity, it attracts the opportunity. I wasn't even conscious of that at the time but that's what I believe now.*

You have more power than you're aware of just by virtue of what you think. It's an aura that you create."
— **Lynn Hill**, extreme rock climber, from *The Learning Project*

Things that are taught are advertised as having one purpose. This is the nature of advertising and it rubs off on the person teaching. It's their job to deliver what's been sold. Teachers narrow the scope of what they teach. But this is not natural to the subject being taught as no subject is born of one idea or for a single purpose.

If you inquire as to why you're being asked to learn the material you'll be told the material is important. They might say, "It's important to know math," or, "If you can't read, you can't make progress in anything." These answers may have some truth, but these don't answer the question.

I asked my middle school history teacher why we were being taught useless, inaccurate information presented as the history of our country. She responded by paraphrasing the philosopher George Santayana to say, "Those who cannot remember the past are condemned to repeat it."

Modern schooling separates subjects into artificially unrelated skills. History is not a sequence of events, it's an evolution of systems and relationships. The changing role of science is as essential to understanding historical events as the dates of wars and the shifting of borders.

You won't be taught about science in history class or history in science class. This arbitrary separation of subjects persists not only throughout all levels of education but continues throughout the strata of professional life in spite of its being a fallacy. This segregated approach to learning skills hinders understanding and productivity.

There are basic skills, and you'll find learning them more palatable if you understand how they can benefit you. Practical exercises are more motivating than isolated areas of separate fields. Living systems have many relationships and applications.

What is natural is what you discover naturally, as a result of curiosity and open exploration. The wider your view, the more things you connect, and the more relevant each becomes. The understanding of whole systems is essential now that the world has become connected. This is what inspires people, and it's the opposite of subject-oriented curricula.

> *"My writing professor, Warren Hecht, was also my student advisor, and I looked at him and I said, 'Should I go on to get a Master's now?' He said, 'No. If you want to be a writer, then you go out and do things. You live your life and you see what's out there. If you want to you can come back later and get your Masters, but first you need to have something to write about! Go out there and do something!' Okay, that was good advice, so I did that."*
> — **Matt Forbeck**, writer, from *The Learning Project*

There is a difference between doing and knowing. When you learn algebra you do it, but you're not learning math; you're being taught to paint by numbers. Math is not a catalog of equations, it is a way of thinking based on measures, consequences, and transformations. It's what math tells you that's interesting, not how you do it.

When you're taught to read you learn to read what you're taught. Knowledge is not in the words, it's in the thoughts. Today, most people read at below 8th grade level so that it's difficult for them to read and understand complex information. More than a quarter of the population is functionally illiterate, meaning their reading skills are inadequate for their needs.

> *"The outside world is moving, always moving—maybe not forward exactly, but in all directions. We have to keep up in our heads—and I have to keep up in my head—so I started making my own worlds. I had to record them. That's what writing is for me: recording the worlds in here, in my head."*
> — **Caitlin McKenna**, student, from *The Learning Project*

Do you recall grammar lessons? Do you recall the details? Well, no one else remembers the details, either. And you didn't just forget the details, you've forgotten everything. You didn't learn grammar in grammar school, you learned it when you started to express yourself in writing, and read others who were expressing themselves.

When I began to learn to write—which I did on my own initiative before graduating from college—it seemed like I had never been taught about writing before. I'd been going to school for sixteen years and I didn't know how to write, in spite of doing quite a bit of writing in college. Most people never learn to write.

> *"Why did I have to learn it? Because I wanted to accomplish certain goals. How did I learn it? Basically by running for office..."*
> — **Phyllis Schlafly,** JD, politician, orator, and social activist, from *The Learning Project*

52. The most important things are not taught.

You cannot rely on schooling to teach you what you'll need to know. You can't rely on college to do it, either. If you're lucky, you'll encounter a teacher who knows you well enough and teaches well enough to insist on your highest potential. Most teachers don't have this skill, and most students aren't looking for it. If you want to reach your full potential, it's really up to you.

"When anything gets institutionalized, the life goes out of it."
— **Laurie Anderson**, musician (Eby, 2010)

To understand why things are the way they are you must ask much larger questions than what's assumed or taught in school. When you ask what others don't ask, meaningful questions come to the fore. When you start to assemble new conclusions the purpose of your original questions becomes evident.

53. Don't lie to yourself.

This is misstated: we all lie to ourselves and we do it all the time. There is no single self within us to tell a single truth; we are made of many selves. There is no one voice that speaks a single truth for all of our selves.

The question, then, is whether or not we know our lies, and, quite often, we don't. It's not for lack of trying, it's because we try so hard. We want to know what's true and right for us, so we mutter our resolutions, click our heels, shut our eyes, and hold our breath hoping truth will prevail, and, when it does, we hope we'll see it.

111

Unfortunately, for most of us, truth is not what we want it to be. In fact, truth is not a thing that exists "out there," it emerges from situations and changes with them. Lying to yourself is insisting on one truth in spite of what you know is your limited foresight and ability. The truth will be what you live, not what you claim. Accept many truths and understand the arguments for each.

> *"Quit lying to people, you know? Accept responsibility for your own actions. And that's where knowledge is so much more important than schooling. These are things that aren't offered in education, it's something that you have to seek yourself."*
> — **Simon Daniel James**, filmmaker, from *The Learning Project*

54. When commitment fails, truth fails.

People have a greater or lesser grasp of reality and, because of this, they come with a greater or lesser commitment to truth. We think of truth as a matter of fact, but, in life, truth is a matter of action. And while fact may be a matter of yes or no, action is a matter of degree. As a person's commitment to action begins to fade, so does their connection to their truth.

Most of what passes for truth has the structure of mutual consent based on rank, authority, expectation, obligation, and need. For most people, these elements are the basis of truth and the limit of their commitment. The deepest truth lies in the certainty of oneself and there lies the deepest commitment. This is emotional; truth is emotional. Strive for this and try to explain it to others.

"The truth of an idea is not a stagnant property inherent in it. Truth happens to an idea. It becomes true, is made true by events. Its verity is in fact an event, a process, the process namely of its verifying itself, its verification. Its validity is the process of its validation."
— **William James**, philosopher and psychologist, from *The Meaning of Truth* (James 2019)

55. Everything is a network; look at the connections.

Look for the networks. Look for the details that connect people, places, actions, and ideas. You'll find that there is far less independence of thought and action than everyone would like to believe. The choices you are given are not free, and your responses are not taken to authentically reflect who you are. The network not only determines what's offered to you, it determines how your actions are understood.

Everything has a context and everyone operates within some context. Because we're so unaware of the full extent of the context we live in, most people are unaware of how their environment determines who they are, what they think, and when they act. The networks become our language and we see ourselves in them. But your real self? That's another matter.

We're born with no awareness of our past and take sole credit for who we become. Everything we see comes from around us, and everything we feel comes from... who knows where! As semi-individuals we each have a special resonance and unique effect. If it were not for the networks we share, we would have no effect on each other, and no means to affect ourselves.

If you grab an insect and shout in its face, "Wake up!" It won't do any good. But with a human being, you stand a chance. If they don't hit you, they might listen to you. And if you make them feel safe enough, they'll may try to understand you.

Benefits

56. Thinking big allows for more possibilities.

What you might do is limited by what you think you can do. For many of us, that limit is imposed on us by our having allowed other people to define us. Acquiring knowledge takes time, but feeling able, allowed, or worth the effort does not take time. Before anything can be accomplished you must define yourself as someone who can do this. What you think you might accomplish is limited only by what you think of yourself. Think of yourself as full of possibility; think of yourself as big.

There is always some boundary, the boundaries of what's reasonable, possible, attractive, familiar, or something else you'd look for in a good project. There is always some boundary defining your thought. Even ideas that are larger, more general, more important, and associated with more things are still limited by your imagination.

The boundary of your thinking is yours to set. Thinking big doesn't mean learning is easier or progress is assured. It doesn't mean you'll succeed. It only means you're seeing the relevance of your work.

"You may often be alone, but you're never, ever, ever lonely until you allow yourself to be lonely because everything's alive. Our ancestors walked under the same sky that we are looking up at... and we're going to live, and we're going to die, all staring at the same sky, under the glow of the same sun, sleeping under the same moon and stars. This earth

that we're walking on has been walked on by so many animals, and so many people, and so many spirits blowing through the wind, and that is so special!"
— **Jaz Lin**, traveler from *The Learning Project*

57. There is always resistance to change.

The most annoying resistance comes from other people. People who create dissonance with how you're thinking, who obstruct, contradict, or try to redirect you. Whether or not they're right, they're infuriating. Recognize that it comes with the territory.

If you aren't annoying a certain number of people, then you aren't trying hard enough. It's a natural part of blazing your trail. You don't get a choice, but you do get to decide how to deal with it. Learn how to safely remove yourself from unsafe people. Be prepared for it.

It's easy to see the obstacles in front of you, especially in others, or in those conflicts of which you are a part. These seem important, even critical, but they are not. The real obstacles are your inclinations to accept these conflicts and to inflate their importance. Your feelings of what you're worth or what you deserve, which you project onto the judgments of others, are greater obstacles.

You give your challenges meaning. You project these important issues onto people and situations outside yourself because, when you do this, you can separate yourself and reduce the problem to its components. You can better see, manage, and define problems that exist outside yourself. External problems are persistent and repeatable, giving you the illusion that they're real and essential.

This is can be a weakness. Projecting can help you see in black and white terms, but the source of your problems and the true nature of your obstacles is not black and white, not easily named or assigned, and not outside of yourself. The source of your problems lies in how you define them or, in many cases, how others have defined them for you.

You are playing a game whose rules were invented by the system you're a part of, for the benefit of those who designed it. Playing by the rules, while it is the safest route with the least resistance, is not your game to win. The rules are part of a system whose winners win because they are accorded special rights to play. Understand what's expected of you, your resources, and what you may win before you invest in playing the game. There is truth to the warning against selling your soul.

58. If you don't have control, someone else does.

If you don't make the rules that affect you, then you're either playing according to someone else's rules, playing in conflict with someone else's rules, or not playing at all. Most people with control wield it with limited insight, make poor judgments, and don't take much responsibility.

It would behoove you to gain authority over your affairs by any means. Consider this an act of self-defense, finding your niche, or protecting your resources. You need autonomy if you're going to own the returns that accrue from your efforts. Without autonomy, your direction and the products of your labor will be diverted to someone else.

The benefit of gaining control is the power to set your own goals and values. There is no shortage of people interested in setting goals and values for you. Their arguments may be convincing and we're led to think we should follow the advice of those with more power, connections, and experience. Lacking these assets for yourself is only to be expected, and every learner should recognize that they have the right to try to create power for him or herself.

It's not that you're entitled to succeed according to the criteria of others, or that you will. It's rather that you only grow through the process of trying. Without self-ownership, you cannot be or feel yourself to be successful.

59. Explore standards.

There are many standards and all are relative to specific situations and personalities. Everyone who presents a standard has made an investment in it and, to varying degrees, will defend it. These standards will not fit you unless you accept the values on which they're based. And if you do accept their values, then you'll find yourself invested, and further directed to follow their requirements.

Standards determine goals and values. They are embedded in situations and personalities and they are often hidden or obscure. You can see this more clearly when you are able to see the overlapping layers in anyone's personality, or the overlapping layers of privilege in an institution.

Comparisons are not tests. If you allow your growth to be guided by where you score the highest, then you will find you have been turned into a resource. Objectivity is a fallacy; there is always a personality behind every judgement.

My father was an insecure overachiever, and so am I. I have learned— and can now feel—that putting other people down can fortify one's ego. It's a game of diminishing returns as your gain is never as large as what you take from others. In almost all cases where I was graded, I could feel an element of ego that was partly my own and partly that of the person or people doing the grading. Humanity is lost, and with it goes human opportunity. Notice the difference between grading and empowering.

Explore standards and compare yourself to them. Understand why people accept them. Our evolving, complex society is a game of musical chairs in which everyone aspires to "level-up" to compete for better and more scarce rewards.

No one can be motivated, and nothing can be sold unless a system of values, risks, and rewards is first established. It is a typical ruse to feel morally compelled and personally rewarded by another's value system. This is the "carrot and stick" of grades, role models, and promised opportunities.

60. Learning is an exploration of feelings.

Teaching is mostly about how you should feel and think. The logic behind these judgment systems is rarely understood or investigated. Do you not think it odd that no one examines the validity of system by which students are judged? Fairness is a primary issue in the workplace but never discussed in schools.

You're discouraged from examining alternatives by being discouraged from wanting to examine alternatives. The unquestionable nature of authority and conformity is not argued according to fact, it's based on feeling.

The conclusions you're expected to reach, and what you should share with others, is not so much a thought or a rule, but a feeling. At their root, choices are grounded in feeling, not reason. We're taught never to question what's sacrosanct.

You might say that it would take too much time, and it would hinder our ability to perform or react if we stopped to consider every decision we made or rule we followed. And while this is true to some extent, notice that there always seems to be some purportedly clear reason behind the choice you're asked to accept. People believe what those around them believe, especially if it is said repeatedly.

If something feels wrong, we must address it. The reason big lies can be easier to foist on people than small lies is that big lies come with big promises, high pressure, and dire consequences. In that situation panic and shock outweigh reason. The most authentic decisions you will make are those you make with care and full responsibility. How many of your decisions have those properties?

People explore the reasons behind their choices in a search for something that feels right; to connect facts with beliefs. An emotional person will explain their actions as being based on their feelings, and an intellectual person will be guided by facts but, ultimately, actions rest on the feelings that define values. As becomes obvious when you examine today's major social issues—religions, border disputes, environmental effects, social behaviors—these rest on values, not facts.

The "material" of education is values. The subjects taught in schools, colleges, professions, and institutions make more sense from this point of view. What's taught is the evidence that supports the values: family values, self-value, appearance, competition as well as professional, national, cultural, and personal identity. These are the things we're left with at the conclusion of our schooling, and which stay with us—not the facts.

Needs

You are born with certain needs, others are taught in infancy, and others develop over the course of your life. Certain needs are built into you, or emerge in you through your ancestry, as inclinations and predispositions.

It was once thought that genetics determined skills that were innate, as well as physical aptitudes such as your intelligence and physical stature. It's now understood that genetics determine latent skills and aptitudes that remain unexpressed until they're exercised. What is expressed more reflects your environment than your genetics.

The need for skills in your environment will alter your genetics in as little as two generations. For example, grandchildren of grandparents who have survived deprivation are more robust and better able to survive deprivation themselves. The constant shifting of emerging skills and aptitudes means you don't know what you're capable of. As you struggle to become more capable now, your descendants may benefit from your efforts, later.

Who you are is not entirely clear as you will change according to your tasks. The measure of your success may not even emerge in your lifetime! What you need, then, is a combination of expectations of what you've inherited over generations and projections of what will be needed over generations. In effect, you are not just who you are in your own life, but a being extended over time, running a relay race through the generations. How do you know what you need, what you're capable of, and what to develop for future generations?

In the interests of simplicity, we'd like to say we can simply look after our own needs, for our own lives, but that doesn't work. We can't be sure of what we're capable of since new efforts may yield new results. Unlike how we're taught, progress isn't linear: breakthroughs happen all the time. That is the nature of complex systems, of which we are one. Also, in terms of finding personal meaning, we are selling ourselves short if we measure ourselves only by the standards imposed on us.

61. Your greatest insights into yourself reside in your feelings.

Emotions are your broadest form of intelligence. Recognize that the pressures you feel in the situations and people you encounter represent conflicts and opportunities over many time scales. There are no certain arguments regarding what you should or should not do as all involve different definitions of scope and measure. Protect your emotional integrity. Find the deepest sense of being grounded and in control of your feelings.

In terms of our evolution, our limbic system controlled our actions, which it did through our emotions. Much later, our brains developed the ability to reason. This began with the emergence of an individual self, which is expanding to a collective self. We're still developing this. We don't emotionally grasp these larger identities—political, cultural, ecological, and environmental—so we have to think about them, and therein lies our weakness.

We have to learn how to think about our larger identities, and we don't all learn, or learn the same, or at the same rate, and we don't all come to the same conclusions. Our conclusions, such as they are, are fed from our outer brain to our inner brain, from the cortex to the limbic system, from our intellect to our emotions. It's a feedback system: emotions trigger our thoughts, which form conclusions that are fed back to our emotional system.

Teaching, reasoning, and experience can input anything at the top level, which is the intellectual level. What comes out at the bottom level, which is the emotional level, will reflect the quality of these inputs. Getting a grip on your emotions is your key to judging the quality of your conclusions.

You can't hope to vet and verify all the information that's fed into you, especially now that information systems have flooded our world with data. But you can compare the emotional indication of social actions with the personal values you trust. This depends, of course, on having trustworthy personal values. The point is, feelings trump data.

There is a tendency to contain and specialize people. There is a contest between serving the community versus developing individual opportunities. The more closely you are aligned with institutions, the more institutions will make these decisions for you.

62. You find abilities where you give yourself permission to look.

You find your ability in those areas where you give yourself time and permission to look. Don't expect to be recognized for insights or abilities you've never exercised. And don't expect the insights and abilities that you're just starting to exercise to display the skills they will develop with exercise. Let yourself develop as you feel the need to develop, in accordance with the opportunities you create, not the opportunities you're given.

If you've never really thought procedurally then you won't know how proficient you are at math or engineering. Similarly with poetry, art, activism, or archeology. You are free to redefine or reinvent any field, and you do not need to be hired to do it. Whether anyone will listen to you is another matter.

You may naturally object and bring forward arguments of what's affordable, available, or otherwise rewarding. You cannot yet conceive of the benefits that await you. Grant yourself the most opportunity. Open yourself to whatever appears.

> *"I took advantage of the opportunities that came my way, but they came my way because of who I am and what I was doing. I didn't realize there was much value to these things; it's really hard to quantify. In the end, people seem to find inspiration in the fact that through determination and focus I have been able to do things that other people haven't done."*
> — **Lynn Hill**, extreme rock climber, from *The Learning Project*

63. Find novelty.

Play is essential. It is the process of discovery and brainstorming. Just as electricity turns atoms into molecules, play turns cells into minds. All forms of discovery are play. Good inventors play, and great inventors play all the time.

Consider how little play our schools allow. It lacks the spark of mind and, consequently, its products are mindless. While students may be productive, they are not adaptive unless they have room for invention. Discard the routine; insist on invention everywhere.

I am a novelty addict because I'm curious, and because novelty triggers meaningful and curious reactions in me. Writing this book, for example, triggered strange dreams conflating characters from my past, whom I barely knew, with projections of futures I'm hardly able to understand.

Truly strange people saying truly strange things, stranger than anything I could make up.

Writing this book is a transformative experience because what I'm doing is becoming me. It wasn't always this way. It has only developed in this direction as I have spent more time pursuing what I'm called to do. This applies to other people, too

> *"Play! Invent the world! Invent reality!"*
> — **Vladimir Nabokov**, writer and poet

64. Take charge.

You have to make it happen. Nothing is given to you, and if it were, it wouldn't be worth it. Your change is in your hands.

You may think this book is a vehicle to another state of mind, a ticket to another landscape. We have indeed taken off and you are comfortably seated, but now I offer you a parachute. We are flying over the territory that is your destination, but we are not landing there; we are heading back to port. I open the door and there is nothing outside. Put your parachute on and jump. What's the worst that could happen?

When my clients are ready to invest in a new way of thinking about their lives, their view of themselves changes and their world changes. Prior to this, they are stuck in the container of their understanding, a container that lacks an exit.

This reflects a general attribute. Most of those seeking outside assistance are looking for something they cannot find. One would expect other people—those who can see a path—to pursue these without assistance. This suggests I play an essential role which I believe is false. These people have sought me out because I am the tool that fits their needs. They know there is a path, they just can't reach it.

I do not transform people, rather, I beat on the lock that binds them. Neither the teacher nor the therapist is essential; you can beat on the lock yourself. I am not the surgeon, you are—I'm just handing you the tools. People ready to sustain change take responsibility for it. This is a prerequisite for learning, too.

65. Do what's different.

Do what you're bad at. Handicap yourself in what you're good at. Exercise the usual cautions. Part of the exercise is seeing those things in front of you that you've overlooked. Pursue interests you've never explored or, just as profitably, engage in things that cause you pain and aggravation, especially when these pains and aggravations reflect your judgments.

> *"The more pain I train myself to stand, the more I learn. You are afraid of pain now, Unk, but you won't learn anything if you don't invite the pain. And the more you learn, the gladder you will be to stand the pain."*
> — **Kurt Vonnegut**, from *The Sirens of Titan*

Rather than avoid trouble, call forward conflicts you feel you can resolve, and then try to resolve them. This is a wonderful exercise. Explore conflicts and see what control you have over them. As long as you exercise basic standards of honesty and self-respect you won't hurt yourself, and you will uncover new understandings.

A typical and easy example, available to all of us, is the questioning of social attitudes and the confrontation of sacred cows. Most politically correct attitudes are built on flimsy reasoning or none at all, and most people's adherence to them or reaction to their violation is reflexive.

You will find yourself disrespected or disapproved of for violating unspoken standards. Even here you have an exercise in presentation because much of the information about your intentions is inferred from cues you present unawares. The reaction of others becomes a mirror for deeper insight not available through other means.

Start a conversation with someone you normally wouldn't converse with. A dollar will easily purchase a conversation with a panhandler on the street. A sincere interest in the wares being sold or service rendered by a shop owner easily opens a conversation. Most people are dying to talk. Be ready for an earful!

I have friends with an amazing ability at starting conversations with anyone. It's not a skill I generally exercise, but when I do, I am rewarded. One needs a certain "street smarts" that comes with practice.

> *"I am always doing that which I cannot do, in order that I may learn how to do it."*
> — **Pablo Picasso**, artist

66. Engage with people who do things that interest you.

Advertise yourself. As crass as that might seem, do it. Make yourself easily available by simply standing up to speak for yourself, or speaking for something you're interested in. Many people do this in the safe circumstances of their church, friends, or family, but—as you can appreciate—cycles of expectation develop that restrict expression and discovery. Cultivate your skill in attracting and engaging with the kinds of people you'd like to have around you.

The focus of this chapter is the context in which you learn. This mixes elements of other discussions, and this should be appreciated. See everything you do as an opportunity to do something more or to integrate more of what you do.

What you need, what other people need, and how you define your role are all open to interpretation. In interpreting these things, you'll naturally remain within your preconceptions, and those are what you want to move beyond. Endeavor to see your limits and go beyond them.

Skills

The benefit of learning to use various materials lies in gaining a clearer vision of what you can accomplish. What is important is how you combine your skills and what you might accomplish with them. This presumes you understand your skills and needs which, generally, you won't. Until you do, a personally meaningful path through anything will be difficult to find. That's why we spend most of our lives looking for it.

It's difficult to know what special ability you have because, by the definition of being special, your skill won't fit a standard. It seems that many of the people with unique gifts don't appreciate their gifts. And if a person with special gifts cannot appreciate themselves, it's most likely that others won't, either. This is the Catch-22 of needing to fit in when you don't.

67. Have a personal standard.

Have personal standards that you believe in. Your standards are entirely yours; you define them for yourself, and it's up to you to tell people about them. Base them directly on feelings; avoid reasons or opinions. Your standards should be open to discussion but not dispute.

Have some idea of how to state what you believe in. Being able to state your beliefs helps you to know them, it provides guidance for others to know you, and it helps others know their own.

Your standards are requirements of basic integrity that you follow and you insist others follow. You should enforce them as if they were checkboxes: if people don't check the box, don't share your space with them.

Every organization has standards of behavior that are stated, standards of performance that are suggested, and standards of belief that are assumed. No matter what your level in the organization, you'll be asked to accept and be expected to enforce these standards. This is true with people, too, but people's standards are rarely made explicit.

Standards allow civil discourse, smooth function, and control. They are the checkboxes that ask for your approval before allowing you entry to a subscription, website, or application. You won't know what they mean because you won't read them—and even if you did, you wouldn't know because they're coded in legalese—but you expect them to be compatible with your values.

People who live by their own standards are grounded people. They will be emotionally stable but their material conditions could be anything. Don't judge people by their looks. Independent-valued people are not quickly rewarded.

Mavericks, iconoclasts, and idealists are always looking for their tribe because they don't have one. The successful ones I know are people who have built a safe place for themselves and sold something—in one sense or another—to the larger community. The path of innovation and entrepreneurship has a relatively low success rate. It takes more work to be rewarded for being different than to be rewarded for being the same.

68. Avoid compromise.

A compromise is shared dissatisfaction. Compromise is the goal of people who are only empowered to lower their expectations. A compromise affirms the lack of shared standards and the lack of common, beneficial solutions. Compromise today; resentment tomorrow.

Successful negotiations are not based on compromise, but on an understanding of the disagreement and a vision of collaboration. Both parties must agree conflict is a dead end, abandon the idea that the winner takes all, and accept the idea that something valuable is created through collaboration. Compromise divides the spoils; collaboration creates something new.

If one party sees the potential in collaborating and the other does not, then no agreement is better than some agreement because time will favor the better plan. Every new idea can be seen as a struggle between conflicting points of view, even if the conflict is inside you. Therein lies the benefit of patience and tenacity.

69. Understand integrity.

As a noun, integrity means the stability of the structure, the process, or the situation. As a verb, it is the process of building stability, reliability, and strength. Integrity in action consists of integrity to yourself, to those around you, and to the context in which you're embedded.

Having integrity requires knowing who you are. Because this is a dynamic process and self-knowledge is never complete, self-integrity is always deforming and reforming as the system grows and changes. Yet, even as our standards shift, there is still honesty, responsibility, and concern. Know who you are at your core in order to respect yourself.

Acting with integrity to those around us requires that we learn how we're understood. This is made difficult by the multiple personalities and multiplicity of the standards of others and within each of us. To continue to be seen as honest, we must understand how others see us, which they advertise in ways we often don't recognize.

By responding to others who model integrity, we create integrity in our network, which is why you should make every effort to surround yourself with people of integrity. Integrity makes collaboration possible. By holding to your vision, you create your consensual reality.

Accommodating those who lack integrity—no matter how much you may love them—harms them and degrades yourself. Like a virus, a lack of integrity breeds illness in a relationship. Distrust spreads like a fever. When integrity is lost, betrayal is the outcome.

70. Create truth.

> *"Mine eyes have seen the glory of the coming of the Lord;*
> *He is trampling out the vintage where the grapes of wrath are stored;*
> *He hath loosed the fateful lightning of His terrible swift sword:*
> *His truth is marching on."*
> —**Julia Ward Howe**, first verse of *The Battle Hymn of the Republic*

The truth is not marching on. The integrity of your circumstances is always decaying because situations and intentions are never entirely clear. Growing disorder in unattended systems is a law of physics so, to maintain balance, you must always be shoring up integrity. You may not feel you are dishonest, but what you mean and what others think shifts with circumstances. Everyone must be aware of the need to clarify truth and contribute to continually clarifying and reaffirming their feelings and intentions.

You will find questions of your action in the eyes of others, or your own eyes. It's not about truth or blame, it's simply the inevitable disorder of a changing world, and you want a changing world because change is the source of creativity. Failure is not only inevitable, it's necessary, but it need not be damaging.

Become adept at taking responsibility. Projects are like rafts descending the rapids: if you wait for directions, it's too late. Be aware and be proactive. Harness the power of negative thinking: what you did a moment ago may be the opposite of what's needed now. It's not a question of apology but revision in changing situations.

71. Pay attention to the asymmetries of your body.

Your body is an antenna that receives and transmits. There are many communications that we're not aware of: effects that grow on us or in us, the feelings of which we're unaware but which accumulate in our tissues. An antenna's transmission is a result of the information flowing through it and of its shape. As our shape changes over time, so our messages get distorted.

Your shape both broadcasts your underlying intentions and is formed by what you receive. Like a cathode over time, your body is worn down by the information it receives—which you cannot perceive at any moment, but which you can discern if you examine your body.

Examine yourself carefully. How does your body reflect your feeling? How do changes in your posture affect your feeling? How does your movement affect your communication? In a private place reform your posture, the position of your limbs, and the set of the features of your face. How would you look if you expressed the way you really feel? Look at your postures and expressions and make them extreme just to see what it feels like. What messages do they convey?

Most people develop asymmetries over time, usually in adulthood. You may be aware of old injuries, or they may have become so habitual that you're no longer aware of them. Many people develop asymmetrical faces such that their left side carries an expression different from their right. Look at yourself in the mirror, covering one side of your face and then the other. These asymmetries are not a coincidence. See if there are differences when you're engaged, curious, happy, angry, or sad.

People develop dominant sides: right handed, left footed, right eyed, and so forth. From these develop asymmetric abilities. The left side of your body is controlled by the more holistic and associative right side of your brain, while the right side of your body responds to the more definitive and reductive left side of your brain. This laterality is true for over 90% of us, but not for everyone.

The next time you think that the world is not as you like, consider how much of this might be due to asymmetries in your perception, asymmetries that you might discern and work to correct in your body.

72. Develop situational awareness.

Situational awareness is knowing what's going on around you, and it largely refers to what's physically around you at the moment. It is a combination of central and peripheral focus, though "peripheral focus" is somewhat a contradiction in terms.

Situational awareness is what you need when you're managing one task while, at the same time, you are vulnerable to outside events. These outside events are not evident, ongoing, or even occurring at the moment, but they might enter unexpectedly and quickly become important.

It's more than simply being broadly aware, it involves prioritizing things that are not immediately relevant. It involves briefly incorporating, or expanding, your focus to include a greater number of factors with the explicit intent of immediately replacing these factors with others. It is a temporary state of heightened acuity that cannot be sustained for long. It comes with practice.

Situational awareness is important in situations where the important events of the moment have their origins in seemingly unimportant events of the previous moments, or of moments that will soon arrive. This could be something that was proceeding normally seconds before but is about to appear on a collision course. Or something that was fine under previous conditions, but conditions have changed.

You need situational awareness when landing an airplane, running an obstacle course, or maneuvering in a risky situation. You need situational awareness when crossing the street, or opening your car door.

Awareness may be a particular ability of mine. It's hard to tell. We have few objective measures of awareness. If I am more aware of my surroundings than other people, it would be because I have explored more environments that required greater skills.

Flying demands a kind of 360-degree awareness that being on the ground does not. Scuba diving challenges ones awareness because one's senses are so limited. Mountaineering, like all wilderness exploration, requires looking forward in time and imagining the consequences of what you cannot see. Physical and psychological extremes open one's awareness. Training brainwaves clearly shows that much of one's awareness is subliminal. One can expand and refine this awareness through various forms of brainwave training.

Awareness is something to which our culture pays little attention and gives little reward. It's not on the syllabus and it's not on the test. A person's level of awareness can be seen by the depth of their insight, but this is something Western culture does not teach.

I believe this reflects the degree to which industry, technology, and our culture has made us indolent and indifferent, as well as unhealthy and small-minded. Time and again we encounter native cultures that have skills, insights, and understanding far beyond our own, yet we discount them. More than that, we destroy them.

73. Develop strategic awareness.

If situational awareness refers to awareness of events with potential impact at this moment, then strategic awareness refers to an awareness of related events that unfold in different time frames and contexts. Events in the present affect—or are related to other events that affect—specific events in the future.

Another way to describe this would be "broad temporal awareness," or, you might say, "being organized," but it is more than just arranging things in order. It might refer to planning for the future, or being a detective in understanding the past.

You need strategic awareness to organize an event, and the larger the event, the more strategically aware you need to be. This event could be a birthday party, a vacation, or a business plan. It will involve weighing costs and benefits, risks and rewards, and there will be uncertainty. You might be planning your day or planning your life.

My friend Jean organizes the New York Village Halloween Parade. Each year, she coordinates tens of new initiatives, hundreds of organizations, thousands of volunteers, tens of thousands of dollars, and millions of people. There are issues of profits, financial obligations, contracts, transportation, expectations, personal and public safety, and the delegation of responsibility, all of which need to be arranged, coordinated, effected, monitored, evaluated, and reported. All this for an event whose purpose is humor, exuberance, creativity, aberrance, and chaos.

Strategic awareness was required for the planning of our mountaineering expeditions to places no one had ever been, and of which we were generally unfamiliar. These trips had high risks, no access to resources, would put us out of all contact for weeks at a time, and there was no back-up.

All of that needed to be put into place just to support the approach to a potentially impassable route. In spite of all of our planning, training, and preparation, we still made massive mistakes, such as underestimating the size of the mountain! It was the epitome of eating your own cooking.

While these examples may seem unusual—and about as attractive as waging a foreign war— they are similar to the project of how we live our lives. If you don't see that, then you are not seeing all the forces and opportunities around you, which may be out of your field of vision. While you might like to live a peaceful life and avoid a foreign campaign, you don't have a choice: the campaign of your life will unfold, and you will either be the master of it or not. And if you are not, then someone else will be. Be strategically aware.

74. You're aware of what you're engaged in.

Awareness is proportional to engagement. If you're engaged in conversation, you're aware of the details of it. If you don't speak the language and make no attempt to, then you'll never make progress in understanding what's said. If you never look at the clock but pace yourself according to the needs of your body or the light in the sky, then you'll have a completely different experience of time passing.

Selecting what you're aware of, and being in control of what you're aware of, are fundamental to your experience and sense of self. People who have lost control over how, where, and when to focus their attention have lost control of their lives.

Allowing children to have control over their own environment enables them to grow their minds. Yet at any age, insisting on your own control enables you to perceive more broadly, understand more deeply, and react more effectively. Align your awareness with your engagement.

5 – Paths

Starting Out

75. Truth, trust, and honesty are all different.

Truth is something that is always the case, and is either agreed upon or allowed by all who are truthful. I know of no truths. The closer you get to truth—such as in physics or theories of mind—the farther you get from human relevance and direct understanding.

Absolute truth is not applicable. It's relative truth that's important and ubiquitous. Relative truths are the things in real circumstances that lead to results. Those of us who live in the same universe should be able to agree on relative truths, but not all of us do.

Trustworthiness is related to honesty and is fluid. It's fluid because every agreement has many perspectives, but only a limited amount of time in which to appreciate them. Add to this vagaries of language, uncertainty of emotion, feelings of vulnerability, and conflicting facts, and you're left with whatever faith you have in another person's intention.

To be honest is to fully reveal your intention and to do your best to achieve it. Honesty—the most relative and least confirmable of these traits—is most important in relationships. Truth can be beyond reach and trust can be subject to interpretation, but honesty is a personal imperative. Its violation lapses into betrayal—considered the most degraded of all moral failures.

Since most adults don't have a deep or formative relationship with children—that is not to say there are not a few great role models, but we need more—it is impossible for them to convey a clear and guiding truth on important matters of personal development.

In many cases, the answers to the questions that young people ask could only have been provided by years of positive role modeling and, when the question is finally asked, the necessary framework of rapport and understanding is not there.

It's not the intention of adults to be untrustworthy, it's just that they have not learned how to be honest, and our society has not given them that chance.

John Dewey was the leading educator of the 20th century and he was quite clear that the intention of the state is to remove children from the influence of their parochial, small-minded parents. His intentions were not evil; he was trying to counter racism, prejudice, and xenophobia in an increasingly dynamic, interconnected, and multi-cultural world. This prescription has succeeded according to plan, but that plan has many downsides, perhaps the greatest of which is that your individuality and your ancestry is sacrificed. Times change.

Trading

76. Accept a stalemate.

In *Never Split the Difference: Negotiating As If Your Life Depended On It*, top FBI hostage negotiator Chris Voss (2016) advises against compromise. In a compromise, the situation remains adversarial. Where a compromise is cobbling together unreconcilable needs, a stalemate is agreeing to look further.

Clearly, a better agreement later is better than a worse agreement now.

Reframe a conflict as two parties working together to extract what's best for both from the resources available. A stalemate gives everyone more time, and with more time more options emerge, giving the contesting parties other chances of understanding each other.

Time may be of the essence, but a lasting solution is worth waiting for. If one party cannot appreciate the benefit that comes from a more meaningful agreement, then perhaps they are not really interested in one. If that's the case, their haste should be part of the bargain, and they should pay for it. The best agreements are the deepest agreements.

77. Aim for emotionally positive opportunities.

Intellectually, we think truth is based on facts, but no one believes what doesn't feel right. You might say you do, but when push comes to shove, you'll follow your feelings. If you're going to live your truth, then your truth had better feel right!

Intellectual ideas are narrow, relative, and lifeless. There are an infinity of logical, reasoned, and intellectual truths about any situation. Any conclusion can be intellectually justified; any truth can be argued and supported. This is essentially the price you pay for the opportunity of freedom and free will.

Truth is an emotional thing. People who cannot fully feel, or who arc shut off from their emotions, live in a world of falsehoods. They cannot express or appreciate the truth and, because of this, they cannot be trusted. Trust resides in emotions.

Aiming for emotionally positive opportunities is a form of seeking truth. Here you'll find truth's family of emotions: trust, dependability, authenticity, and love. Few opportunities are purely positive, and you're usually offered lesser truths clothed in reasons and compromises. One's life course is a series of compromises, but compromising truth—while it may pay money—yields few spiritual assets.

> *"The worst thing you do when you think is lie—you can make up reasons that are not true for the things that you did, and what you're trying to do as a creative person is surprise yourself—find out who you really are, and try not to lie, try to tell the truth all the time."*
> — **Ray Bradbury**, author

We're taught that by applying logic and reason things become increasingly clear, and this may be true for simple things. But if you're making it up as you go along, then the process of following incorrect reasoning will end in conflict. The best reasoning can do for you is lead you to a contradiction, which is a relief, because then you know you must invent something.

78. Fail often, quickly, and in small ways.

When you don't know what will work, aim to find out what won't work. Develop skills with small projects. This is the realm of model building, games, simulation, brainstorming, and crackpot ideas. Sketch, plan, write, stand up and speak. This is experimentation. If you have not failed or made a fool of yourself, then you are not trying hard enough.

> *"Experimenters search most diligently, and with the greatest effort, in exactly those places where it seems most likely that we can prove our theories wrong. In other*

words, we are trying to prove ourselves wrong as quickly as possible, because only in that way can we find progress."
— **Richard P. Feynman,** PhD, physicist, (Feynman, 1965, p. 158)

Your fears will not get smaller as you accomplish more, they will get bigger because you'll have more to lose. If you opt for safety, then your innovation will suffer. Be fearless to the limits of what's safe. The best failures define the right decisions. This works as much in the realm of relationships as it does in the material world. Welcome the heartbreak; don't discard the results.

Almost everyone has an opinion. Some are right, some are wrong, some are well-meaning, and some are not. Most are a tangled combination, some of whose aspects will be of value to you. To untangle them, get involved and test them for their agreement, resistance, and benefit.

Your opinions are important, and your most important opinions are about yourself. These are also some of the most tangled. Just because they're yours does not mean you should trust them or even believe they are well meaning. We all have self-destructive, self-opinions that are significant barriers to positive change.

79. It's worth losing the battle if that's what it takes to win the war.

You have the idea that to go from A to C you have to pass through B. It is your belief that getting to B is necessary. But maybe it's not. And if it's not, then why fight for B at all? What if B is a sticking point in an argument, but it's irrelevant to the outcome? Will an apology or a concession get you an agreement, and should you really care about the value of what you're giving up? After all, which is more important, reaching your goal or establishing that you were correct?

In the January 2014 issue of *O, The Oprah Magazine*, Dr. Phil repeats the oft-quoted dictum of marital conflict resolution: "Do you want to be right or happy?" Before I became a therapist, I used to think this was an insightful question. Now, I think it's superficial and misguided.

Putting being right in conflict with virtue is a tendentious way of implying your need for being correct is in conflict with your goal of being emotionally balanced. This could apply to anything, and it could go either way: being right might or might not be necessary. It also implies that by accepting being wrong you will be happy, which is far from assured.

Aim toward being right and being happy, not right or happy. If you can't be both, then it's work that's needed, not surrender.

An equally useful bit of relationship advice, which also applies to any dispute, says that if the relationship is unsound, it's not going to work. In that case, it doesn't matter whether you're right or not, you shouldn't be there. This advice falls along the lines of, "Wake up and smell the coffee," or similar admonishments to cut your losses.

80. Practice thinking about several things at once.

Thought is richer than language and one of the dangers of talking too much is limiting your thoughts to words. Feeling and sensations are inherently nonverbal, and thinking is nonlinear—to which your dreams can attest. To subscribe to the prejudice that thinking should follow a narrow path is to reduce yourself to an adding machine.

You can think of several things at once. You cannot express them in one voice, but you can create different voices in yourself to carry different opinions. These voices are the key to maintaining a multi-tiered conversation in your head. They are the key to a deeper understanding, which requires that you hold conflicts in your mind and see things from both sides. It is the definition of a simple-minded person that they cannot hold conflict in their mind. The person who should always get your vote is the one who carries forward the largest number of different opinions.

Thinking multiple things helps you to match a world which does not have a single thread and does not follow a single line of cause and effect. For the most part, the world does not even follow any system of reason that we know. We're constantly chasing events to understand them, to make sense of them, and no sooner have we made sense of one thing than a contradictory thing appears.

The best way to model this chaos, or the splitting of the paths, is to follow the emerging changes. By recognizing evolving alternatives, playing them off each other, and taking different sides. We do this naturally, and we may do it better than any other animal. But social forces encourage us to think along narrow lines. Doing this kills the development of understanding.

You must see things from different points of view. The most important differences are those that pertain to how different things come together, and similar things move apart. If you develop the habit of holding multiplicity, you will be less sure about what you think, and better prepared to play a constructive in what happens.

"A stupid man's report of what a clever man says can never be accurate, because he unconsciously translates what he

hears into something he can understand."
— **Bertrand Russell**, PhD, philosopher and
mathematician

81. Speak for yourself.

Don't ask others to speak for you, and don't accept
representations of yourself fashioned by others. Don't accept
grades or assessments, they disrespect your essence and take
your power away. Speak for yourself.

Don't speak for other people and don't accept situations where
you're expected to speak for them. In doing so, you take away
their power. The goal of any good mediator is to say as little as
possible and enable all parties to represent themselves.

Enlisting a spokesperson for your deeper feelings preserves a
structure that's not working. It's a temporary coping strategy,
like a splint for a broken bone, or a clamp for drying glue. It is
the desire for guidance without taking authority, and a bad
approach to a long-term, working relationship.

Of course, many of the relationships we have do not work, and we hope
we will get beyond many of the obstacles we face and never face them
again. Sometimes this is true, but most of the time it isn't.

Getting past a border guard is considered a one-time event. You tell
yourself, "If you ever need to do this again, I'll cross that bridge when I
come to it." You will come to it, and if you haven't mastered the crossing
the first time, you'll need help the next time.

If you do not master a problematic situation, the problem will continue to
occur until, eventually, the help you rely on will run out. At that point you

may realize it would have been better to have mastered the situation at the first opportunity.

82. Take More Than Your Share of the Responsibility.

Taking more responsibility than is within your power is not fair, but it helps others if you do. The safer, freer, and less worried others are, the more effort they can put into fulfilling their responsibilities. This is also the best way to see another person's greatest ability. What they do when free to act is a measure of their courage and imagination.

On the other hand, feeling compelled to take responsibility when it is not enabling, respected, or appreciated exploits an imbalance of power and exhausts available resources. It's really a question of synergy: take more responsibility when it generates greater productivity and reward.

Altruism is a selfless concern for others, but that's not what I'm talking about here. Taking more responsibility is practical and goal-oriented. It fosters goodwill in a collaborative situation, broadens the safety net, and gets more done. There is nothing particularly selfless in that.

83. The best way to resolve your differences may be to blame someone else.

Blaming someone else is a more memorable way of saying, "The best way to resolve your differences is to reframe them as shared goals that you pursue by different means." What you have in common, then, becomes a source of emotional bonding; what sets you apart are details of circumstance, history, and other people's points of view.

This may seem like you're debasing yourself, but it's an opinion. As long as the other person is not gaining an advantage at your

145

expense you're not prostituting yourself. You might still feel you're selling yourself short, and that may be true, but you're making the best of a compromised situation.

Chris Voss recalls coming to an agreement with a murderous terrorist to release hostages. He and his adversary's goals couldn't be more different as Voss didn't care about politics and his adversary didn't care about lives. However, they both agreed to blame society as the source of their differences and, in that way, built a larger agreement that saved lives and affected politics (Voss, 2016).

Markets

84. Don't believe the advertisement.

Few paths are correctly labeled. Life is like a strange city in which all the street signs are mixed up. Most signs are placed by people who insist it identifies the path they're on, paths to one form of success or another. There does not seem to be any preexisting path to personally meaningful success. Each person must discern their own. Know the path you're on.

The advertisement applies not only to what we might choose, but to where we are now. It is advertised that we're in a golden age, that we're in a just society, that medicine has never been more effective. There are strong arguments in support of these assertions, according to psychologist Steven Pinker (2018).

There are cracks in these arguments and in these cracks you'll find large, unanswered questions. Environmental pollution may show the lie to our "golden age." Wars make a mockery of justice. The failure to appreciate our general lack of mental health puts Western culture in jeopardy.

"I decided that I would try this out on schizophrenics at the state hospital in Manteno, Illinois. At that time I was a psychiatrist. I had a girl who was 17 years old, crawling on the floor like a baby, drooling. She'd been that way for the last four or five years. She barely talks at all, just mews like a sick cat, and crawls along on the floor because she can't walk. I decided to give her the treatment.

"Eight breaths and then she wakes up a perfectly normal 17-year old girl. She talks very clearly and she could remember the condition she had been in. Over the period of the next 10 hours she slowly, slowly declined. It lasted about 10 hours and it raised the question: what the hell was going on? The State of Illinois forbade me ever to use that treatment again."
— **Jerome Lettvin**, MD, PhD, psychiatrist, engineer, and neuroscientist, from *The Learning Project*

Chess grandmaster, José Raúl Capablanca, said to succeed, "you must study the endgame before everything else." In chess, you know the path you're on. The problem in most things is knowing when you've gotten to the endgame. That may not be so much different from situations where you don't know where you're going.

Your life is a unique game played with unusual pieces by unusual rules. Over time, both the rules and the pieces change. The instructions are to play by the rules. Sometimes you will and sometimes you won't. You need to study your own endgame.

85. Establish a beachhead for a push to future success.

The under-appreciated saying, "First find a market, then find a product," is more to the point than its more academic version, which says, "Begin with market research." It is much easier to give people what they're looking for than it is to present something they don't want, and then to try to convince them they should want it. Find someone who wants what you have, and then let them know you have it.

Once you have a market for something, such as the market for "get rich quick" schemes, your product simply needs to meet expectations, it doesn't even have to work. And, in the case of "get rich schemes," it never does!

I invented a more flexible accounting system. I designed, patented it, created, and installed it. I marketed it as a software package called "4th Quarter Accounting," but I was not successful at selling the product. I had the proof, but my prospects couldn't understand it. They were not assured of the benefits. My product was like a better ski for people who didn't know how to ski.

> " ' *The challenge is that to move people a large distance and for the long term, we have to create the conditions where they can move themselves.' Ferlazzo makes a distinction between 'irritation' and 'agitation.' Irritation, he says, is 'challenging people to do something that we want them to do.' By contrast, 'agitation is challenging them to do something that they want to do.'*
>
> *"What he has discovered throughout his career is that 'irritation doesn't work.' It might be effective in the short term. But to move people fully and deeply requires something more—not looking at the student or the patient as a pawn on a chessboard but as a full participant in the game. 'It means trying to elicit from people what their goals*

148

are for themselves and having the flexibility to frame what we do in that context.' "
— **Daniel Pink**, from *To Sell Is Human, the Surprising Truth About Moving Others* (Pink, 2012)

86. Become aware of how you set your direction.

You create your future based on the world you're aware of, the judgments you make, the paths you consider, and the ideas that occupy your mind. All together, this is the environment you see, through which you weave a path.

The more you interact with others, the more you invest in the constructions made and maintained by others, the more you will become an organelle within these structures. Be aware that the meaning of language spoken within these domains is specific to them. You must retain the ability to speak and understand other world views if you are to move outside these domains. And if you want to create a world of your own, you'll need to build your own meanings.

Each world view understands things slightly differently, using different words, phrases, associations, and shades of meaning. These small differences add up to the segregation of people, selective skills within groups, and prejudices between them. If you listen to people of a different social group, age, and class—even within the same culture who speak the same language—you'll encounter radically different ideas, meanings, and expectations expressed in identical dialects.

For example, bankers speak the same language no matter their mother tongue. Similarly, scientists, industrialists, monarchists, managers, criminals, teenagers, and children can speak among themselves and translate their expressions across languages at no loss of understanding.

Life paths are constructions of your imagination that exist with the consent of those around you. Your future coalesces like crystalized sugar: your actions melt it into existence from a network of people who are linking their lives together.

Your past is of a similar provisional nature. It exists to the extent that you identify yourself with it, remember and recount it, and act in ways that are extensions of it. You are what your stories make you be and if you forget your stories, through a stroke of complete amnesia, then who would you be?

These are your memories but you can change them. You can remake yourself fairly easily within the confines of your environment and, if courageous, beyond them. Most people can't break out of their container because it has become too much of a habit, and they've been trained to fear their own autonomy.

> *"A focus on our strengths urges us toward a desired future and stimulates an openness to new ideas, peoples, and plans. In contrast, spotlighting our weaknesses elicits a defensive sense of obligation and guilt, closing us down."*
> — **Daniel Goleman**, from *Focus, the Hidden Driver of Intelligence*

87. Pay attention to how you're answering the world.

Make an extra effort to be aware of what you attract in the world around you. If you have a social presence, be aware of what you attract in others and what others you attract. Take seriously how others respond. It partly reflects what you portray of yourself, as well as aspects of yourself of which you're unaware.

Do you respond with gratitude, invitation, and appreciation? Or do you wait for things to come to you? If you are honest in presentation, welcome what arrives. You may feel your honesty deserves a greater reward, but what you've gotten is authentic. Don't debase your presentation for more sales; find better prospects.

We all wish we were quicker or smarter in order to respond in better ways. You can be, if you deepen your awareness. Become aware of the layers of meaning in every person's presentation. Be present, listen deeply, and sweep first impressions from your mind. Your insight lies in your second impressions. Let them rise to the top.

I asked a stranger what her story was. She said she didn't have one and then spent the next ninety minutes detailing her life from childhood. When she was done she said, "I feel so guilty that I told you all these things!" I was about to admonish her not to feel guilty when I stopped myself and said, "Enjoy your guilt!" Briefly taken aback she relaxed, began to smile, and said, "I will!"

Albert Einstein was a lonely odd-ball, wandering the morning streets of his Princeton, New Jersey home in his housecoat and bedroom slippers. He worked on his own and didn't follow the work of others. There were others where he worked who were just as odd, interesting, and congenial but—according to Freeman Dyson who was a young man at the Institute at the time—most people took pains to avoid Einstein.

Claude Shannon—a younger colleague whose work was as original and influential as Einstein's—passed Einstein each morning. They waved to each other but never met. Einstein even wandered into one of Shannon's lectures but didn't stay to listen.

Einstein maintained his privacy by looking odd. Shannon—who always wore a suit and tie—secured his by blending in. Both were odd-balls, but neither found each other. If you are unique, don't expect to be understood even by those whom you'd like to attract.

> *"It is strange to be known so universally and yet to be so lonely."*
> — **Albert Einstein**, PhD, physicist

88. If you invent a better mousetrap, the world will not beat a path to your door.

There is a saying, "If you invent a better mousetrap, the world will beat a path to your door." We love this kind of encouragement. It motivates inventions, but it's laughably false. The world most definitely will not beat a path to any invention that claims to do better at something an established product accomplishes to an adequate degree.

Consumers are generally unqualified to judge the risks inherent in a new product, and they know this. A better mousetrap must first establish itself, then people might accept it. Establishing a product is wholly different from coming up with it in the first place.

Selling doesn't even require a working product, as we see from the many highly valued, technology start-up companies that never produce a profit. Or from the many elected candidates who don't deliver on their promises. What's needed is relief, and what's sold is hope, not a guarantee. Once the fear is relieved, the problem is solved.

I moved into a house whose previous owner thought it had mice, and they placed mouse traps in judicious locations. They never caught any, but the mice went away. The reason they never caught any was they never baited the traps. And the reason the mice disappeared was that they were never there in the first place. People solve a lot of problems this way. For them, the old-style mouse trap works just fine.

89. It's better to be not understood, than to be misunderstood.

People are looking for confirmation of their prejudices and preconceptions. These are the things they've invested in and, in their life, they usually have no "Plan B." Our errors are embedded in our prejudices and preconceptions, and these errors become our biggest obstacles.

People's first desire is satisfaction, and their second desire is a path to it. People want confirmation both of the rewards of their likes and the success of their plan. Their least desire is a change of assumptions. The most useful thing you can do is to provide honest reflection. I can certainly see myself in this picture.

Your conversation will be heard in the context of these filters, and your message to others will be rewritten from their point of view. You will be understood from another person's frame of reference both in terms of what you say and what you mean. That is to say, the respect they accord to you will be tainted by their prejudice. Few people see who you are or hear what you say. At times like these, you'll do more good if you're not understood and, instead, are heard as a new voice with a new message.

90. Opportunities are like auctions.

An auction has bidders and sellers. Nothing has a value in an auction outside the scope of the bids and the asks. Value only exists in terms of what people want.

Think of your opportunities as trades: giving up one thing to gain another. The value of the thing is what you pay for it, and just because you've bought or sold it does not mean the market is closed. The market of your opportunities continues until you leave it, and up until then you can pretty much trade anything you want. Few decisions are final.

The value of an object is determined by two people making opposite plans. The seller prefers the cash while the buy prefers the asset. The value they agree on represents two different views of what's being traded.

There will be other pairings of buyers and sellers at different times and places, but at this time and place the buyer and seller's agreement is considered as true as anyone else's. The real value of some asset—be it a thing, an idea, or a course of action—only exists in theory. Value depends on agreements crystalized through action.

If you engage in the trade, then your action is one of the two components of the commodity's real value. Conversely, the opinion of someone who does not engage in the trade may be useful, but it has no value.

Resources

91. Do what you find hard to talk about.

Given that you only learn what you experience, there are many things that you cannot experience—and so cannot learn—by talking. These are emotional and physical things, things that embody contradiction, and things that cannot be described effectively, like love and hate.

My most formative experiences were rich and complex. I would switch from one hobby to the next before getting proficient in any of them. Most of this was due to my own limited resources, but I also wanted to sample different pursuits. I was fascinated by slot cars, competitive diving, archery, soldering, skate boards, fly-fishing, sling shots, paper airplanes, skiing, the French Horn, veterinarians, and working as a stagehand. Don't wait to be encouraged. Pursue your interests.

If you are not annoying some people, then you have not reached the limit of creating for yourself the best environment possible. There are people who will teach you if you show an interest, and others who will just be annoyed.

Cubist painters described their form as an attempt to see the world from many angles at once to represent its multiplicity. But rather than appreciate a larger worldview, the public received cubist painting as ugly and distorted. The real world does behave in ugly and distorted ways, and people don't want to see it. It's easier painted than described.

92. Imagine the details.

Every goal begins with a vision, and that vision is of something whole. At the same time, every goal is reached by many steps and many parts that play supporting roles. Keep your broad vision and leave yourself time to fill in the details.

Develop the discipline to look inside your vision in order to recognize the ingredients. This will likely take you beyond your comfort zone, but you must go there. No one else can imagine the details of what you envision.

> *"Opportunity is missed by most people because it is dressed in overalls and looks like work."*
> — **Thomas A. Edison**, scientist, inventor, and entrepreneur

This is the realm of play. The guts of a project involve a lot of "doodling around." You may have no idea of how to solve certain problems, cross certain bridges, or attract the right people. You can't head off in every direction, invest in every possibility, or commit yourself to the first person who shows up. There is going to be trial and error; you don't want to get committed to any experiment.

Any new formulation involves innumerable, unavoidable, dead ends. Conceive of these not as failures, but as sketches, tests of ideas, and the unearthing of related answers. You need this information.

Breakthroughs come in little packages, and most little packages are not breakthroughs. Don't raise your hopes, but don't prejudice the outcome, either. Thank every failure, don't pay too much for them, and let each one leave you feeling a bit wiser.

93. It's usually counter-productive to ask why-questions.

It's easy to reach beyond what you know, and to see the ignorance of those around you. Most people feel threatened by ignorance and react defensively when errors and uncertainties are exposed. Exposing the ignorance of authorities gets a quick reaction, which is too bad because most management is done by guess-work. Managers should welcome real observations.

Whether you're dealing with managers, teachers, or bosses, if you expose their mistakes, you'll need to reassure them that you are not undermining their authority. Develop this as a skill because you need to ask these questions and they'll take it the wrong way.

I remember three instances when, as a student, I was angrily rebuked by senior scientists for pointing out their implausible claims. In two cases I was asking obvious questions. In the third, I knew what I was talking about because I had done new work. Ego interferes especially in those areas where egos are rarely challenged.

I have yet to master the art of exploring other people's minds. I can do this as a therapist because I'm welcome, but among scientists and practitioners I'm not. That's why I work alone. The scientific community is supposed to be a forum for discovery but was always way too small for me. The brightest scientists never seem to find community. I believe the secret lies in being patient, but who has the time?

"And then the head of the department, Professor Rabi, a very famous physicist, a Nobel Prize winner, came into my office, and the person who was going to be the next head, Professor Kusch, who also got a Nobel Prize, came into my office. They came into my office and sat down and said, 'Look! That's not going to work. You know it's not going to work. We know it's not going to work. You're wasting the department's money—you've got to stop.'

"Well, that's the picture, you see. A lot of people don't always agree with you, especially if you have a new idea. Fortunately, I had tenure. That is, they couldn't fire me just because they didn't agree with me! So I said, 'No, I think that it has a good chance of working. I'm going to keep going.' They marched out of my office kind of angrily. And we kept going."
— **Charles H. Townes**, PhD, on his invention of the laser, in *The Learning Project*

Isaac Newton credited his success to the giants who preceded him, but none did, and he knew it. With the exception of the celestial data of Tycho Brahe and Johannes Kepler—who died before he was born— Newton invented everything he used: the theory, math, and the data analysis. He was an intolerant man who made this famously deferential statement about seeing further because he stood on the shoulders of giants because—in addition to being a physicist, alchemist, economist, and theologian—he was a politician.

94. Learn to use resource materials.

A librarian is the most useful person you're likely to encounter in compulsory education. There is a wealth of material available to people who need or want to understand a field, and a librarian can help you find it. It used to be harder to judge the quality of this material, but now it's become easy to get and to judge and to find reviews of anything.

Learn of the prerequisites from the original research, then go to texts to learn the details. Don't attempt to learn everything because that will take forever; it's not all needed, and you'll lose your sense of purpose if you try. Don't learn prerequisites for their own sake; learn them to accomplish something.

Not all librarians are helpful. There seems to be an old-guard bureaucracy that sees itself as protecting the information from the unwashed masses. These librarians seem more like up-tight school teachers and less like circus magicians. They prefer to produce worksheets rather than rabbits out of hats.

Textbooks are generally awful. The material in advanced textbooks is also poor—with notable exceptions—because knowledge does not grow in textbooks. Textbooks are often written poorly and with political prejudice. Some textbooks have derailed education, as is the case with elementary school readers that teach reading by word memorization.

"If I sell you my first reader, then I don't have anything else to sell you. I don't have any second reader. But if you buy Dick and Jane, or Alice and Jerry, you've got to go from first to second to third, and the publisher can sell the series... within a couple of years, 80% of the schools had the Dick and Jane readers... the consequences are obvious: people can't read."
— **Phyllis Schlafly**, JD, politician, orator, and social activist, from *The Learning Project*

Monographs are more accurate and useful, but are mostly a compendium of resources rather than an explanatory resource. They are great for getting up to date, but you have to know the field.

Advanced texts are increasingly directed toward training for employment, playing the role of instruction manuals. They rarely mention unanswered problems as it is unlikely that you'd be asked to answer them. Saying too much about something that's poorly understood could be seen as a lack of authority, dating the material and impacting sales.

I have never encountered a textbook that attempts to reveal the flaws within its field. On occasion, we're told these issues would be confusing... as well they should be! It is these disconnected points that define the future. For these reasons, it's imperative that you read original, disputatious authors invested in advancing their fields.

Walter Pitts, a scrawny boy growing up in a tough Detroit neighborhood, escaped into the public library where he taught himself logic, mathematics, Latin, and Greek. After reading the magnum opus of one of the world's leading mathematicians he wrote to its author, Bertrand Russell, of several errors he had found. Russell responded by inviting Walter to come study at Cambridge, but he couldn't. Walter was only 12.

Actually, the Walter Pitts story is a cautionary tale. Walter was so unique, sensitive, and advanced that he didn't need and never bothered to get any degrees. He created the mathematical foundation of modern neuroscience, then became disillusioned, burned all his notebooks and, not long after that, disappeared. It is a sad story, but it would be unfair to blame the library.

Expectations

95. Be attentive to what you're getting.

Your goals will start to manifest through the appearance of elements within them. You may be looking for a finished package or a well-defined result, but what you'll first get are aspects of it, others who are interested in it, or the sprouting of what's possible. Nurture and encourage these. They may not be part of your final vision, but they will be indications that aspects of it are starting to form.

Opportunities arrive like apples shaken from a tree. What you're looking for will appear in small and partial form and without great fanfare. Your achievement will not come knocking at your door like a knight in shining armor. More likely, you'll pass it on your way to work. You'll see various pieces, each with potential.

Creating something is a difficult process. You need to be both discriminating and accepting. You're not looking for what you initially set out for, you're looking for the bits and pieces from which you'll fashion a vehicle to get there. You'll need to develop a sense of the process and to play an interested but uncommitted role. Take small opportunities and resist taking off in their direction. You have to determine what fruit to pick, when to pick it, and what to do next.

96. Be careful what you ask for.

More often than not, you get some version of what you ask for, so look carefully at what you get. Imagine in as much detail as possible the thing you asked for. Fate is a busy, short-order cook who cuts corners. If you want to be happy and successful, then don't just ask for success, ask for success with happiness. Otherwise you won't get it. Be sure to check what you're served.

It's also likely that what you've imagined is less or different from what you need. You bear some responsibility for what you get, even if you didn't choose it, and you bear all the responsibility for what you accept. Quite a few things that we're served we cannot return, so be careful.

Setting goals is a risky process. You're aiming to create something that does not yet exist. Your path to discovery will be guided by you. There will be many decisions that you have not thought of but, when taken together, will have a large effect.

The temptation is to disregard the small things and focus on the big thing: the final goal. But there is no final goal, there is a scattering of possible stopping points. If you have a goal, your only chance of reaching it is to manage its acquisition every step of the way.

97. Be grounded in the future.

Make the future a reality in your mind. See the future as you want it to become, then act and live from that place. In this, you are in the present because there really is no point in time other than the present for what you make as your reality.

At the same time, it is the future that is coming toward you. Make as your reality something you believe in and that you are in love with, and if you are not in love with it now, make it something you will be in love with in the future. Your purpose is to make the future unfold as the encompassing reality you imagine.

Being fully in the present while grounded in the future is hard to do. It's clear that you should avoid living in the past and we're admonished to be fully in the present, but the present is as much of an illusion as the past or future. You live "in" the reality you manifest. You live it now, regardless of what you believe, or what others tell you to believe at this moment.

There is a difference between being "in the now" and being aware of what is coming toward you. You must do both. You can drive a car "in the now" but you cannot drive a car without being aware of what is coming toward you. Time may be an illusion, but it contains objects that are moving toward you, and some of them are coming directly at you.

Your body lives in and responds to the present. At the same time, your body has rhythms that extend into the future to varying degrees. Your heart is aware of its next beat, your lungs are aware of your next breath, and your digestion is aware of your next meal. What your mind is aware of is your choice. Chose it to be what is healthy for you.

98. If you hope to make a difference, don't expect to know what you're doing.

Schooling through the master's level is aimed at delivering a product. People who want to create something new, often cannot find and do not acquire the skills they need through school. If invention is your goal, then you'll be making up your path as you go along. Most likely it will be a rough road with many learning opportunities. It will also be a risky path with many chances for failure.

> *"Chuck Strobel… came up to me at the Applied Psychiatry and Biofeedback conference and said, 'You know Nancy, you and I… we're really the pioneers of the field. We are the foundation. That's a big responsibility.' And I'm thinking, 'Who, me? I don't even have a clue what I'm doing!'"*
> — **Nancy White**, PhD, neuro-psychotherapist, from *The Learning Project*

Jobs exist to create things for which there is a market. New inventions, almost by definition, have no market. In some cases, and at some times, fields of novelty are full of applications, and in those times you can be hired to be creative without too much regard for the immediate value of what you produce. It's assumed that almost anything will find a use.

Some organizations are so rich they'll buy almost anything, including things of no immediate use. Such was the case at Bell Labs in the 1950s when Charles Townes worked there. Such remains the case with the US military, which is why so many advances are funded by the military.

I took my mathematical background to a job interview at Bear Sterns, an investment firm dealing in the subprime bond market. I was told that I would not need to actually do anything of value because simply displaying complicated graphs would sell new customers. I didn't get the job, Bear Sterns' stock price tripled and then went to zero with the subprime fiasco eight years later. I would not have lasted long.

Times like those are unusual. What's usually wanted is a version of what is known. The market buys improvements, and students are trained to provide them. Schools train what people buy.

99. Most people are looking for the wrong thing.

People stubbornly use their rational minds to identify and pursue their goals. When they encounter an obstacle, they press ahead regardless of the resistance. What they see as their problem usually doesn't have the solution they're looking for, or any solution at all. Not everyone does this always, but most of us do.

In truth, we're unaware of either our goals or the underlying means that we're employing to achieve them. We are only focused on the obstacle. This is a reflection of our narrow awareness, limited options, and the nature of reasoning which typically accepts certain unknowns and insists on putting them together. Simply having a chance to verbalize and reflect on what we assume and how we're thinking is often the most useful thing we can do.

Some of us break through this barrier. It may be an epiphany or a gradual awakening. We don't need to be enlightened about everything, and there's nothing wrong with being stubborn and bull-headed. It's for the big, deep goals you that you want enlightenment.

Enlightenment isn't a big thing, it doesn't explain anything. Enlightenment is just a spiritual clarity that extends to your root. It's a scoring across the rind of life that spiritually orients you by letting a little light in.

100. Hope nothing; trust no one.

Hope is unreasonable faith in the future; trust is unreasonable faith in a person or thing. Base your expectations of people and circumstances on what you know, and if you don't know enough, then inquire, investigate, and learn.

Hope is the last step before delusion or despair and, as a coping strategy, it's better than either of those two. But it's only temporary, and if there is no more to it than wishful thinking, then the currents toward delusion or despair will take you in those directions when hope runs out.

Trust is hope's equally emaciated twin. It should exist only in the realm of handshake agreements and cross-your-heart promises, both of which need better foundations than trust alone. If you're not verifying those things in which you place your trust, then you are selling yourself short; you are committing a kind of abuse of yourself. Don't expect someone else to accept a losing situation because of a trust agreement they should not have agreed to. If you're the beneficiary of such an agreement, then you are being exploitative.

If you find yourself trusting something but can find no evidence to support it, then what's really going on? Events unfold due to the natural scheme of things. Do not trust that someone else will act in a fashion that is out of balance, thereby putting themselves at risk, simply because they owe you.

True friendship is not based on hope or trust, it's based on knowledge. True friends don't let other friends take a fall alone not because they believe in reciprocity, but because they have a feeling of shared identity.

Back up trust with tests and verifications. Even better, understand that everyone wants to be rewarded. If the rewards are understood, then you don't need to rely on someone jeopardizing themselves later because of an earlier commitment made without knowing what they were risking.

101. Talk about what you find hard to do.

Talking about what you don't know how to say can either be ignorant or wise. If the subject is deep, it can be both. Wisdom embraces ignorance, ignorance as in not knowing, not ignorance as is stupid. When you really know and understand a great deal, you realize how many things you have little understanding of.

Talking about what you find hard to do boils down to trying to express yourself on difficult matters. There are things that are hard to do because you cannot do them, or cannot do them yet, and other things that are hard to do because you don't want to do them, or are not allowed to. All of these things are worth talking about.

The things that are easy to do are the least worth talking about. It is unfortunate that most people talk about the easy things: they complain, boast, and gossip in order to bond and entertain. None of these amount to anything other than solidifying preconceptions and identity.

The next time you're among people in conversation, listen to them. Compare what they say with what others talk about. Compare what they say with what you would talk about. Then, think about what is important in your life. It would be fair to assume that these same topics are important in the lives of other people. Who is talking about what's important? Who is exploring difficult situations?

> *"People will come to adore the technologies that undo their capacities to think."*
> — **Neil Postman**, PhD, author, educator, and media critic

Judgments

102. Align your vision with the interests of others.

Compulsory schools align individuals with institutions and assume you will be assimilated. Few of the agents of education recognize what they're doing. Few people are aware of the social role they play. People don't like to think of themselves as unwitting agents, it's uncomfortable.

How you present yourself depends on how you want to be seen. Create an integrated appearance by recognizing that your posture, energy, dress, attention, speech, breathing patterns, and even your unspoken thoughts will have an effect. Just as you can dress in a school or business uniform, so you can dress in a school or business attitude. It doesn't have to be your only change of clothes but, whatever you do, try not to be in conflict with yourself.

Your goal is engagement and a crafted rapport. Don't struggle; it either works or it doesn't. It helps to know what you want to say and how you want to be heard. Sell what you need as something that advances the interests of others. This will help you get what you want, make allies, and be seen as a provider.

I didn't do this in my youth as I was too narrowly focused to see these opportunities. I was personally invested in establishing my autonomy, which was not an option that anyone was making available to me. I once wrote a letter of apology to a school principal whom I had offended. That made me appear mature in his eyes. I should have capitalized on his goodwill but, instead, I was angry.

If you're too flexible, you may get run over. There are some people whose interests you don't want to serve regardless of what they offer. A mountain guide named Ginger hated Americans so much that he nearly killed me. I should have abandoned his services. Years later, a professor basically demanded a bribe in return for a passing grade. I refused and he failed me, but that time, I did the right thing.

103. Always ask, "How is this useful?"

There are many useful things to learn, but if you don't see the point, you won't learn them. How can you, when there is no context? The failure of most teaching lies in the useless form in which the material is presented. We might blame the teacher since presentation is their responsibility, but it's your life and your time spent. You would do well to make up for their shortcomings, or else the time you spend will be wasted.

A commodity is a useful raw material that can be bought or sold. When you're learning, you're investing in the commodity of knowledge and, whether you know it or not, you're speculating in the market.

The value of knowledge, like the value of an agricultural commodity, is the combination of what it's worth now and what it will be worth in the future. The current value of the knowledge taught in conventional programs is next to nothing—it's presented without any relevance—so its value largely resides in its potential.

> *"Well, we were being, ... uh ... we weren't holding ourselves accountable for our own actions. We thought that since we were all prior service we were special, and Sergeant Cook told us one day—he never really yelled, he never got upset—he told us, 'In no other job that you ever have does it matter if you sit through the class, day dream, doodle, or what-not, but if you don't remember this stuff then somebody dies, and it's your fault because...'—and he wasn't saying it to me, he was generalizing—'because you didn't want to pay attention. This truly does matter. This is life or death...'*
>
> *"Ever since then, when it came to medicine, if I heard it, then it clicked. It was almost at an autistic level, but if I heard something that had to do with medicine, then it clicked. You could have told me one thing five years ago, and if it pertained to medicine, then I would remember it to this day."*
>
> — **Dave Williamson**, US Army Medic, from *The Learning Project*

The future value for knowledge is determined by what you make of it. The main market for knowledge centers around employment. This doesn't answer the question of what's most important to you.

The primary purpose of compulsory education is socialization: the training of feelings and values. What you're taught in that regard is not a raw material but protocol and conditioning. Nations are powered by industry, and the availability of workers to support it depends on their compliance.

"According to John Dewey, the father of modern education, the whole purpose of public schooling is to socialize children, not to educate them. So there may be different motives, but the result is obvious. The latest adult literacy survey is on the internet—I pulled it off just about two or three weeks ago—and it's depressing, it's devastating. If you can't read, you can't learn."
— **Phyllis Schlafly**, JD, politician, orator, and social activist, from *The Learning Project*

Judging from the two or three years it takes an unschooled person to learn the material presented in the whole of K through 12 compulsory education, most of the thirteen years provides no material value, nor does the socialization part that's aimed at making you employable. Rather, it creates in you a desire to be part of the system—a need to be part of the system—and the inclination to police yourself in that role. This is training, not teaching. Most teachers are trainers in the sense that they're not providing knowledge, they're inculcating behavior.

Two conclusions can be drawn. First, most of the time, you're not learning anything in compulsory education programs. And second, those who are teaching you are not teachers in the sense you may suppose. They're not supplying knowledge at a serious, formative level; it's not their job.

I was frustrated with my tenth-grade science teacher. I was so interested in the subject that my parents hired him to tutor me, but I never learned anything from him and I couldn't understand why. I have since realized it was because he didn't know anything beyond the textbook knowledge he taught in class, which was insufficient from any perspective. He was perfectly qualified to teach, but he didn't know anything.

104. Being alone is productive.

Regardless of how it makes you feel, being alone allows you to grow in your own reality. For most people, this fosters strength. Solitude is a process of tying up loose ends and cleaning house. You will appreciate essential and neglected aspects of yourself amid a large collection of useless ideas. Building the first and disposing of the second will seem daunting, even painful, but such is the process of becoming wiser.

Our modern society teaches that you are unable to live without it: not able to live alone, work alone, or be alone. By becoming essential, society builds you into it, and builds your dependence on it. It's true that you cannot build the products you want for the low cost offered at WalMart, but what you can build for yourself—which no one mentions— has greater force.

It's easier when you share your goals, feelings, and troubles. Conversation generates a fog of palliative support, but you'll find more solutions if you work by yourself. You'll be more likely to come up with an original idea if you avoid the diluting wash of conversation. Words dissolve the power of feeling. Wise people avoid banter not because they can't, but because it does not serve them.

> *"I live in that solitude which is painful in youth, but delicious in the years of maturity."*
> — **Albert Einstein**, PhD, physicist

Different fashions of social behavior come and go, along with our social minds' various fascinations, fixations, and opportunities. We get sucked in to these cultural celebrations, but they are not for our benefit. Today's obsession with social media reflects the uncertain self-identity we've bought into. The enticement of fantasy avatars rests on our own low self-esteem. This is less than a zero-sum game because when the game is over, your power is gone.

105. Don't be depressed by the negative.

Negative thinking is the power behind the idea of "Trust but verify;" to prove something's not wrong before accepting that it's right. Human brains are better wired to recognize the negative than the positive. In fact, the positive, by its nature, doesn't call attention to anything outside itself. Positive situations are self-contained, and this provides no protection. Negativity means, "focusing on the potential for outside disruption."

The dichotomy between good and bad may be an illusion when seen from the vantage point of the whole, but as long as there is a good, it can only be defined with reference to the bad, and the bad will always be easier to find. To successfully apply negative thinking, explore negativity without becoming negative. You are a scout patrolling a perimeter looking for what you don't want to find.

Debugging software requires that you do everything to make it fail. Writing software requires that you do everything to make it succeed. I find it difficult and tiring to hold the goals of creation and destruction in my mind at the same time. This kind of work requires a protected, negative space: a space in which you are immunized from the negativity you conjure.

Ironically, immersing yourself in the negative can rescue you from negativity because, if you cannot find it, it is not there. The same goes for fear, as most fears are inflations of the unlikely. The same does not go for depression. Depression is a predisposition to see everything as negative, which is an abnegation of truth.

172

Considering the negative enables you to correct it; you emerge from negativity by fixing what's negative. In contrast, depression is a mistake itself; you emerge from depression by changing your reality.

> *"I cried because I had no shoes until I met a man who had no feet."* — **Sa'dī Shirazi**, poet, c. 1210

106. Decisions are like children.

Decisions create opportunities and responsibilities that uphold a version of truth. You make a commitment when you make a decision: you commit to your opinion as long as the underlying truth remains. A decision without a commitment has no future.

Decisions are not made out of thin air, they're born and they inherit from their parents. See them as living things—as if the decisions themselves are alive—things that need your protection and nurturance. The best decisions are those that grow into things with a life of their own and—like the child of a good parent—become part of the family.

If you approach your decisions as potentially life-changing, then you should expect to be taken seriously. If you are not taken seriously, or are not treated seriously, then the decision is not being raised in a healthy env ironment. As in the raising of all children, hold yourself to a high standard.

A person who makes no decision puts forward no truth. That person becomes irrelevant or, worse, survives on the commitments of others. A person who makes too many decisions overcommits themselves. They commit themselves to more truths than they can affirm, creating personal and spiritual obligations they can't uphold and debts they can't repay.

107. Distinguish criticism from dislike.

When you're proud of something, you're personally invested in it. You're also an easy target. Critics find it difficult to distinguish between judgment and action, between who you are and what you've done. As recipients of criticism, we also find it difficult to keep the two apart. However, if you take your work seriously, then you must welcome and consider all warnings of its weaknesses.

We've all experienced unfair criticism from people who did not like or understand us. We are especially vulnerable when our work reflects feelings important to us. However, even criticisms that you judge wrong at first glance may have important, underlying truth. First, take the poison out of any criticism, absorb its benefits, and discard the rest.

"You have to know how to disagree with other people. If somebody disagrees with you, if it's a serious person, you want to think carefully about what he's saying. Think carefully about whether you are really likely to be right or not."
— **Charles H. Townes**, PhD, physicist, from *The Learning Project*

Quite a few people who feel powerless or unappreciated find reward in knocking down anyone who has built themselves up. This sociopathic tendency guides people into professions of authority. Many teachers, managers, and bosses are guilty of this, even the well-meaning ones. Unhelpful personal traits get out of hand where feedback is prohibited or suppressed.

174

As I tell my therapy clients, "Everyone is crazy." You have to expect it. People often build their dysfunctions into their lifestyle and when they do, their shortcomings become chronic. As you get older, you learn to protect yourself and to withhold trust, pending verification.

108. Don't believe everything you think.

You can't explore the consequences of an idea unless you first accept some aspect of it. You cannot protect yourself from negativity if you don't understand the negative. Learn to follow the thinking of ideas you don't believe, in order to better understand them.

If you don't accept bad thinking at least for long enough to trace where it comes from, then you won't recognize it when it arises in yourself and those around you. And if you don't, then, at some point, you'll find yourself drawn into the thinking you're trying to avoid.

Get in the habit of thinking things you don't believe, of trying on foreign thoughts for size. A thought is not a statement. It can only be understood along with the feelings that underlie it. Just as the power of negative thinking protects against negative events, so too the power of negative thinking protects against negative thoughts.

Most thoughts underlying unpleasant actions are reasonable and some are hard to dispute. Many of the underlying feelings are twisted and unresolved. It's the feelings that explain the actions, not the thoughts. You want to understand the feelings, and you can only do that by exploring them, as repugnant as they may be.

I imagine myself believing every idea or action I see expressed by others, especially those that are frightening and abhorrent. I don't take them far, but I try to understand how they resonate with other ideas I've encountered and may have accepted. This makes me vulnerable, and it explains why I refuse to subject myself to extremely negative writing, film, and people. I can get too caught up in it.

Racial, cultural, and gender prejudices are widespread. By considering these behaviors you can better understand how other ideas contribute to them, and how some people can take prejudice and antagonism to extremes. The more you entertain unwholesome ideas, the more sensitive you become to them, and the easier they are to avoid.

It is an illusion of our legal system and fallacy of our notions of mental health that good and bad thoughts are distinct, are held by separate people, and are easily distinguished. There are negative enticements everywhere. If you don't explore the negative terrain, then you won't know how to get out of it when you take a wrong turn and find yourself in it.

109. Don't believe everything you think about yourself.

Low self-esteem leads to self-dislike, regret, and self-destructive actions. These self-perceptions feel reasonable and authentic— if you don't know any better—but are a breeding ground for illness and trouble. Something like a virus infects Western culture, causing us to think badly of ourselves. This is not shared by all cultures.

It's unclear who benefits from this, as there is no evident pathogen or parasite, but something does. There are large industries within our economy that benefit from the sale of self-esteem to those who buy it. Even more deeply, this is built into their personal value of money.

Some things you think about yourself are your own and others are things you've been told. Most of these were incorporated into your self-image before you were aware of the self you were developing. You had, and probably still have, difficulty in determining what things about yourself are true. None of them are objective, entirely your own, or well defined. What we know about ourselves is nebulous.

We have reasonable ideas about who we are, and we have feelings about ourselves. Most likely, your ideas support your feelings. You can cook up a reasonable argument to support whatever emotional feelings you have, in spite of whatever evidence might exist to the contrary. Be skeptical of these arguments.

I suggest your problems are rooted in your reasonable feelings, because you shouldn't have any. You can have reasons that stand on their own strengths, and you can have feelings that just are, but you don't need reasons for feelings. Both are essential and different. Reason and feeling are not oil and water, they are sand and air. They coexist but do not provide justifications for each other. Ad hoc justifications provide bad foundations.

What you feel is important, because it will determine what you believe. You may be skeptical, and your feelings may be incorrect, but you can't deny them. Holding feelings loosely is a skill that is as important as disciplined reasoning.

Quite a few feelings would be unhelpful were you to act on them, even quite destructive, but they are valid, nonetheless. Being able to disconnect from feelings can greatly improve the quality of your life. In extreme times, it may even save it.

Adults are not very untrustworthy in the character-building advice they give to children, and children trust adults more than they should. There may be a silent majority who try hard to be good parents, but, from what I see as a therapist, many don't try at all.

Children should not depend on adults as role models; they should be instilled with more confidence and given more opportunity to learn on their own. Confidence may depend on knowledge, but self-confidence does not. Don't confuse the two. If you grew up learning from nature and people in the real world, you were lucky. If you grew up in institutions—day care, health care, religious or secular schools—you were not.

Your parents were never taught how to be parents, and most likely never learned. Kids lack self-confidence because their parents lack self-confidence, and they're rarely given the chance to learn it for themselves. This is why the virus of low self-esteem continues to run within the culture.

Grade schools supplant parents offering confidence on a conditional basis. These conditions are determined by performance and on one's relationship to institutions, class, and privilege. This does not build self-confidence. Much of my work as a mentor and therapist involves helping people reform themselves. It's never too late to rebuild your childhood.

110. Evil is an enigma.

Bad situations require a combination of forces before they "ignite" into reality. They require a combination of perpetrators, victims, arrogance, indifference, fear, and a history of trouble. This is especially true of what we call "evil."

To know evil requires your participation. It can't be understood from afar, it must be experienced. Some deny evil and explain it as "painful steps toward progress," others see it in black and white terms. I think of it as a necrosis that's eating into our brain. I know a few people I consider evil, but they're the last people to even entertain the idea that evil might describe them. Evil exists in a realm of delusions.

"Wartime propaganda in various material forms permeated the national mindset, making reality increasingly remote... As the dominant reality became in a certain sense fictional, Kusama remembers trying to confirm the actual existence of things by counting innumerable pebbles on the riverbank."
— **Midori Yamamura**, describing life in Japan's Imperial State at the start of World War II (Yamamura, 2015)

The evil people I know are pleasant and well-liked. I'd like to say they're only pleasant on the surface, but they're actually well-meaning below the surface, too. They cannot see how their thoughts and feelings generate evil, and you will be hard pressed to indict their motivations. There are unreconcilable kinks in their chains of reasoning, and the devastation and sorrow they leave behind is unmistakable.

Dennis Rader was a stamp-collecting, dog-loving, badge-wearing, code enforcement officer, family man and father of two, who somehow found time to be a Cub Scout leader and church council president. He also found time, from 1974 to 1991, to bind, torture, and murder ten people— two of whom were children—before being exposed in 2005.

There is something truly amiss in an evil personality and it's located where neither you nor they can see it. If you want to find it, then you must become involved at a deep level, being sensitive, open, and non-judgmental. What you find will be disturbing, disconnected, and unfathomable. Gaining this understanding is difficult, unpleasant, and crucial.

111. Judge people by their intentions.

We're told to judge people by their actions, but actions are not the whole result. In any situation, a lot comes between the initial intentions and the final result. To judge on the basis of actions is to assume the result was intended. This is never exactly true.

An outcome involves many steps, each with its own decision. Big intentions are built from smaller intentions, each with their own character flaws. Life moves too fast for anyone to control it completely. We're flying by the seat of our pants.

We hope that skill will connect intention with outcome, but few skills guarantee a result. You can predict the result of well-planed skills, but the more uncertain the skill, the less you can presume the outcome, regardless of the initial intentions.

If all you can see is the result, then you must base your judgments on it. The presumption is that, all things being equal, the same result will follow from the same intentions. On the other hand, if you're involved in the process, then you should also be weighing intention. In that case, your judgments are based on the potential of what could happen next time, not simply on what happened last time.

Sometimes it's best to judge people by their intentions, other times by their actions. The most correct judgment may lie somewhere in between.

"There is no shortage of people telling you what you shouldn't be in life. And why is that so? Like, why do they

even give a shit? Why should someone go out of their way
to tell you what you can't be?"
— **Neil deGrasse Tyson**, PhD, astrophysicist and educator,
from *The Learning Project*

112.Winning a rigged game makes you stupid.

School is a rigged game. Most computer games are rigged
games. Institutional advancement can be a rigged game. Any
situation that presents challenges that are not the real
challenges misleads you.

School pretends to prepare you for life beyond school, but
doesn't because it is disconnected from the real world.
Institutions encourage performance but reward nepotism
because the relationships that develop within them don't exist
outside of them. In most learning situations you're not working
for your own advancement, you're working for someone else's
advancement and, outside of that context, what you learn may
have no value.

It's certainly valuable to know how to insulate yourself from,
insinuate, pretend, supplicate, defer to, and reward others.
These skills are essential in dealing with others, but they're not
usually the skills you've come to learn. If you want to capitalize
on your strengths and build your insights, you need to play a
fair game.

I wanted science to be a fair game, the game of understanding, but it is
more a game of personality. It took me decades to get beyond the
nepotism and irrelevance built into the schools I attended.

I found mountaineering made me wiser because it was not a rigged
game. That's not to say the odds were always with me, but at least,

when I cut it close, I could dance along the edges. This is what you need to do with difficult problems, you need to risk the void of ignorance without having to worry about someone stabbing you in the back.

"The supreme quality of leadership is unquestionable integrity."
— **Dwight D. Eisenhower**, Five-star general and 34th President of the United States

"The worst thing about being lied to is knowing you weren't worth the truth."
— **Jean-Paul Sartre**, philosopher

"Relationships are about trust. If you have to play detective, then it's time to move on."
— **anonymous**

113. Playing a rigged game makes you successful.

Collaboration, networking, alliances, personal introductions, private arrangements, patronage, privilege, and all sorts of arrangements based on situations outside the present are a form of rigging the game. Tipping the odds in your favor is the first thing you try to do. The alternative of fighting your way to the top—being ranked on the basis of merit alone—is considered unseemly if not unintelligent.

The only person who makes no use of their connections is a person who has no connections. That person is suspected of either having a poor record that gained no support, or of being an outsider who isn't part of the culture.

School endorses personal accomplishment and equal treatment, but the real world endorses privilege, arrangements, and alliances. Evaluating someone's merit solely on the basis of an isolated measure, such as grades, is unwise because there is no good isolated measure. The whole notion of ranking people according a theoretic measure makes little sense. In the real world, your school record is irrelevant.

The sensible and generally successful way of getting ahead is to take every advantage, tip the odds, and game the system. Playing a fair game will make you better at playing the game, but playing a rigged game will get you closer to the real goal whatever that is. You'll get farther with the resources you have if you make the best use of them.

This is the reason successful business people dislike schooling. Schooling teaches the wrong lesson. The successful person finds the most efficient path to success and doesn't waste time learning a commodity skill set. They do not play the game or follow the rules; they make the game and set their own rules.

114. Look for what's wrong with the facts.

There are no objective truths in the manner that most people expect. The reason statistics are so widely derided is because that's all that most truths rest on, and people don't want to admit it, so they blame statistics.

Even the best of truths rest on untestable assumptions, although these assumptions may be far down the chain of reasoning, so far down that they're never questioned. The closer you get to the assumptions that underlie people's beliefs, the easier it becomes to see the fallacies.

Most assumptions can't stand up against scrutiny, and our most strongly held assumptions are no exception. All of our core beliefs are unprovable. To assume the benefits of medical care, education, and government is to rely on statistical evidence, at best.

If you do not understand the statistical evidence in support of these assumptions, then you cannot justify them. Yet almost everyone hates statistics, and that's because they have no competence in its use. And still we never learn—and are never taught how to learn—what's going on.

We discourage children from incessantly asking, "Why?" But who is being taught here, the children or the adults? Children's why's are valid: they want to know; the answers given by adults are inadequate. I've found the same to be true in my own studies; the lack of good answers is nearly universal. If I ask "why" three times in response to the answers I'm given, I usually reach the point where there is no answer.

> *"I'm a garbage picker-upper as a mode of science: I focus on the garbage truck. I look at the parts that others choose not to pay attention to. It's interesting, the number of things that are not paid attention to... absolutely astounding."*
> — **Jerome Lettvin**, PhD, MD, psychiatrist, engineer, and neuroscientist, from *The Learning Project*

115. Take all criticism positively.

It's hard to give criticism that's taken positively, and it's hard to take criticism positively, but it can be done. You have to clean it, like you clean a fish. Remove from it the personal opinion, implications of personal value, and whatever feelings of inadequacy you carry. You must whittle down the critic's standards to your own standards.

In many cases, the criticism applies to goals you don't intend to reach, you don't care about, are unfair, or for which you're ill-suited. It's the part that's left that's useful. Find in the criticism the bits that you should have noticed yourself. They are things you could have done something about, and can do something about now or next time.

Useful criticism is about focus: what you wanted to do but failed to do because of misunderstanding, misjudgment, or inattention. Focus on those things that you're aiming for. The other things? Maybe.

It is often the case that your critic does not want to discuss their critique. They feel entitled to their opinion. I received an unsolicited criticism that began, "Thanks for your email. I am interested, but your email copy is boring as hell. Just some pointers from a guy that analyzes 10-20 sites a day..." It went downhill from there. It was self-serving, and I discarded it wholesale. Sure, there may be grains of truths in it, but it's not for you to sacrifice yourself in order to find them.

When a critic will engage you substantively, their input is valuable. They have considered what you've done, expressed their judgment and understanding, and are willing to accompany you to a deeper level. Such people are rare.

At the same time, if you have been given criticism in good faith, accept it in good faith. Don't attempt to score points, defend your honor, or put your critic down. It is fear of this kind of reprisal that inclines critics to avoid discussion and leads them to regret offering their opinion in the first place. Honor a well-meaning critic; those who are not well-meaning are better off disregarded. If you think there is some merit buried in distasteful comments, discuss these with someone you trust.

116. Clear criticism so it does not clog up your mind.

You would like all advice to be positive and well-intentioned, but even if you're careful in what you listen to, you'll still hear much of what you would rather not, and you'll never know for sure unless you consider it.

Good criticism clears away the bad parts and empowers you. Bad criticism is like a clogged toilet and must be flushed away. Even though it's sewage, you can't just ignore it. Just because it's obviously wrong doesn't mean it doesn't hurt. Bad criticism is meant to hurt, it's meant to injure, and it does, and that's something you need to heal.

The value of criticism is determined only by what you make of it. Few people who criticize really care all that much. Careless criticism is invariably someone's opportunity to voice their opinion in the guise of righteous advice, saying to you privately what they would not say in public.

Of course this includes teachers, managers, and bosses who, for the most part, apply an artificial standard that is not aimed at enhancing your opportunity. Poor criticism is unhelpful, and I have found that to be close to 90% of what I receive.

One important exception is craftsmanship, which is where there is a clear standard that you're trying to meet. When you're learning a skill, especially one whose success will be determined by what other people think, the opinions of others are essential.

I was never taught to how to write well; I don't think anyone really tried. It was only when I hired a private tutor to help me with my writing, in my last year as an undergraduate, that I finally received instruction. My tutor was another student, and with his help I started to learn to write as other people would read, and not according to what I wished to say.

117. The only person guaranteed to support you is yourself.

We'd like our parents to defend and protect us, always. Our parents can't, even if they would like to, nor can anyone else, either. Support and protection is what a well-adjusted mother does. There is a time after which it should stop. Once we mature, we must learn to be responsible if we are to continue learning on our own. Even the most supportive partner in your later life should hold you responsible.

We often find support from people who are less closely attached than family, and whose agendas are less complicated. We get to choose our relationships with friends and partners. It takes a lifetime to develop the skill of knowing whom to trust.

Learning to trust requires making all manner of mistakes and, when it comes to relationships and people, the number of mistakes seems endless. Recovery from some of these mistakes can take a long time. Recovery from business mistakes can take several years. Recovery from a failed relationship can take a decade.

In the testing of people and relationships there is only one standard that you can rely upon, and that's how you feel. You may not always be right, but you are the only person who deserves your unconditional trust. You are the only person whose interests are always your own.

There is an exception. Some of us have been so disabled, confused, or misdirected that we are at war with ourselves. Most of us have several people inside of us and some can be self-destructive.

If you ever feel weak, self-effacing, or self-destructive—and most of us have these feelings at some point—then recognize that these parts of you—while they may need your help—may not deserve your trust. What I tell people to do, if this is the case, is to build an alliance with the strongest and most trusted aspects of themselves so they can better recognize the less able or less reliable aspects within them.

This is not an issue of alliance versus enmity, but of recognizing more and less mature voices. Hearing these voices clearly and knowing where they come from is a mature ability. It begins in childhood when we see in someone else the reflection of trust from inside ourselves. If you have a trusted inner guide, nurture them. If you don't, find them.

118. There are five parts to every solution.

The five parts to every solution are opportunity, vision, idea, argument, and consequence. The opportunity is the platform you stand on. The vision is what you believe needs to be done. The idea is how you propose to go about it. The argument is your step-by-step solution or proposal. And the consequence is, basically, why anyone should care. Of course, once you've achieved the solution, there is still more work to do. But that's another story.

Opportunity

Start with the opportunity, as this is often given to you. It's something that precedes the project. By the time the problem is clear, the opportunity is already in place. You will have worked to get yourself there.

Vision

The vision is what the project means to you. This is your personal investment and how the solution will affect you. The vision should contain your motivation. It might be incorrect, but it cannot be wrong because it is yours to define. It is always your right to have a vision.

Idea

The idea is how you state the problem, which connects your argument with the consequence you foresee. Your idea might be unlikely, unwelcome, or unwarranted, but unless it's completely confused, it usually has some merit. It is the value of your proposition.

Argument

The argument is the detail, form, and novelty you're presenting. You can have a new solution without a new argument; you can solve a problem using old tools. The direct approach always uses old tools, but the most celebrated solutions create new ones.

Consequence

You have the right to your own opinions about the consequence of your work, just as you do regarding your vision. Your vision is what you think is important, the consequence is what you propose to do about it. Big consequences provide big motivations but are naturally more vulnerable and harder to defend.

New ideas are often criticized because they deviate from the norm. It's frustrating to defend work that has been attacked on the basis of its failure to meet a standard it didn't aim to meet. I have a biology article that's been rejected from peer-reviewed journals on grounds so frustrating that I refuse to read the criticisms. This is fairly typical of the headwinds that new ideas face. Resistance can have positive results but not always.

Two common lines of criticism are that the details are in error, or the technique is not appropriate. Most criticism is directed at one of these aspects of a work. It's the easiest aspect to criticize and the easiest kind of criticism to substantiate. Any time you propose a new argument, it will first be seen as a target.

When cubist painting was introduced in the 1920s, it was criticized as being skill-less and ugly, both being criticisms overlooking the vision and the idea. The critics were secure because art was expected to be whatever the critics expected.

In the rare case that you solve a problem that has defeated everyone else by using the same tools as everyone else, you will immediately gain recognition. Such people become celebrities in their field and unknown outside it.

Most people opt for small consequences as most people prefer lower risk. This creates the mistaken illusion that there are few ideas of large consequence available to you, which is untrue. It's just that most people are afraid of ideas that have big consequences.

Every solution applies resources to an issue. Often, the inspiration for a solution emerges from your advantage in access to, or understanding of, the resources. This may include the problem itself as most resources exist in close association with the tasks for which they're used.

It pays to have insight, experience, and access to all aspects of a problem, not just those that others consider necessary. Most of the brilliant people I've worked with were multi-talented and cross-disciplinary, often combining talents that most others in their field did not have. It's even more powerful if you're multi-passioned.

Our culture loves heroes, which often means people who do something a saner person would not do. People like this kind of person because they feel that if someone who's remotely like them can do it, they might do it, too. Why else would anyone really care that Richard Branson ballooned around the world, Aleix Segura held his breath for 24 minutes, or Wim Hof climbed Mt. Everest in his underwear?

119. Trust your judgment.

You may not be right, but unless you find out why you're not right, you won't learn. Building judgment is a dynamic process of rewards and consequences.

Your judgement includes what you think is the cause of things, the present intent of things, and the future consequences of things. In addition, you may have a greater sense of how things fit together: the meaning of things.

Emotions represent judgments and these can be complicated. Use your emotions as "the writing on the wall," and recognize that just because you see it "written" doesn't mean it's true. It means that one part of you feels something that the rest of you should be aware of.

These parts of you are important. They will continue to inform you. You cannot argue them, rather, you must allow each part of you—each aspect of your intuitive intelligence—to explore the consequences of its own way of thinking. In this sense, trusting your judgment does not mean that you believe you're right. It means you have sufficient faith to follow your inclinations and learn.

Some of our ideas should not be followed or made real. Nevertheless, these ideas are important too. They are insights into what we don't need, don't want, or is fundamentally wrong. These are difficult ideas but necessary in order to build discernment. Faith is your capacity to hold onto an idea that doesn't make sense. Judgment is your capacity to embrace both the good and the bad, and to understand the difference between them.

"A casual stroll through the lunatic asylum shows that faith does not prove anything."
— **Friedrich Nietzsche**, philosopher

6 – Encounters

Learning is like business, you can be an employee or an entrepreneur. It's your choice, up to a point. As in a business, employees with upward mobility define their jobs as they progress, but most employees think like students as that is the relation to authority with which they're most familiar.

It's useful to explore the latitude this perspective may afford you. How much freedom of thought does your job or position allow? What kind of thinking is expected of you and those around you? You would be surprised at how narrowly these questions are conceived. It's important to know how other people think. You'll get part of the answer by asking.

120. How is skill recognized?

What does your teacher, supervisor, boss, or authority think is skillful? What they think defines the opportunities they offer you. Performance reviews, tests, and scores of various sorts are the standard, and they're what most students shoot for. High scores raise your status, but they rarely open new opportunities. They may take you to what is advertised as the next level, but they won't take you out of the system.

If you rely on someone else's standards, and they rely on a standard even further removed from you, then there's little chance your skills will be recognized. In an institutional context, individuality is rarely valued.

A test is backward looking and offers nothing educational. Carefully devised tests provide insight, but these are tests of a different kind, more like real-life experiences. It's too bad we don't have a word to distinguish these types of tests. Rites of passage is the only word I can think of, but that expression has fallen into disuse.

In a larger sense, a test is an experiment and you learn something when an experiment fails. In terms of gaining experimental insight, we're always looking for a test's failure point. Is it not strange that this productive notion of testing has been abandoned in school?

Tests, in the sense used in school, are rare in business because they're demeaning. In business, the job is the test; what you do which speaks for itself. What counts is how you react to what you don't know, not what you've been taught. Reflect on how different this is from tests in school.

> *"When Richard Branson was four, his mom drove him miles from home, let him out of the car, told him to find his way back on his own and drove off. He did. That was the making of him, he reports in his autobiography. He was given his turn and he pulled it off. Nothing would ever daunt him again... This is how you get private moon rockets built, by giving future builders a turn at four."*
> — **John Taylor Gatto**, from "Don't Worry About College: A Letter to My Granddaughter"

Community

121. Learn for your own benefit.

Imagine there was a written test to evaluate your preparation for a rite of passage. You need to prepare for this event, certainly, but you would hope your skills would be understood in the same way you are understood. This is where tests fail: they do not understand you, and they do not aim to.

In a rite of passage one rarely fails. You are prepared for the test and it's given when you are ready. A rite of passage presumes you are on a path and as long as you remain on the path you will eventually secure passage. It may not be now, it could be later. You could find yourself held back or moved forward, but the notion of being ranked, numbered, and assigned is foreign. A rite of passage is a ceremony in honor of your achievement; a final exam is a sacrifice of you to someone else.

Learning to drive is a rite of passage. Once you've learned to drive, you can drive. Testing your driving is something else. Testing your driving is a sacrifice you're asked to make for public safety. You might learn from your driver's test, but that's not the point.

Similarly, learning to fly is a rite of passage. There is a written test and a practical test, but it's the practical that's considered definitive. In every field where there is a real need and a real risk, to know is not enough, you have to be able to do it.

Do you understand why tests must be administered individually? Do you understand why working with another person is considered cheating? We have been trained to take this for granted, but what is the result? The result is that we fight with each other, and we do not learn how to work together. We are anti-socialized.

122. Work toward collaboration.

Collaboration transforms a test into a learning experience. A cohesive group works together. Individual performance matters, but the result that matters most is the result achieved by the group. We use the word team to indicate a group of people working in collaboration, but a team has come to mean something quite structured, in which roles are assigned. It is surprising how little collaboration goes on, how little community-building actually takes place.

A collaboration—which is the word we might as well use—is a group focused on a goal, not a structure as you find in teams, squads, and clubs. You wouldn't call a group of hikers, scholars, or friends a team even though they all may share a common goal. Collaborators have autonomy.

Form collaborations of friends, companions, neighbors, and travelers who recognize shared goals and common obstacles. When you form your own communities, all your efforts are meaningful. The result is an increase in synergy, effectiveness, and reward.

The most educational course I ever took was a numerical analysis class in which class members had to collaborate to solve a problem that required a unified effort. Every week we were given a new problem too big for any one of us to solve. We were told that we would have to work together, and we were left to our own devices.

We could form teams, collaborations, or work alone. The answer consisted of a few, multi-digit numbers, and each person was responsible for handing in the same set of numbers. If, for some reason, you were not able to find a number or found the wrong number, then you lost credit. There was no policing and there were no rules. There was no partial credit for each number, which was either the right number or not the right number.

The class was really about the process of working together, taking apart the problem, proposing different approaches, understanding the alternatives, arguing them out, delegating tasks, and finding answers as effectively as possible. Every week was like another "Manhattan Project."

The teacher, Eyvind Wichmann, gave lectures but played no role in the solutions. Sometimes I'd speak to him and he'd scribble things on the board that I hardly understood. I think he was intentionally being opaque because he always seemed to be chuckling to himself. Wichmann was Finnish, and it is probably no coincidence that Finland has the best educational system in the world. It was the best class I ever had.

> *"The modern university... is an efficient mechanism for developing and transferring information, but it is not well-suited to addressing the complex, multifaceted problems of our times—crime, addiction, unemployment, discrimination, ethnic hatred, and so on. Were we to design a university in response to such needs, it almost certainly would have a more flexible, interdisciplinary structure, where students and professors from various fields could more readily work together in task-oriented teams."*
> — **Thomas R. Fisher**, Dean of the School of Architecture, University of Minnesota (Fisher, 2000)

123. Choose the thoughts you expose yourself to.

I have trained myself not to read advertisements which is generally safe, but not always. I will not read journalism, listen to music, or watch videos without screening them first. I will not listen to or agree with people who think badly, according to my judgment.

You cannot avoid thinking about an idea once it's in your mind even if you don't want to think about it. The primary role of your personality is to filter your environment, to accept what's good and reject what's bad. Use this filter. Be discerning.

Other people's ideas usually reflect their personal agenda. Those ideas that are broadcast most emphatically usually have a slightly pathological intent. Many widely consumed images, emphatically embraced behaviors, and generally endorsed attitudes contain a streak of mass pathology. The psychologically twisted intentions and subliminal mechanisms in commercial advertising and public discourse go far beyond what's considered fair and appropriate. Just because consumers "buy" the story in no way certifies the product.

Once someone else's ideas have been put into your head, it's too late. It's hard to remove an idea that's coated with subliminal attractions. The best you can do with bad ideas is to learn how to avoid them and recognize how you are manipulated.

"What you do, what you own, what you plan, what you believe, who you think you are, what you want, and so much more are the result of beliefs and values you've been trained to have, to be, and to want. Some of this is simple enculturation, but when it takes on the intent of deliberate manipulation, then enculturation per se is an inadequate term."
— **Eldon Taylor**, PhD, therapist and coach (Taylor, 2009)

Robots

The tech revolution illuminates the difference between what teachers teach and employers need. The skills needed in a turbulent world—where opportunities are found by exploring change—are not those taught or recognized in a predetermined world of segregated subjects. Innovation is disruptive, and the students most suited to prevail today are the ones most likely to be excluded: the disruptive ones.

New York University's program in integrated digital media was the first university program I noticed to completely break the mold of linear learning. The students whom I knew in the program had learned outside of school, building computers in their basements and playing on-line games, often to the dismay of their parents and teachers.

Digital media programs combine "artistic inquiry with scientific research and technological practice to explore the social, cultural and ethical potentials of emerging technologies." Rather than follow decades-old textbook material students "work in small teams… collaborate on intensive, four-month projects, often with industry clients for real-world experience," as described in a program at the British Columbia Institute of Technology.

These disruptive tech media programs started appearing around 2005 and now, fifteen years later, are widespread. They have had a bleed-through effect in digital engineering but little on traditional education. Most teachers and administrators outside of these programs are not aware of what's happening.

124. People project their feelings, issues, and visions.

Everyone projects their internal world onto their external reality. That's how we generate the feedback we need to understand ourselves. We project these visions onto the surrounding environment in order to understand what works and why things don't work.

When the issues are complex and the dramas we create fail to enlighten us, we recreate the same issues repeatedly and eventually, maybe, we figure it out. Sad to say, speaking as a therapist, these re-enactments usually lead to the same conclusions. We're so good at recreating our problems without adding any new understanding that we keep getting the same results. Learning is absent in these situations, but if we are going to find a solution, learning is crucial.

Projecting is normal. Not only does it happen all the time but it's necessary; if your neurons cannot recreate a resonance in the present with a situation you've experienced in the past, then you won't know what to make of it. Understanding what you're projecting is a question of how accurately you project from your past experience, but you must stand back from it. You must realize that you are creating your situation; it's not fate. You have the power to change it.

We resent the projections of others, especially where there's conflict, but we project on others, too. Much of the time, we don't even see other people for who they are, we see them only in the roles they play for us. If the cycle is to be broken, something must change.

When you see yourself taking a hand in creating your reality, look for the purpose. Much of it is automatic. It's done without thought or awareness, and your reaction to what you experience is what's drawing you to explore. It may have little or nothing to do with you personally; it's simply a reaction to a confluence of circumstances in which you are involved. In therapy, I draw out a person's feelings so they can recognize the role they're playing in what appears to be something independent of them. It's not; you always have some hand in making your world real.

Combative people always seem to find each other and, when they do, there's combat. I'm on a community committee with another member who is authoritarian. Being anti-authoritarian myself, we have opposing views. This person criticizes me in dismissive ways. This has nothing to do with my decisions, it's about my general attitude. It's not business, it's personal!

200

The criticisms are this person's effort to find confirmation of their point of view, and they're frustrated because I don't provide it. I cannot reform them; there would be no benefit in trying. Our ability to conduct business is hampered by our personal views, and—though it's selfish of me to say it—I don't care. Were I more invested, I would confront the issue, but neither of us will change our opinions. One or the other of us will leave the committee.

125. Social attitudes have a life of their own.

Trends of social thinking—or memes, if you will—have a life of their own. People are carriers of these attitudes, as if the memes attract actors to play out their drama in search of a resolution. And the idea, if it's successful, multiplies in others and mutates, like a living thing. If the idea is profitable, it spreads. If it contains problems, then many are enlisted in resolving them. If a resolution is found, we're given a new script, which we follow, hardly noticing a change.

Your reality is a stage on which you have created a story. Your story combines your unique experiences, enculturation, expressed genetics, and developed aptitudes. It is the common ground you share with others that conflates our personal stories into social memes that reflect common issues, traumas, and needs.

Help others by taking full responsibility for your projections and more than your fair share of theirs. Recognize and support people's needs. One hopes they will relax their compulsion to follow social scripts and contribute personal insight. This does not happen without practice.

We create spectacles and we're willing to pay money for it: political contests, celebrity intrigue, social darlings, tabloid romance, sports competition, superstars rising, lottery winners and hidden conspiracies. We weave these stories to make our consensual reality with which we interpret the world. This happens unconsciously and is to be expected.

There is little point in explaining the fantasy nature of these stories because those who are enmeshed in them are wedded to them. It is in the nature of our reasoning mind to distort explanation to fit our purposes. You should expect this. You would be flattering yourself to think you are above the fray. You create dramas for yourself, too, for your own purposes.

This process can get out of hand. People take things literally and lose sight of the learning role these projections play. If this happens, people identify with their religious, national, racial, cultural or other projected roles and become less personally responsible. When metaphor becomes real, weapons can become lethal.

The world is currently experiencing the COVID-19 pandemic. Many people are practically hysterical. Others are attempting to control the situation without knowledge or insight. The result is layers of misinformation, misunderstanding, fear, pugnacity, and ignorance in everything from casual conversation to pseudo-scientific policy. People don't know how to use what little they do know in order to find their way out of ignorance.

126. Discover what others see as your strengths and weaknesses.

Know the latitude you're accorded in the role you're given. You will rarely be seen in the way you expect. This is partly due to how little effect you have in being seen for who you are, and partly due to how little interest others have in knowing you authentically. You have greater power than can be expressed in the limited opportunities made available to you, so play the largest role in shaping how you're seen and in creating more opportunities.

> *"Paul made me realize the person who wants it the most is the one that's going to win. The person that's not afraid to go out there and do it. So wrestling, in my life, even my parents saw it... by the time the end of this season came around they're, like—they didn't know who I was—they're, like, 'Who are you? Where'd you come from?' And I changed."*
> — **Mike Short**, student, from *The Learning Project*

You cannot easily change what other people perceive, but you can inquire as to how other people see you. Learning to understand others is a skill that isn't taught and isn't simple.

There are many levels to the ways people communicate, and everyone's method of communication is slightly different. Words are a loose container that is estimated to convey a surprisingly small 7% of what people are trying to communicate. Body language conveys more intent than spoken language, and there is an astounding amount of subliminal information that we hear, see, and otherwise perceive and register but are entirely unaware of.

When you inquire, put yourself in listening mode. This is not because your own views are unimportant, but because agents of authority are generally poor listeners. The Buddha said, "If your mouth is open, you're not learning." I assume he meant that you're not learning if your ears are closed, because explaining to others is the best way of learning of what you speak. Partly, it's the feedback that teaches you, but also you learn by listening to yourself. In any event, if you're not being heard, don't bother talking.

> *"What you think you become. What you feel you attract.*
> *What you imagine you create."*
> — ascribed to **The Buddha**

127. Thinking is in conflict with a full and meaningful life.

Feeling and thinking cover the territory of experience from different perspectives. Thinking considers situations in order to understand their consequences. Feeling is an experience of many consequences that engage you at a visceral level. You cannot argue your way to a different way of feeling, and you cannot change the facts by feeling differently. A full and meaningful life depends entirely on how you feel, and not on what you think.

Because most facts are really stand-ins for feelings—that is, you accept facts according to what feels correct—rearranging the facts won't change your feelings. What feeling can do is lead you to think that some facts are no longer important, such as when a person completely misunderstands a situation and wrongly ascribes intentions to others.

Even if your facts are shown to be entirely wrong, it can still be hard to change how you feel. Such is the case with heartbreak where you really want to feel one way, but all the facts indicate something else. It's easy to foster illusions when those illusions are attractive or satisfy a deep need. The greatest chance you have in changing your thinking is to discover new thoughts that have new feelings. If these new feelings prevail over old feelings then the new thoughts will prevail over the old thoughts, and you will change your mind.

"It's easier to act your way into a new way of thinking, than think your way into a new way of acting."
— **Jerry Sternin**, author of *The Power of Positive Deviance; How Unlikely Innovators Solve the World's Toughest Problems*

Jerry Sternin, founder of the Positive Deviance Collaborative, advocates looking for what does work, not what should work. He has approached big problems—such as slavery and malnutrition—by focusing on practices that work, not on theories of what should.

It can be scary to take a new approach when you think you know how things should work out. There is wisdom in relaxing into things as they naturally develop, rather than trying to change the course of history because you believe you know better. If people took this approach, it would be difficult to fight a war on the basis of an ideology.

Before we were intellectual animals, we acted emotionally. Our intellects evolved in order that would could discern the consequences of what we see. Our emotions are still there, connected to our larger sense of things; connected more to the whole than to the parts.

We identify with thinking because we have more control over it, but emotion underlies thought and there's little we can do about it. When emotion doesn't serve us, we think it must be wrong. This has been the cause of much conflict, subjugation, waste, and destruction. As the saying goes, "The road to hell is paved with good intentions."

We identify more with intellect because we feel we are free agents, a control that mostly consists of the filtering out of what we want to exclude—a reduction of the multiply-connected, holographic world to something linear. Spiritual, emotional and other disordered experiences are important because they make the world bigger.

205

"Never express yourself more clearly than you are able to think."
— **Niels Bohr**, PhD, physicist

128. Don't attempt to solve what you think is the central problem.

The credo of the positive deviance approach asks you to turn away from the expert and toward the facilitator. This is opposite to the trend that killed the "witches"—who were healers in a communalist culture—and installed the doctors—who were agents of an authoritarian state.

We see this sort of turning-away happening today. It is the logically and socially deviant practice of grass-roots activism, social disobedience, creative license, alternative medicine, extreme sports, crowd sourcing, unschooling, and common sense. It involves power-sharing with non-experts and the abandonment of central control.

Deviance is embraced at the highest levels of science but largely in private by the few who follow their intuition. Jerry Lettvin, a neurophysiologist who held court with the greatest hearts and minds of his time, advised me, "Don't do the research first, write your papers first. Do the research later." As a poet, Jerry recognized that insight comes from the heart.

129. Pay attention to how you're being heard.

Learning to communicate is arguably your most important skill. It's a skill that cannot be explained because a large part of what you mean—one might even argue all of what you mean—transcends what can be explained. I don't mean that what you

206

intend cannot be adequately explained, but that it cannot be fully explained. There's always a compromise.

How you're being heard will determine the opportunities you're given. As is so often the case, how well you're understood is not determined by how well you explain yourself, but by how much you have in common with the other person.

Students deserve more latitude than employees because they should benefit from their own efforts, but when the syllabus is paramount, this opportunity is lost. In traditional schooling, the object is not learning but grading, ranking, and certifying. The skills you'll need are not what you're taught.

The Greco-Roman thinking—which lies at the root of liberal arts education—held that all free men needed the verbal arts of grammar, logic, and rhetoric, and the four numeric arts of mathematics, geometry, music, and astronomy. Women were given no formal education, and slaves were only taught the servile arts.

While times have certainly changed, you will notice that most of compulsory education focuses on training one to be of service. As college education has become more widespread, it too, has shifted from the liberal arts to professional training. Most of the essential things I know I've learned myself. This is also true of most of those who mentored me.

"Just because a teacher tells you something, that this is what you're going to see or do,... no, medicine doesn't work like that. Life doesn't work like that either. You will most likely see the complete opposite... You start with a foundation and you build on it. After you've built on that, another problem arises and you build on that, make that

problem your cornerstone and keep building,... and build, and build, and build... I get in there and I engage. I make sure that I have some sort of understanding about what's going on. There is no excuse, no excuse for failure to engage."
—**Dave Williamson**, US Army Medic, from *The Learning Project*

130. Efficiency is not enough.

Efficiency means not wasting energy, but if your task is a waste of energy, then you're not being effective no matter how efficient you are. Being effective takes a more farsighted view, it presumes a goal, not just a means. And while your goal could also be a waste of energy, at least it completes the plan. Have a plan, not just a means. Know what you're doing and why, not just how.

Having a goal is a dangerous thing. If you're too efficient, you'll be through the forest without seeing the trees. There's a lot to be said for being inefficient in accomplishing a goal where the best to be achieved is the creation of opportunities and a broadening of understanding.

This is the most important lesson in learning: you should never be so sure of where you're going that you fail to learn from the process. After all, in any real process of discovery you really don't know where you're going. As a result, getting there as fast as possible makes the whole endeavor a waste of time.

"Well, I persuaded a student, Arno Penzias, to work with me and look for Hydrogen in inter-galactic space. And he worked hard at it. We made a maser amplifier to get great sensitivity, and he looked. He didn't find it. Well, that still

made a thesis for him, he got his PhD and he got a job at Bell Labs and he wanted to look some more. And so he made a good maser amplifier and he had a very good antenna at Bell Labs.

"And he and a friend of his, Bob Wilson, looked. They didn't find Hydrogen, but what did they find? They found the Big Bang: the origin of the universe... What a wonderful discovery... So he didn't find Hydrogen, a great disappointment maybe but—wow!—he made one of the most important discoveries in the world."
— **Charles H. Townes**, PhD, physicist, in *The Learning Project*

Your goal is being effective, not being efficient. Efficiency targets the processes while effectiveness addresses the whole. Your goal may be high performance, but will efficiency take you closer to your goal? If you cannot distinguish between efficiency and effectiveness, then you'll have a short-term plan but no long-term plan. There should be both.

Stimulation

131. Read too much.

When you're ready, don't just read a little so that you want to read more, read so much that when you're finished reading you need to start doing. Read so much that you light your imagination and then, when you run out of reading, you'll find yourself on fire.

Reading should be enervating. Avoid reading drudgery that wears you down. One has enough of searching through haystacks when you're trying to get your bearings. Inspiration is not that.

"I read my eyes out and can't read half enough...the more one reads the more one sees we have to read."
— **John Adams**, 2nd President of the United States

Don't read at all until you're ready, but when you're ready, let it bloom. Some bloom early or late, and some are slow or fast. It's a transition kids go through as neural structures come online. Having a school syllabus that teaches reading to everyone at the same age and at the same pace is criminal.

Girls develop these circuits sooner than boys, and you cannot rush it any more than you can ask a legless tadpole to jump. It's staggering that mainstream education systems fail to recognize this and, as a result, permanently turn many people off from developing reading skills ever.

Not everyone is ready to read. It's an issue of vocabulary and imagination. We think with mirror neurons that recreate in our imagination experiences we've had before. From this comes metaphor and, from that, imagination and creativity.

"To be a master of metaphor is the greatest thing by far. It is the one thing that cannot be learnt from others, and it is also a sign of genius."
— **Aristotle**, philosopher

There is a fine line between the flash of insight and the scars of too much information. There is an important difference between child and adult material, and there's much more in this nether zone than simply sex and violence. This is a subject beyond this book, but evil is something that manifests in people, and it can be fostered in children.

I encountered deeply disturbing material as a child when I stumbled on Matthew Brady's photo essays of the Civil War, chronicles of American racism, and photos taken during and after the holocaust. As a result, I felt more in those images than what was on the page. They changed my life and I still remember them. I can't say whether the effects of this exposure was good or bad because it remains unsettled, but I still feel a sense of injury from them.

132. Don't read too much.

Before you become comfortable with reading, don't read. As you become comfortable reading, read a lot. After you're comfortable reading, stop reading and start doing. Reading is worth nothing if it does not cause you to act.

Eugene Wigner was one of the more saintly people I've known: patient, smart, humble, and good-humored. He was an inspiring mentor. Easily excited, he would literally bob up and down for emphasis, admonishing me, "Don't read too much!"

He was speaking to me as a fellow researcher—though I was hardly even a student—and in research, reading can become a huge drag on productivity because there is an endless amount of material. Reading must bring you to the surface, like you're ascending from the depths. You need light; you need air. If you don't reach the surface quickly enough, you drown.

First, as procrastination, reading too much lends to the never-ending feeling that you need to learn more. It fosters the illusion that unless you have a massive, well-supported point you have no right to speak. And second, reading other people's ideas will quash your own by loading them with arguments, doubts, and criticisms. Few ideas can grow beneath the suffocating black plastic sheet of other people's opinions.

You are a person of action—if you are anything—and every action is a new frontier to some extent. Get accustomed to taking the initiative. That means doing things for your own reasons and needs, without the support of justification of others. Don't read too much!

> *"Books are fatal: they are the curse of the human race. Nine-tenths of existing books are nonsense, and the clever books are the refutation of that nonsense."*
> — **Benjamin Disraeli**, Prime Minister of the United Kingdom, from *Lothair*, a novel

That being said, of course, I read too much. I try to keep it under control. At certain points I say to myself, "Enough is enough!" and force myself to write, think, and create. I've learned to read in different ways so that I am not hijacked by lesser material. In reading—as in conversation—if the person talking to me cannot speak or write well or cannot get to the point, I cut them off.

> *"The intellect is a great danger to creativity because you begin to rationalize and make up reasons for things instead of staying with your own basic truth—who you are, what you are, what you wanna be."*
> — **Ray Bradbury**, author

133. Inoculate yourself against computerized entertainment.

Being fixated on video products—news, entertainment, and games—is a waste of time. They're generally dopey, repetitive, and irrelevant. Some contain valuable lessons... but it's not valuable if you do it over and over. If you're attracted to puzzles, learn quickly, and move on. If you're attracted for entertainment, have fun, discern their lack of value, and move on.

These stimulants are designed to be addictive. They create a cult following for the profit of others, and they take more than they give. Cults never serve you. These forms of media halt your growth, drain your power, and interfere with your control of attention. From both a neurological and social perspective, video is an opiate of the masses.

As with viral infections, the only sure way to gain immunity is to encounter and to survive the illness. Maybe a vaccine will be invented some day, but today the only certain cure I've seen for video and game addiction is to immerse oneself completely. The only people I know who are fully "cured" of video addictions are those who were, at first, addicted and let it play out. As a result, they have put these things in their place.

The First Step

Writing outlines is important. The purpose of an outline is to quickly reach a point where it can be thrown away. Outlines are mostly garbage, and that's what you want them to be. They are filters that catch all the detritus attached to a topic. You fill them in and, when you're finished, that's all they are: largely filler.

134. Outline a lot.

We naturally outline when we think. Most thinking is shallow outline-thinking. It's necessary: we think, review, and revise. Do a lot of thinking to yourself. Remember the good thoughts. Replace the bad.

You want an outline that's got all the garbage so that you can distinguish between what's related, what's relevant, and what isn't. You want to see as much as possible, and an outline is a survey of the everything.

My first outline for this book was a fantasy. Most early outlines are, and that's a great way to find direction and confidence when setting out. It would lead to a disaster if you followed your outline without revision, but it is not a waste as long as you don't waste time on it.

I'm reminded of a Boy Scout troop heading onto the trail, weighed down with everything they could possibly need. They don't get far. As alpinists, we started out with the same list of needs, but brought the minimum, which was less than was comfortable. Traveling fast and light, we got by with just enough.

135. Don't overlook the details.

Don't underrate the importance of long-term planning but recognize that *The Big Picture* is made of many little pictures. There are many stories of tunnels being dug that come out in the wrong place, master plans that accomplish the wrong result. A big project is like a marriage, and the success of marriage lies in the details.

I spent a year running hours of code on an expensive supercomputer, only to spend a final few days to discover that the equations were wrong. I married a woman on the basis of mutual affirmations of raising a family, only to discover—after we had a family—that we disagreed on what a family meant.

Prior to our expedition to climb a new route on Alaska's Mount McKinley, we studied the details carefully. We knew every step of the route according to our high resolution, aerial photos, but after the bush pilot dropped us at the base of the mountain, we found critical features of the route were five times larger than we had thought. We had assumed the wrong scale, and it now appeared impassible. Wisely, we changed our route.

136. Do the most with the least.

Get the most out of everything. This isn't just efficient, it's effective. Using something fully gives you both the short and the long-term benefit. To fully understand something you must understand it at all scales. Ask questions, question answers, turn over rocks, and look under the hood. If you're not being annoying and ripping a few stitches, then you're not asking enough questions.

If you're interested in cars, then learn not only the models but also the tools, fuels, manufacture, repair, social, national, and economic roles, their creation, use, and disposal. Learn how you can and can't drive them. Understand roads, accidents, laws, and behaviors. Learn how they affect the environment and people's thoughts and behaviors. Follow all the aspects of automobile celebrity, exuberance, failure, status, economy, and ecology. That will teach you something!

Louis L'Amour is the quintessential mountaineering author, not because he wrote about mountains—most of his 105 books are Westerns—but because every aspect of his books is useful to the project. My friend Fred Beckey taught a generation of us how to consume them: read them during storms for their calm, time-passing effect. As you read each page, tear it out, crumple and stuff it into your jacket for insulation. In the morning, burn the pages to make tea.

"Five lines where three are enough is stupidity. Nine pounds where three are sufficient is obesity. To know what to leave out and what to put in, just where and just how—At, that is

to have been educated in knowledge of simplicity."
— **Frank Lloyd Wright** (Wright, 1992)

Perspectives

If you collect everything into *The Big Picture*, you'll quickly see what's missing. What's more, you'll see what's important. With that information, you stand on the verge of making a difference.

137. The more important something is, the less straight forwardly you can think about it.

Clarity is often in conflict with completeness. Clarity means reducing something to a well-understood, essential picture. Completeness includes a regard for all things and their consequences. Clarity can be inaccurate in some particulars, and inappropriate in its generality. The purpose of clarity is having a context to do a few things correctly.

A complete picture is a picture of the whole that hangs together. The purpose of completeness is to justify the whole event or approach, usually because some kind of wrap-up is wanted.

The connections between things are rarely straight. Appreciate confused thinking as having a validity that complements, and is often more accurate, than clear, straight thinking.

My physics dissertation required a number of solutions to unsolved problems and I was the only person on the project. Every night I would fret about these obstacles until I'd come up with a vaguely plausible solution. I would then relax and go to sleep. I never remembered these solutions in the morning, which was just as well.

"How wonderful that we have met with a paradox. Now we have some hope of making progress."
— **Niels Bohr**, PhD, physicist

138. If you have your own ideas, expect resistance.

Expect resistance both inside and outside of yourself. Move along the edge of it, rather than letting it overwhelm you. Imagine resistance as a wave that you want to ride. Orient yourself to the directions from which this resistance comes and find a path that flows with it. If you can't flow with it, then recognize that you're fighting against it and you may well fail. Make your decisions based on the long-term and what insights you have of it.

Use resistance against itself; make it an ally. A wave is just water, but it has the weight of the sea behind it. More than that, there is not just one wave. Resistance is a source of energy and evidence of your engagement with something real. Instead of rejecting it, bring it toward you and help it flow to its natural conclusion.

"It's not what happens that counts, it's how you react."
— **Bruce Lee**, martial artist and actor

139. Endeavor to make a difference.

If you see what's needed and you have an idea about how to obtain it, then your idea is good. Even if it turns out you're not the first, or someone else has already found an answer, you're still ahead because you understand why something is important. You can distinguish the strengths and weaknesses of partial solutions.

All solutions are partial solutions. All answers turn out to be partial answers when you understand the larger scope of the question. It's often the case that the larger scope is hidden in the details, and it takes a questioning mind to find it. It's hard to see beyond the details when you're focusing on them.

> *"Believe in the good things... believe that it's worth at least to save one thing for future generations. And it's worth it, that's something important. And you don't lose that feeling. When you're adult and you haven't learned that, it becomes very hard to keep believing in things when you see that nobody else does, or everything's against you."*
> — **Gudrun Sperrer**, teacher and wildlife conservator, from *The Learning Project*

Exploring the details and asking, "Why?" can be rewarding, but is rarely encouraged. The reception you get in asking these kinds of questions can distinguish a good opportunity from a great opportunity. It's the difference between doing what's on offer, and questioning what's on offer. Question what's on offer.

140. At its root, every tool is a compromise.

You don't have to master your tools in order to understand what they're good for, but you'll learn more about them if you do. Usually, there are several purposes for every tool. Some are obvious and others are obscure. Some functions are hidden by a tool's difficulty of use, such as that of an airplane. Others are revealed in what a tool accomplishes, like an ax. Understanding a tool's full scope reveals the problem it solves at a deeper level.

You can't explore new territory until you get there, and these boundaries are not entirely geographical. For some reason, people think pushing any limit is impressive. In most cases it's just pathological, to which the entries in the *Guinness Book of World Records* will attest. There is something innately human about doing new things. Every tool is an invitation to explore some limitation.

Every subject can be seen from either of two sides: how it's understood and how it's not understood. Every project or product has the same two sides: what it does, and what it can't do. Seen from the opposite side of what can be done, every project contains the seed of a problem to be solved.

In today's cross-disciplinary and interconnected world, important insights can come from any direction. Celebrity and wealth are on offer to anyone who can make the rich richer and the powerful more powerful, but even small ideas can make big changes: zip-lock bags, container ships, LED's, and perhaps medicine's greatest invention: washing your hands. After decades of trying to prove my intelligence, I have succeeded: I have found a better way to tie my shoes.

141. When you get something new, try to break it.

This is what kids do naturally, as do monkeys. Breaking things has been the path of our evolution and is the meat and potatoes of scientific exploration.

One of my father's favorite comments was, "Shall we read the instructions, or break it first?" Reading the instructions is like reading the spoilers. Solve the puzzle yourself. Unfortunately, as children, we're told to stop this insightful approach, and that's too bad. It works so well!

"I went through the entire house and took stuff apart. My Mom got mad at me because I would always forget to put it

*back together, and there would be stuff that kind of works
and there's stuff that straight-up doesn't, like our phone."*
— **Hamilton Shu**, student, from *The Learning Project*

Some discoveries are deduced, but most are accidental, perhaps not entirely, but rather the result of a thousand accidents. You circle through what's likely when searching for the truth. If it's your passion, you keep looking.

Innovations for survival are another matter. There would be more such innovations if invention was more essential. When your survival is the issue, you won't have the resources to mass produce your innovation.

142. Inspiration, practicality, and value are separate aspects of innovation.

Any puzzle will have aspects—different approaches that illuminate it in different ways. There is a creative aspect that requires innovation, a practical aspect that generates material results, and a contextual aspect in which a solution's value can be considered.

Any problem, any puzzle, can be intriguing. You can categorize people by the kinds of puzzles they're attracted to. Some people seem to be attracted to nothing. They act like they're awake but they're asleep.

Approach puzzles broadly. See them as a reflection of your ability, a situation, an opportunity, and a need. Every puzzle is a thought experiment.

I don't know of any comprehensive list of puzzle types, but at any point in time it seems that certain puzzles are recognized and popular. One's need directs one's interest and attention, and, for that reason, practical puzzles have always been popular. That includes mechanical, intellectual, emotional, physical, and social puzzles. Every field has its own puzzles, but there seems to be a smaller set of underlying types.

143. The benefit of being childlike.

The benefit of retaining one's childishness lies in being curious, open-minded, attentive, and unprejudiced. These are valuable qualities we can retain as adults without returning to a juvenile state of mind.

We barely remember our early childhood, and few of us can recover a childhood mentality. Most talk extolling children and childhood is misleadingly, sounds attractive, but has no follow-through. For many people, childhood is a sad and troubled period which everyone would like to remember fondly, but few do.

In my experience as a scientist and therapist, those people who retain positive, child-like qualities have retained this connection always. Curiosity, open-mindedness, attention, and lack of prejudice are valuable skills that should always be practiced. I doubt that people who have lost these qualities are likely to regain them.

"Children are also better at seeing the wholeness than adults. This is, I believe, because the wholeness comes to us, it is visible at all only when our minds are open. It is words, and learning, which have the power to distort the wholeness, and to prevent us from seeing it... It appears that it is not easy for an educated, 'modern' person to recover her or his natural holistic perception."
— **Christopher Alexander** (2002), from *The Nature of Order*

I work with many therapy clients whom I help revisit their childhood. They don't return to being children and they don't regain their childishness. They return to childhood to remember, resolve, reassemble, or forget traumatic memories. This can be an essential therapy, but it is not aimed at recovering one's childhood skills.

Certain benefits of childhood are extolled and I believe it is essential to preserve these in ourselves. However, people who have lost or discarded those qualities and who have "become adults" will not regain some version of them short of a life-changing transformation. And what one might regain, such as through birth, death, and transformation—is not really of a childish origin but rather a return to one's fundamental growing nature.

Children are imagined as valuable, important, privileged, and protected across all cultures. Children are actually disrespected, disregarded, unauthorized, and abused across many cultures, more so in modern than traditional cultures. This reflects the greater role of family and community in traditional cultures as well as the greater importance of continuity through ancestry that exists in traditional cultures (Christakis, 2013).

Our character is largely developed in childhood. Many of our traumas and emotional strengths and weaknesses are rooted in our childhood experiences. There is widespread and general endorsement of children, childhood, and children's ability to learn. In general, these attitudes have not change our culture's indifference to, and lack of understanding of children and childhood.

"When I was a child, I spoke as a child, I understood as a child, I thought as a child: but when I became a man, I put

away childish things."
— **Paul**, 1 Corinthians 13 (KJV)

"I tell you the truth, unless you change and become like little children, you will never enter the kingdom of heaven."
— **Jesus**, Matthew 18:3 (New International Version)

144. Make toys.

We don't hear much about toys. They're considered childlike, but this is a mistake. Toys are simple examples of complex puzzles, and every complex puzzle is first solved in the context of a toy representation of it.

Toy builders are inventors and geniuses. You will never meet a toy builder who does not have a twinkle in their eye. If you want to understand something—anything—make it into a toy. Build toys.

Toy building is a multi-faceted exercise. You're trying to distill the essence of a problem, and you're trying to distill the essence of its excitement. I find that when a problem is reduced to its essence, it is always interesting but not always exciting.

"It seemed like such a wonderful idea, that you could build a wing, that you could take off and go down the hill... I got interested in building gliders, man-size gliders that I could operate, 'cause on my grandmother's farm, where I lived, she had a hill there of about a 30° grade. So I'd pick up this glider and get running, and jump off the edge and glide down to the bottom. Sometimes successfully, sometimes not. And of course, being that young, a lot of the practical side just went out the window!"

— **Donald Dubois**, machinist, inventor, from *The Learning Project*

I design games that combine rules and actions. As an exercise, I will take a boring system and see if I can find something exciting in it, or conceive of something exciting and see if I can distill it into something pure. I've designed games that simulate systems, are geometrical, kinetic, political. Games that are visually attractive or morally offensive.

"I'm a little child... You know the emperor's new clothes? I can see the naked emperor, just because I'm a little child-minded person. I'm not smart. I mean, good scientists are like that. They have the minds of children."
— **Clair Patterson**, PhD, geochemist

Plumbing is vaguely exciting, so I designed a plumbing game. The idea did not develop into what I expected, but maybe it could. My game is not yet satisfying to me, so there is more to explore. I called the game *The Fruits of Plumbing*, and you can see it here: https://www.mindstrengthbalance.com/alternative-education/games-system/#fruitsofplumbing

"I started making toys right away, using wire as my main material as well as working with others like string, leather, fabric and wood. Wood combined with wire (with which I could make the heads, tails and feet of animals as well as articulating parts) was almost always my medium of choice. One friend of mine suggested that I should make bodies entirely of wire, and that is how I started to make what I called 'Wire Sculpture'. In Montparnasse, I became known as the 'King of Wire'."
— **Alexander Calder**, artist, inventor

145. Be your own ally.

There are personalities within yourself that excel at certain tasks. The more subtle or difficult the task, the more support these personalities need. Innovation, by its nature, generates novelty. You must be grounded in something in order to maintain your direction as you pass through unfamiliar territory.

Learning is a collective activity that requires various parts of yourself to create, release, discern, criticize, inspire, admit, cajole, relax, and find enjoyment. You are a system, and innovation requires all your skills and many of your weaknesses. You must be your own greatest supporter.

The great artists have a measure of stability; there has got to be some determination in order to remain focused. It's typically called compulsion or necessity. Great scientists have a measure of instability, that tends to be emotional or conceptual, and it's typically called insight or inspiration.

Great innovators are rarely supported; their creative process is rarely understood. If they're pleasant people, they will appreciate any opportunity for sincere sharing. Getting such people to open up to you is a skill you should develop.

"I didn't have an allowance of any sort, but my parents would give me a couple of bucks every so often and I'd go to book sales... I started building radios. I'd electrocute myself 20 different ways with these power supplies. I was building tube equipment, and everything was 600 volt B₁.

"I could make regenerative receivers and do wild stuff. I began to realize this was a language, just like the language in the books, except this was a language with materials, and I just started to manipulate materials. I was doing this

*all the time, not paying much attention to my schoolwork
because I couldn't stand it. I drifted off into this alternate
world of exploring stuff."*
— **George Plotkin**, MD, PhD, engineer, neuroscientist,
inventor, from *The Learning Project*

146. People don't listen to unimportant things.

We have three kinds of vocalizations. One is to broadcast a
message—to be heard. A second is to elicit a response—to
interact. And a third is to take up mental space. This third
distracts our intellect so that there's room for new feelings and
ideas to emerge. These three channels exist in how we interpret
what we see: the foreground, background, and context. These
divisions are a feature of our brains.

Manipulating each channel is an art form of which great
presenters are masters. The richest interactions skillfully
combine all three so each makes an important contribution.
Our skill-less interactions are dominated by only one form, lack
purpose, and become uninteresting. To be more effective, be
aware of these.

You bring different levels of honesty to each form and the more
honest you are, the deeper the truth that you will convey. The
truth lies in your accepting what cannot be clearly said. The
deeper your truth, the greater your sense of purpose.
Communicate with a purpose if you want others to listen.

I attended a concert at a large concert hall in Berkeley, California, where
David Munrow, leader of the Early Music Consort of London, sat alone
on a folding chair in the center of the stage. He played a simple penny
whistle with such energy that not a single person stirred in an audience
of several thousand. I've never seen anything like it before or since.

147. Try to understand the struggles and successes of other people.

A deep learner is an innovator. They employ skills that are different from someone who depends on the stability of their environment to support their profession, social role, and personality. The difficulty of innovation isn't appreciated by those who don't do it.

The people who offer us the most reward are people who think like we do. The people who offer us the most insight think the least like we do. As a therapist, I join people in exploring all levels of their minds. I encounter people whose thinking process I cannot understand and which I have never heard described. We assume a lot about the world in order for us to understand it, and not everyone has this understanding.

If you plumb deeply enough, I believe you will come to that mysterious level beyond which you can't make sense of the world. It is a territory that is not entirely safe, and some people are stuck there. Some are mentally unable, but others appear quite able, but are looking for something. You can't learn this from a book. You can't describe this in words. You can't learn this unless you go there.

We surround ourselves with a membrane of judgments, and we use these judgments to orient and direct ourselves. We're normally attracted to the positive and repelled by the negative, but through the action of our inquisitive minds we can explore other directions.

I've met and learned lessons from many people with whom I could not establish a positive, personal relationship. Some of these people I found unpleasant because of who I am or what I did or said, and some of them are known for being unpleasant in general. These people injured me

227

but, over time, I learned to bear their scars. I developed the self-confidence to be immune to their depredations, more or less. I also developed the skills to remove what I needed from the domain of personality. I learned to see their bad behavior as their weakness, even in those cases where I was wrong.

Being wrong is part of the learning process. If others are not helping you avoid being wrong, then they should be helping you endure it. People who don't help you do either are either indifferent or exploitative. Some of these are creative and productive people, they just lack interpersonal skills.

If the novelty is educational, then it's best to experience it with as little judgment as possible; safety being the only criteria that one must always apply. Novelty is usually disconcerting, and scary in the extreme. Most things that seem bad are reflections of things already inside us. If there was not something inside us that we connected to, then an experience of complete novelty would have no meaning at all.

148. Be gentle with new ideas.

There are only three fair responses to a new idea: "I tried that," "I don't get it," and "That's interesting." These are judgments of having an idea, not judgments of the idea's result. In most cases, new ideas are not recognized as simply ideas. Instead, ideas are presumed to be a means to an end, and it's these ends that are judged.

New ideas are embryonic and do not have a final form or any form at all. If, in a given situation, a new idea is not respected for its potential, then probably every new idea will be disrespected. Many industries or situations perceived as idea incubators are hostile to new ideas.

Invention is an illumination of darkness, and almost everybody is scared of darkness. People's prejudice for preconceived order, combined with the pervasive insecurity in many fields, results in a generic hostility to new ideas that is not even recognized. But you'll recognize this hostility if you're the one presenting a new idea! Recognize this and you'll be better able to have and to protect new ideas.

Emotions

Your emotions combine with your intellect and identity to form the whole of you. Emotions are at the core, playing the role of your critical organs, while your intellect is like the muscles and your sense of identity is like the skin of your body. Your intellect does the moving and your identity protects your boundary, but it is your emotions that perform the functions that sustain you.

149. Protect your emotional identity.

Just as you have a personality, you also have an emotional self. Your personality is your thoughts and attitudes which you think you can control, and can control to some extent. Your emotional self is what you feel and don't have much control over, at least you don't think you do.

You guide your personality like you're driving a truck: making wide turns and struggling to wake yourself up or settle yourself down as circumstances require. Sometimes your thoughts are unclear or conflicted; sometimes they seem to be going in the wrong direction.

We hope our emotional selves will follow along like a trailer, supporting us in happiness when things are good, and helping us understand grief or sadness when they're not. We're taking a lot for granted, and it's somewhat of a miracle that our emotions comply as well as they do. From this, we develop the illusion that emotions are secondary, or that they're just a consequence of our experience.

You can be sure you won't always understand your emotions, and that is as it should be for a growing person in a dynamic world. Your emotions are your sense of direction, a collection of compasses, and their needles direct you according to the different measures they provide.

> *"We'd be in Boston one day, the next day I'd be moving equipment down to New Jersey, and then out to Pennsylvania, and then back... I'd run that truck damn near round the clock.*
>
> *"I had the best radio money could by in that truck. I'd put the windows down, crank that radio up; I could go 24 hours, baby! Wind blowing and the music playing. (laughs) I could really stay awake, stay awake, stay awake. Maybe I'd go three, four days, and then I'd have to crash and grab 8 hours of sleep. Oh man: go, go, go. I really loved that job."*
> — **Tom Kellogg**, landscaper, logger, excavator, and heavy equipment operator, from *The Learning Project*

150. Emotions are not secondary.

Emotions are a guiding force; they drive the trucks of our experience. You will see and understand the world in ways that are consistent with your emotions. If you are glad, then you experience happiness. If you are fearful, then you experience fear. If thoughts are the lenses that focuses our experience, emotions are the framework that orients us.

The power and autonomy of emotions becomes clear when you deal with people whose emotions do not function properly.

These are people who are depressed or elated without reason, who cannot engage appropriately, or who cannot understand how others feel.

What is it that leads you to trust that anyone will behave reasonably, honorably, or honestly? There are a million reasons to do anything, reasons that are for or against any action. We certainly don't scrutinize everyone's every action before we trust them, we hardly scrutinize our own. We trust people's behaviors because we believe we know how they feel.

151. You have emotional control.

You can improve your emotional control if you are honest with yourself, respect your feelings, and work with them. Your emotional self is like your power animal: if you treat it well, it will be your ally. It seems to have a mind of its own.

Abuse your emotional self by repressing or acting in conflict with your feelings, and your feelings will band against you. A person with a fundamental dislike of themselves is revealed by a broad dislike of their circumstances and distrust of others. Hide your feelings and others cannot make authentic contact with you. Show your feelings and they can.

We're often pressured to display inauthentic feelings, or we're made to feel it's unsafe or inappropriate to display our feelings. Enable other people to understand your feelings if you want to establish a meaningful engagement with them.

Feelings of vulnerability, impotence, or insufficiency are feelings of a different sort. You can reason with the thoughts of vulnerability but not the feelings. Problematic thoughts call for a solution, and you can take steps to solve these problems. Problematic feelings don't call for clear or immediate solutions. They are difficult to express and resolve. We tend to intellectually ignore or erase vulnerable feelings, but they will remain and grow larger over time.

Recognize that your feelings are a more authentic and less changeable reflection of who you are. Protect those feelings and build an environment that protects, nurtures, or heals them.

152. Allow yourself your inner conflicts and ensure the space for them.

You feel the need to change your mind before you change your mind, and the same goes for your actions and intentions. The force that creates new thoughts is not reason, although reason may have played a role. It's not emotional, although it may be accompanied by feeling. Being flexible requires that you give yourself the chance to explore the need to change.

There are many situations in which you are not given the latitude to think or act differently. You are given a directive, and it is necessary that you follow this directive. You won't learn much about what drives you in situations like these. You may learn how to perform your task, but you won't learn if you should, or why.

Agents, functionaries, and subordinates find themselves in this position. Students are put in this position. It undermines one's ability to learn. In order to learn you must have the latitude to decide, to go ahead or turn around, to succeed or fail.

Situations where you cannot or should not fail are not learning situations. The learning must be done before those situations. There are certainly many valid and necessary situations of that sort: driving a car, healing a wound, or even crossing the street. In those cases, follow the plan.

However, in real world situations and more complex problems the protocol is approximate, there is no plan, or the plan is flawed. In many cases, you'll find yourself in conflict between performing and learning.

On two occasions, I climbed major, sheer-sided mountains alone and unroped. Some people make this a sport; I did it on only twice. I'm glad I did it then, and I'm glad it went smoothly as there was no room for error. Not knowing exactly what I'd encounter, I planned as carefully as I could. I had the narrowest of focus and not a single distracting voice in my head. Life had a different priorities then.

The Golden Rule in any project is that if you are responsible for the outcome, you should have the authority to decide how to perform the task. Then, you know you're fully responsible, and the entire outcome is to your credit or your blame.

Breakthroughs feel emotional. Your words and actions are the point of an arrow, and your intellect forms the shaft that provides momentum. Your emotions are the bow that starts the arrow flying, and it is your emotions that are released upon conclusion. Without healthy emotions, your arrows will fly off the mark, or the will not fly at all.

153. Be emotionally connected to everything you do.

What you do has personal meaning when it evokes emotion in you. If your life is to be as meaningful as possible, then everything you do should be meaningful. That's not to say that everything has meaning in itself, as there are many tedious and unwelcome tasks, but none should feel inconsequential.

Everything you do should have some connection to who you are.

I've been a professional as a physicist, a software consultant and programmer, and a counselor. In every field, the majority of the people I meet project their dissatisfaction onto those whom they see as a threat to their security or self-image. It's often the most powerful and widely respected people who are guilty of the most indifferent and injurious behavior.

This is a destructive kind of emotional connection; it is destructive to all involved including those who instigate it. You will meet these people wherever you turn, and you most likely already have. They are beacons of guidance, lighthouses marking the shoals of cruelty and indifference. Watch them carefully and engage them if you can. They are living examples of what you don't want to become, and this is especially important because many of them hold positions that you aspire to.

Their emotional dysfunction is not unique; it comes with the territory. The forces that twist the spirit of people in positions of power, privilege, and authority are not personality flaws although they are linked to personality weaknesses. These forces are built into the system and create rot throughout the system. Think and feel your way forward carefully if you are following in their footsteps.

A pair of physics Nobel Laureates at Harvard University are suspected of unethical and libelous action in their attempts to derail the career of a less well-known colleague in their field, Ruggero Santilli. Santilli claims and has brought lawsuits to the effect that these and other scientists conspired to destroy his reputation and suppress his work (Santilli, 2017).

I know both of the Nobel Laureates—one quite well from working with him as a graduate student—and I'm intimately familiar with both their work and that of Santilli. While the work of the Laureates is technically beyond reproach, I have found these two to be arrogant and dismissive of generally everyone. In contrast, Santilli's work is foundational, inspiring, and can fairly be termed heroic. Forty years after the initial conflict, Santilli's work has survived. It is receiving acceptance and could potentially found the next step in the revolution in physics that started at the turn of the twentieth century.

It doesn't matter who is right or wrong in the end, what matters is the pernicious influence of corrupted personalities. The lives and livelihoods of thousands of physicists have been affected by this kind of skulduggery, and there are other instances like this that I know of but of which I am less well informed.

The public would be surprised to know that progress in science is greatly retarded by systematic, personal corruption. Scientists themselves, as a class and as a profession, are famously aloof and indifferent to the social forces that support them and, to a large extent, forge their own personalities. The systemic flaw is the lack of an emotional connection, it's something hyper-rational people tend to lack both to themselves and to others.

154. There are larger movements afoot than you know.

It is a beautiful thing when everything works out right and—if we carried no legacy and the universe was a garden of Eden— our good intentions would flourish. But we do carry a legacy and the universe carries one too. There is chaos and work that needs to be done for the balance and betterment of ongoing affairs. Greater positives come with greater negatives. You can't get away from the risks, but you can adjust them.

Everything has a context, and every context exists within a larger context. The ultimate context provides the ultimate reason, but we'll never know that, and it doesn't matter. We deal with what we see, and by doing so we see more.

We understand everything we do within some limited context, and that may be the only context you need: family, work, or health. When soldiers go to war, they're not supposed to question the context. When you're tested, you're not supposed to question the context. When you question these contexts, you find more is happening than you are first led to believe.

There is a kind of permission to fail—or to derail things—that's inherent in the right to ask questions. Asking questions is exploratory, and exploration is a decision-allowing process. You may not like some of the answers, and there may be negative consequences to some of the decisions you make, but you need the freedom to understand the possibilities.

I remember as a child pouring boiling water on ants to watch them die. This was pathological, and I wish there was someone around to help me understand what I was doing. Perhaps because of this, I have a respect and fascination with ants. Somewhere buried in the context of my childhood lies the explanation for my actions. I feel penitent to this day for all the ants I killed.

Many decades later I worked with the famous jazz trombonist Roswell Rudd. Roswell was an odd and affable person, and he loved to kill ants. He would crush them between his fingers. It was a habit of his that shocked me down to my childhood. I could never feel entirely good about him, because of it. I am still working to understand this behavior, sixty years later. I don't fully understand it.

155. The 5-10-85 percent rule.

Let me invent a "5-10-85 Percent Rule" that says five percent of what you can learn is essential, ten percent is useful, and eight-five percent is irrelevant.

When it comes to facts, the rule applies: five percent of what you're taught is essential, ten percent is useful, and eighty-five percent is useless. Unless we are highly focused, engaged, and motivated this will be true even if we're interested in the material. The majority of what we're taught is useless or unnecessary.

By the time you graduate from high school, you know how to read and write at a basic level. You actually weren't taught to write; you were taught to spell. You weren't taught math; you were taught to add, subtract, and multiply. You probably don't remember how to divide. Basically, after twelve years of schooling you knew almost nothing.

How long would it take you to teach these skills to someone? Why did learning this take you twelve years? Do you remember much more of it?

Most of what's taught in school is irrelevant to us and is forgotten. This partly reflects the unimportance of the material, and it partly reflects our lack of foresight in appreciating what we might need later.

Many of us don't know where we're headed. We certainly didn't when we were kids. We should have spent more time exploring this at the time, and probably should be spending more time exploring it now. Your first order of business should be to find direction and motivation. Schools don't bother to do this, so most of what we learn is forgotten and our time is wasted.

Practical skills are value-laden. Things like sewing, welding, and carpentry are full of necessary details. Their tactile learning is different from book learning. Crafts skills are useful in other contexts: attention to detail, mechanical awareness, and design. Physical, visual, and auditory skills foster balance, dexterity, rhythm, and timing. When we develop these deep cognitive skills, our learning improves in all areas.

"The other thing that I see now in education, and it bothers me, is that there's hardly any shops in our school system today. All the stuff that I've done as a student in shop class I used in my lifetime, in Grumman, and in my home. I've put rooms on my home, I've built things, and what-not. It's vital for kids to learn, and I can't believe they abandoned it! You're learning something you're never going to learn otherwise, and it's gone: there's hardly any shop classes anymore."
— **Lou Giani**, wrestling coach, from *The Learning Project*

In high school, I refused to take gym class because I could further my physical learning better elsewhere, and I did. I read extra material in an attempt to make my time useful. My college mentor, Charlie Townes, learned electromagnetism from the same graduate textbook that I used. I don't recall any of it while he famously did every problem in the book. He felt the material was relevant, and so it became relevant. I didn't think so, and so, for me, it didn't.

People active in a field will know and teach the fifteen percent that's necessary or useful. Those people are not teachers, and they are often too busy to teach. Work with them, instead of with the teachers. They'll tell you what's needed, then you can learn it yourself.

The remaining eighty-five percent of what's advertised as essential is not useful. It was background material once, and it played a supporting role then. Either that or it was created in someone's mind as part of a methodology to help you "understand." A lot of nonsense is fed to students on that pretext.

You would be better served if you found what you needed by yourself or —what is the best by far—figured it out for yourself. Once you start thinking things through, you'll be amazed at how far you can see across different fields and into the future.

> *"Since then I never pay attention to anything by 'experts,' I calculate everything myself."*
> — **Richard P. Feynman**, PhD, physicist

156. Engage with the world and do what calls you.

You'll do your best work at what's most meaningful to you. Consider this your calling, or what you are here to do. If you'd rather not be mystical about it, then consider it to be what's most meaningful for others, or what you are most able to bring to fruit, by virtue of your circumstances.

Retiring from a profession is contrary to having a calling in life. Since most of us do have a profession, establish your profession near your calling. Hopefully, someday, you'll make the jump from the profession to the calling.

Don't be quick to reject unattractive opportunities. Everything that glitters is not gold, but many things that don't glitter are. While hardship, difficulty, and pain may not be great teachers— though they'll inevitably change you—they are opportunities.

They occur in just those areas where things should be different and their appearance is your opportunity.

What calls you the most often lies on the other side of what repels you the most. Doing the greatest good often requires confronting the greatest bad and dealing with things that feel the least changeable.

There is wisdom in doing things with minimal effort and maximal efficiency. There is also wisdom in doing things that seem impossible and where you feel you make no progress. It all depends on how it makes you feel. A hard problem is hard for a reason, which probably means there's a different way to look at it that's easier.

Reading, writing, and arithmetic fall into the useless eighty-five percent category. That's not because they're unnecessary, it's because they're presented outside of any useful context. They're absolutely necessary when you need them, but until you have something to say, something to read, or something to calculate they are of no use. Once you do have a need for them, you'll learn them quickly and with little assistance. The aptitude to learn them is wired into us.

The standard justification for teaching these things in schools has been that you need to learn them before you can use them. Have you ever wondered if anyone has proved that? They have not because it's not true.

Like anything, need comes before desire, and until you have desire nothing is going to make much of an impression. It is infinitely easier to learn something after you need it. One uses and learns at the same time.

If you meet an engineer, they will not teach you algebra, they will show you how to solve problems. If you meet a writer, they will not teach you grammar, they will show you how to use words. If you meet a scholar, they will not teach you how to read, they will show you how to think.

> *"One of the cool things that I've kind of discovered in my learning has been becoming more aware of what was going on at the time, like in religion, in literature, I can relate all the different ideas together and things start flowing, and that's cool to me. I'll hear something either in British Lit. or American Lit. and I jump off this deep end of, 'So that's why!' Or I jump off with thoughts like, 'I wonder if he was writing this when...' and I start going on with that. That really helps me be engaged."*
> — **Jessica Henry**, student, from *The Learning Project*

157. When you find the resources you need, you will have to fight for them.

If you're in just the right place and recognized as being able to do what others want, then you'll be given access to the resources you need. But in most cases, what others need and what you want, will not be the same, and you will find yourself sailing into the headwinds of other people's expectations.

One of the resources you need is intuition. You need to find it, follow it, and develop it. The process by which you develop intuition looks a lot like fiddling around. It doesn't look impressive from the outside.

Quite a few great minds have incubated in libraries, nature, laboratories, studios, or on stage. In these places, people will spend a lot of what appears to be unproductive time, having little to show for it. This is an essential part of the process of finding yourself.

A caterpillar needs a cocoon, and you need protection too. The best way to get it is to have allies to secure what you need and give you the time and space to gestate. This is what graduate schools are there to do, though they don't always do it. An apprenticeship can provide someone who will take you under their wing, but good wings are hard to find. There are few allies or enablers for a person in school.

Real opportunities exist for those who are ready for them. Young people are not as incapable, worthless, or helpless as they have been told. If you're lucky enough to wake up to your calling, then know you'll have to find your mentors, allies, and resources.

The Buddhist saying, "When the student is ready, the teacher will appear," conveys the sad misconception that you have no responsibility in creating your opportunities. The teacher might be standing right in front of you, but you will not see them unless you make an effort. Contrary to the aphorism, they won't see you either. These things will not be offered to you. You must find them.

When you have resources and a need to learn, there is little that can stop you. But classrooms are not resources and obligations are not needs. Learning the tools before you have a problem or area of inquiry is like eating without a digestive system.

I really cannot think of a single class I've taken—and I've taken many—whose material I did not have to discard in favor of teaching the material to myself. In most cases, classes never make the real problem clear.

I had no interest in welding until I needed to build a trailer for my airplane. Then, all of a sudden, I was full of ideas and questions. I took a class at a vocational school and was completely intrigued. To this day, I have great respect for and an interest in welding… and I welded the trailer.

Before there were schools—in cultures where people wanted to read—nearly everyone learned how to read. Literacy among Freemen of the American colonies in the late 1700s was close to 100%. Now that we have schools to teach literacy and a society that doesn't require it, literacy rates are below 50%, and few read.

Grades K through 12 span some of the most important years of a person's life. Kids who are not taught according to any program at all, but who are allowed to explore their full natural and social environment, can voraciously learn this material in a small fraction of the time.

Sonya Peters: *"My biggest issue with the world is trying to understand how it can be that when you meet someone and you ask, 'What are your interests?' and they go, 'I don't have any.' That's my biggest issue: how could somebody not have any interests! And the problem is that three years ago I was one of those people."*

Lincoln Stoller: *"What happened there? What is the difference between the interests you had three years ago and now?"*

Sonya Peters: *"It came with the realization that I could actually get something that I wanted. That I could actually learn something. 'Oh, you can sit down and you can read this book and you can learn it, learn what's inside.' When before I thought you needed a teacher to teach you everything."*
— from *The Learning Project*

158. Be flexible and resilient.

Few teachers support deep learning, the kind of learning that is meaningful and stimulating. Deep learning doesn't require much, but few understand it. For most people trained as teachers, learning is a transmission of data. For them, learning is not the invention of meaning or the exploration of oneself.

Your teachers don't have much to teach you, but time is short, resources scarce, and you probably already have a relationship with them, so get some return on your investment. Perform this experiment: can you get your teachers excited about learning?

Anyone who teaches believes they have something of value to transmit. Reflecting on the worst teachers I've had—with the exception of a few who were simply bad people—each one felt they had some valuable lesson to transmit. In most cases, I tried to make the best of it, but I was combative. At the time, I did not have a strategy. I could have done better to manage these relationships but, in any event, the resources and opportunities were scarce.

People are recognized for what they've achieved, not for who they are. If you want support in your efforts at deep learning, you'll need to go beyond a social relationship to something personal. If you're inviting a person you don't know well into a relationship you can't control, you're taking a risk. Maintain your autonomy and don't be afraid to trust your judgment.

159. Don't assume that you know who you're talking to.

As a professional therapist—and as someone who has dealt with people of all sorts outside of therapy—I assure you that few people have a single, integrated personality. Most people have a lot of problems in their lives and with their personalities.

It's a definition of saint-hood that a person is wholly good, clear, unbiased, understanding, good-natured, trustworthy, upstanding, and so on. Everyone has a little of these features— or maybe a lot—but no one is one hundred percent pure.

You may think that the "other mind" of any person is a small voice, an occasional mood, or a minority opinion, but this is not true. Most people have huge "other minds," vast and alternative opinions, some of which are completely contrary to the person you know and who they present themselves to be. This makes sense if you realize that no one is so smart that they can figure everything out from a single, consistent, harmonious point of view that applies to any situation, stress, or conflict.

Our worlds are complex and contain much that's unexpected. We're flying by the seat of our pants. We concoct our personalities so that we have some persona to offer. We expect other people do the same: everyone has to have a calling-card to introduce themselves, and that calling-card is our personality.

You will experience the persona that another person advertises if you fit into that person's world. We gravitate toward a common "normal." As social animals, we're drawn to conformity like the cosmic dust that clumps together to form planets in space.

Our world's have so much uncertainty that we cannot test every other person's merit. We must trust them if we're to get down to the business of getting our needs met. We create the fiction of mutual understanding In order to get things done. In this realm of trust, we make many mistakes.

If you stay close to normal and don't think outside the box, you may get what you expect. If this satisfies you, good for you! You're in luck: society exists to create and protect normality. Normality doesn't make for an entirely healthy, happy, or pain free life, but that's what's on offer. It's as close as your nearest nine-to-five job.

Some people are not "normal." You have to be careful about these people. I know, I'm one of them, and I speak from experience when I say that it can be hell thinking outside the box. For better or worse it's in my blood, and it would be torture for me to live a life without novelty. Even those things that engage most people—like video games and movies—repel me. They're so predictable! They're boring! Some of us are constantly sailing off to find the edge of the world, and when we get there we jump off.

There is a role for the odd-balls. They write books like this one, which help you navigate uncertainties. What you need to be concerned about —what anyone needs to be concerned about—is knowing who you're talking to and how you're being heard. Some people will open their hearts and share their souls. Other people have lost their hearts and souls and will reach for yours. Those who share tend to create community; those who are in need tend to become vampires. Angels are one and devils are the other, and everyone else is in between.

Stress

Stress can be good. Anything that's held together, anything that's in motion, anything that's changing is undergoing stress. There are bad kinds of stress, but being alive is stressful and that doesn't have to be bad.

Do you like to be curious, entertained, comfortable, or exuberant? All of these involve some kind of stress, either to draw you forward or to maintain a shell that protects you. It's struggling that's unpleasant, although you can rise above that too. What we generally define as stress would be better called struggle because virtually everyone who is happy is living with stress.

160. Be dissatisfied with being bored.

Stress lies between boredom and struggle. If boredom is having the life drained out of you, and struggle is having the life sucked out of you, then a healthy level of stress is when your life is running smoothly. Once you open your mind to the benefits of regular stress, also called exercise, you're on a path of increasing power.

I know of two ways to overcome boredom. One way is to find something to do that's interesting. This is the easy way. It eases boredom, but it doesn't cure it.

The other way is to do something so boring that you reach the limit of your boredom. People who take boredom to this extreme actually cure boredom. Once the bored mind is broken, you'll never be bored again.

"The one time that I can remember feeling really bored was the short period of time that I did this retreat in Western Massachusetts, in the Berkshires. I took very little with me to read on purpose. It was boring for four days, but it was a really active kind of bored. It was like, 'I have to get in touch with this boredom!' kind of bored. So no, I don't get bored, I don't let myself be bored."
—**Michelle Murrain**, PhD, neuroscientist, computer consultant, writer, activist, from *The Learning Project*

War has been described as consisting of hours of boredom punctuated by moments of terror, and the same goes for mountaineering. I've known career soldiers drawn to mountaineering for this reason. Of the many hours of excruciating boredom, the time I remember least clearly was ferrying loads across glaciers in Alaska.

A glacier is huge and loads are backbreaking. There are no landmarks for miles, and there is nothing to break the monotony of their white flatness. You're shouldering the heaviest load you can carry, there is nothing to see, you cannot think, and you are in pain. There is no point in even being present.

The only salvation is separating from yourself. With that skill—the skill of being somewhere that you are not—you change your notion of space and time. It's not so much that you're no longer bored, it's that you shrink time down to a point so that the boredom, which would otherwise last for hours, happens in some other world.

Your body strengthens under stress, so you can increase your capacity if you work within your limits. The same holds true for your mind. Under stress, your mind becomes stronger. For some reason, people don't know this.

161. Learn to control stress.

The feeling that you can effectively manage your life helps you overcome stress; the better you deal with stress, the more effective you feel. It's the feeling of control that's crucial, not the actual degree of control. You might feel in complete control of your life as a housecleaner and feel completely out of control as a corporate CEO. It depends how you define your life and the kind of control you need.

Control stress by breaking it down and by focusing beyond it. One gets tunnel vision when confronting stressful things. Stress draws you into this micro-focused state. In this state, the stressful situation feels like it's everything, consuming, and overbearing.

Refuse to allow yourself to be drawn into and onto the anvil of stress. Insist on giving yourself time and space, whether these are physical or mental. Refuse helplessness. You'll feel like you don't have the ability or opportunity to do this, but you must.

A self-efficacious person faces stress more calmly, and overcomes stress more quickly and comfortably, than someone whose less self-efficacious. Different people will develop different levels of stress in the same situation, and they will differ in whether or not they can resolve this stress.

Learn to control stress separately from controlling the things that create it. It's a learned ability; you learn equanimity. I developed the ability to avoid becoming stressed through extreme sports, but it involved danger. It's something that you burn into your character. You can also develop the ability to release stress through exercise, mindfulness, and meditation. It is a mental skill, and approaching it that way is easier and safer.

162. Get mental exercise.

Do things that are hard and at which you may perform poorly. Try solving the Rubik's Cube, cross-word puzzles, watercolors, or something else that you're really bad at. Don't demand improvement, just look for interesting aspects of the process. Exercise curiosity.

Consider things that baffle you. Seriously think about problems you have no idea of how to solve. Think of answers to the great problems and then tear them apart to explore their flaws. Be comfortable with making no progress.

I did this when I first went to college: I talked about problems I had no hope of solving or understanding. No one took me seriously. I was embarrassed, so I stopped. After many decades, I've started again. My solutions are no better, but you have to think about these things. If your lack of answers stops you, then how can you learn to understand the problems?

163. Exercise your body to improve your mind.

Physical exercise sharpens your mind, improves your health, and stabilizes your mood. It acts in obvious ways, such as changing your environment and strengthening your heart and lungs. Sustained exercise increases the growth of brain cells. Exercise improves brain function by improving your immunity to disease and promoting digestion.

Your lymphatic system is part of your primary defense against disease, and it consists of lymphatic fluid that flows through ducts and capillaries. This fluid does not circulate, and it is not pumped by the heart. It is a one-way system in which the fluid is pushed by your muscular movement.

Our intestines are the source of cells and chemicals used by our immune system, as well as much of the serotonin and other hormones essential for brain function. Healthy digestion is essential for brain development and mental function at all ages.

Answer these questions for yourself:
- Why do we have exercise fads but not intellectual fads?
- Why is having a good body attractive, but not having a good mind?
- Why are exercises of the mind and exercises of the body promoted separately?

- Why is learning associated with exercising the mind and not the body?
- Why do we portray learning as something you do with your brain and not your limbs?
- Why don't we appreciate the crossover between mental and physical intelligence?

Integrate mind and body through exercise. Think about what your mind is doing when your body is exercising, and do something with your body when your mind is exercising.

164. Perfect your sleep as a state of mind.

It bears repeating—as I am repeating here—that all aspects of health and performance improve with sleep, rest, and relaxation. Sleeping is not just going to bed for a period of time. Rest does not just mean sleeping, and relaxation is not just taking a vacation.

Sleep is a skill that you perfect with involvement. It has four different levels and you can work with and improve each. You can learn to make better use of your liminal states, the falling asleep and waking up states that are called phase one. You can deepen your non-dreaming states during which your body undergoes physical repair—these are sleep phases two and three. And you can guide, interact, and play an active role in your dreams, which predominantly occur during the rapid eye movement or REM stage of sleep. See my books on sleep and dreaming—*The Path To Sleep* (Stoller 2019a), and *Becoming Lucid* (Stoller 2019b)—for details.

Your body requires periods of rest in order to revitalize. Follow your body's rhythms; relieve stress and tension not only through your daily cycle but at every moment. Test scores, endurance, creativity, attention, awareness, responsiveness, vitality, recovery, sexuality, and insight all increase when you regularly get a lot of sleep and pursue a low-strain, low-stress lifestyle.

Sleep is to learning as digestion is to eating; you literally put things together in sleep. At one level, you consolidate memory so that you are mentally organized. At another level, consolidation enables you to understand your experiences, including your learning experiences.

To encourage sleep deprivation as a demonstration of toughness is foolish. You'll perform worse in every cognitive measure. Sleep deprivation is as smart as alcoholism. An underslept person is more likely to have an accident, make a mistake, hurt someone, and fail at their tasks. Staying awake for 24 hours impairs memory and reaction times to an extent that's equal to what's observed in the behavior of a person who is legally drunk. If you want to be effective, don't just be busy, stop what you're doing, and get more sleep.

The Law of Attraction

The law of attraction says you attract to yourself whatever is in synchrony with your habitual, consistent mental attitude. This is not a law, and it easily constitutes bad advice. It leads people to think they can think into reality anything they want, which is false.

What is possible, however, is that you can think you've made reality into anything you want and, when it comes to influencing other people, that's often enough. Believing anything with enough force and charisma is often enough to lead other people into whatever perceived reality you create for them.

The tendency to attract—as "tendency" is more accurate than "law"—refers to how you filter what you see, and how people interact with you. It's all about focus, direction, attention, intention, actions, and interpretations. There is no law here, just the tendency of others to follow what you model for them.

If you're thinking bad thoughts, a table is not going to rear up and hit you. On the other hand, you may be so distracted that you hit yourself on a table. You are responsible for any interactions you have with objects that have no volition of their own.

You will not get money by thinking money-filled thoughts, but you will be more likely to see the potential for profit. You will not find true love by wishing for true love, but you can be a more attentive, honest, and loving person by virtue of what your thinking about. There is a greater likelihood of resonating with others who have similar intentions.

165. Recognize your role in what you see.

Recognize that what you see in some people reflects what you see in all people, not just those people. If you can't tell how much of your mood is contributing to your sense of comfort or discomfort, then it's contributing to a large extent.

It may seem trite, but it's inevitably true. What you like about what you see around you, reflects something you like in yourself, and what you dislike is a similar reflection. Feeling good or bad about yourself seems to be confirmed by what's happening around you. When you're happy everything glows, and when you're unhappy everything is pale.

There is a middle area: that subliminal area that lies between what we intentionally think and what we unintentionally do. We all have attitudes that are reflected in our bodies and our behaviors of which we are unconscious or only vaguely conscious.

166. Learn your unconscious habits.

There are things you think about, consider in your mind, and express, and there are things you think about but do not clearly consider and yet still express. These are your subliminal thoughts: flashes of feeling, reflex reactions, and fragments of ideas that attach to your presentation and shape the texture of your personality. These subliminal thoughts contribute to how others see you, without your being aware of them.

You can see your unconscious habits by viewing yourself without thinking about yourself, but looking at your image without considering how you'd like to appear, and by listening to the thoughts that bubble into your mind without trying to judge or catch them. If you do this, it will make you slightly uncomfortable because you will be perceiving aspects of yourself that are incongruent with who you think you are. You will be appreciating aspects of yourself that are in conflict with your "normal" identity.

Many of us eat compulsively for comfort for much the same reason that smokers take cigarette breaks. Breaking this emotional connection with food is one of the best ways to change your eating habits, but it takes more than just a resolution, it takes a complete change in how you relate to yourself.

Many of us hold anger in our bodies and express it in our mannerisms, but don't recognize it in our thinking. You can often feel the connection between the physical and the emotional if you release one or the other. The same holds true for other emotions.

Our minds and our bodies work as a team that functions no better than two people in a three-legged potato sack race, but we're so used to it that we are unaware of how ridiculously incongruous we appear. Who we think we are and how other people see us are not the same.

When you consciously focus your attention on portraying a particular thought or attitude, you can change the subliminal cues you give to others. You were unaware of these cues before, and you may be unaware of the changes you're exhibiting now, but people will pick up on them.

Another example is smiling. People who want to influence others learn how to smile, not as an expression of their feelings, but as a means of entrainment. There are hundreds, if not thousands of postural, gestural, facial, tonal, and rhythmic cues that we express and receive without ever knowing it. They are built into our nervous system.

By making an effort to control your conscious thoughts, you also have some effect on your unconscious expressions. At this, some people are better than others, and practice lead to improvement.

We are very reactive; almost everything we think or do is a reaction. We're especially reactive when we're not aware that we're reacting but think we're acting of our own free will. We think we're exerting our free will almost all the time.

This is the "user illusion." It's the result of the small amount of our information processing that is controlled by our consciousness (Nørretranders, 1999). Most of our actions are habits and reflexes generated and supported by our moods and memories. For this reason, we are a source of much of the conflicts that we ascribe to causes in the outside world. We are the source of much of our own abuse.

Abuse

There is abuse that you do to yourself, and there is abuse that others do to you. The two tend to be related, but on the face of it, they appear different. Hopefully, you're aware of your role in causing yourself grief. There are the obvious things like overworking, over-worrying, over-eating, creating a negative environment, and abusing your body through neglect, injury, or excess. Increase your awareness of these habits and their consequences. It's not moderation that should be your goal, it's balance.

The less obvious ways we abuse ourselves are embedded in our personalities in ways we cannot see. We project our personalities on our environment and see in our environment a reflection of ourselves. We attract and repel elements in our environment that are, or are not, in synchrony with our personal awareness. You do it; we all do it.

This goes on moment by moment, not just occasionally. Even a momentary change in your mood will reflect what you see, how you're seen, and how your environment reacts to you. This action might cause an event that will lock you into that mood—such as yelling at someone— or it might pass. This doesn't mean that you create what you are, it means that you create a reflection of yourself that resonates in the world, and that reflection and its resonance can endure.

Then, there is the issue of the abuse done to us by others. You might suppose it's easier for us to cope with abuse done to us since we might see these incidents as someone else's fault. But the most damaging incidents are those we cannot distance ourselves from, which we cannot understand as someone else's fault. These events can cause the greatest psychological damage, fragmenting our personality into unreconcilable pieces. Even such outright assaults as rape not only damage, demean, and disempower, but dissociate a person from themselves. They fragment your soul.

The most destructive abuses are those we don't recognize as abuse, but accept as natural consequences and reflections of who we are. If you did recognize that you were being abused, then you'd have healthy anger that would uphold your self-respect. It's the abuse that we don't have the psychological power to stop that is most dangerous. As young children, we have not separated ourselves from the world. The sickness we encounter through an incidence of abuse is something we experience as part of ourselves.

167. Never compromise your integrity.

Self-respect is a central and necessary ingredient in accomplishing anything. It is essential that self-respect is enhanced as part of any learning program. If you act with sincerity and goodwill, then never allow yourself to feel humiliated, degraded, exploited, dismissed, or diminished. Let suspicions raise a red flag, and err on the side of caution. Anger is healthier than humiliation.

I have not been sexually exploited, as least not much—there was an incident with a gardener when I was about five which I consider to be of minimal importance. As a therapist, I meet many people who have been violated and, in most cases, their memories of these events are vague.

I know college and grad students who have been exploited, and I know two of tho professors who exploited them. I have felt personally exploited in different ways and to different degrees. Non-consensual situations are fundamentally exploitative, and this is the root of the problem: we are required to accept exploitative situations but we are not informed or prepared. From these, situations develop that go over the

line. It only becomes clear after the fact—to those who are victimized—
that the lines of ethical behavior have been crossed.

Developing self-respect is central to all learning. Most school programs
don't recognize this, so you need to. You need to recognize what it feels
like to have self-respect, and you need to be alert to situations where
your self-respect is at risk.

In most schools, the lack of self-respect is so pervasive that there is no
respect of any kind, anywhere. This prevails in institutions where people
are ranked, which is just about everywhere.

With regard to gross exploitation, if it feels bad it is bad. This is not as
obvious as it sounds, as your claims of being exploited are often
dismissed as weaknesses in your character or performance. Exploitation
first arises as a feeling, and feelings are often dismissed for their lack of
specificity, especially when your feelings conflict with the program.

Feeling you are exploited is being exploited, it does not depend, and it is
not made better, according to the intention of another person. You are
the judge and your feelings are their own justification.

Feeling exploited does not mean the other people or person knows they
are exploiting you. The potentially evil thing about doing what's
reasonable is that a person can reasonably support anything. In cases
of subtle manipulation, the exploiter is oblivious to how you feel and
feels justified in their actions.

If you blame another for exploiting you, you are pitting your feelings
against their intentions. This forms poor grounds for argument.
Exploitation, or perceived exploitation, starts with subtle transgressions.
The exploited person feels the violation beyond the context of the
relationship, but you must be clear with yourself: might this

transgression be seen as part of a relationship that you agreed to? This does not mean you need to endure these transgressions; it means you need to redefine the relationship!

The second important point is the role you play. Myths and fables embody many of our attitudes, and the myth of the vampire applies here: the vampire cannot enter your house unless you invite him or her in. The vampire has no reflection or, more accurately, the vampire does not reflect on itself. The vampire is deathless or, more realistically, the vampire's syndrome never heals itself.

This is a metaphor for exploitation: it always begins with an act of consent, otherwise it would simply be assault. In the vampire myth, the victim is unsure of what they're getting into, but the vampire knows. In reality, the vampire perceives your invitation as authentic and acts without hesitation.

There is a threshold beyond which exploitation becomes predation, and predators should be recognized as different from exploiters. Predators know they're taking more than was on offer. They may rationalize why they're crossing the line, but they know they're crossing it. Most of the instances of exploitation that I know of are better described as instances of predation.

You may be the victim of a predator or an exploiter. You may feel the same in either case, but you should refine your feelings because they have different motives and defenses; they have different vibrations. Ideally, you avoid these situations, but, in reality, you have to deal with what you were not able to avoid.

168. If you're feeling exploited, the whole situation is to blame.

It is shortsighted to reduce exploitation or injury to a single action, idea, or event. The precipitating event is rather an aspect, manifestation, or consequence of a larger, negative situation.

The temptation will be to identify and confront the most egregious insult and find a simple and definitive fix. One might say to oneself, "I'll tell them what they did wrong so that they won't do it again." A wiser response is to address and to change the whole situation. But since change can be difficult, slow, or— as applies to other people—next to impossible, your most effective option is to act unilaterally: exit the situation.

Exploitation occurs in situations where the right choice is unclear. There are usually other people being exploited in the environment who are as uncertain as you are. They could well be in a double-bind where they are being forced to aid in your exploitation. They may be given rewards for acting unethically or punishment for acting ethically. Neither situation excuses the actions of an accomplice.

You bear some responsibility for the situation. You are reluctant to admit your mistake because:

- you're invested,
- you're committed,
- future promises justify the sacrifice,
- you think—or others tell you—it was the right thing to do,
- everyone does this,
- you deserve this,
- you didn't do anything wrong,

- to object would be insensitive, too sensitive, demanding, or inappropriate.

These rationalizations help you cope with a bad situation. None will make a situation that feels bad now, feel better later. Rationalizations delay the inevitable, override the danger signals, and hide your need to heal yourself.

By adopting excuses, you endure exploitation more efficiently and less stressfully, but you endanger your health and your long-term goals. Exploitation is a form of torture: if you have to endure it, endure it with the least injury, but it would be better not to endure it at all.

169. You bear responsibility for your exploitation.

Short of abduction, you are largely responsible for your exploitation. You decided—perhaps under threat to life and limb—to endure it. You may not have felt you had a better choice, but you had a choice. If you had said no, then it might have changed from exploitation to assault. If that occurred, it would be different for all parties and things might have developed better for you in the long run.

Don't feel cornered in a situation that's developing badly. Don't expect—and don't let anyone tell you—that you're committed, it's too late, and that you should have acted differently beforehand. You are under no legal or moral obligation to uphold an illegal contract. You always have the authority to leave a bad situation or, if you're on your own turf, to expel the agent or cause.

In spite of what we're told about being charitable and not shooting the messenger, shooting the messenger is a good place to start. The messenger is a paid accomplice, the first link in the chain of compliance and complicity.

Victims of assault also bear some responsibility for the situations in which they find themselves, but avoiding those situations is usually difficult, unlikely, or impossible. There is nothing simple or safe that you can do to remedy an assault. Nevertheless, dire situations require dire actions, and doing anything is better than doing nothing. You may not be able to gain any advantage for yourself, but you may be able to deny some benefit to another. Think longterm.

170. Stress will make you sick.

Stress often feels exploitative, and it probably is to some degree. You want to eliminate stress but, sometimes, this requires changing rather than leaving the situation. In that case, you must decide how much change can be accomplished and how to cope with what can't be changed.

While exploitation is unjust, stress is par for the course. Some stress is good, such as the stress that comes with understanding things better. Coming to see problems better is a prerequisite to solving them, and it will always cause stress.

Instead of thinking of stress as bad, think of healthy and unhealthy stresses. Healthy stresses exercise you and make you stronger. Unhealthy stress causes injury and makes you weaker. This can often be a matter of degree: listen to your body.

171. Recognize three forms of stress.

Bad stress comes from a situation where something is needed that you're unable to provide. It's a situation in which there are no good alternatives, but you feel you have to act. Bad stress arises in dangerous situations you cannot control.

Consider the different forms of stress to better arrange yourself. There are stresses of tension, compression, and confusion, and you can approach them differently. If you see their different natures, you may find better ways to cope with them.

Tension is when you're torn between various options, and none of the options are good. Pare your options down to those that feel like they offer the best outcomes. Work to improve these and then pick the best.

In compression, you're pressed to do something that's insufficient and you don't see other options. You're being pressed to do something that does not feel right. Recognize what's missing and insist on creating something in that space.

Confusion is when something is coming at you and you can't orient yourself. Step back and gather information. Playing stupid is a time-tested approach because most situations insist that you take a role. Declaring yourself unable to do anything usually causes something new to appear.

172. Recognize your stress limit.

You bear some responsibility for the stress you endure. Draw your own line between the stress you can handle and the stress that's excessive. No one else can tell you how much you should accept.

Be wise in setting your limits. Stresses don't exactly add, they tend to multiply because they set each other off. Also, while one only has one emergency at a time on average, the more stressed you are, the more likely there will be an emergency. Give yourself a good deal of room and remember: you can't burn the candle at both ends for long before everything goes to hell.

Your teacher, employer, superior, partner, or colleague may impose consequences if you don't play their game. Stress emerges from a conflict between parties, and in that conflict, the other party judges their need to be greater than yours. They may appreciate your struggle or they may not, but if they're stressing you out, then at a certain level they're saying, "I don't care."

You retain the right to set the limit of what you need and what you'll endure. It is the typical mistake of young people to believe that they're entirely independent and that no one depends on them. This is shortsighted because, in most cases, both parents and your siblings depend on you to a greater degree than they may even be aware. Think of how you affect others when you're well and when you're ill. If the stress gets too much, then assert your right to leave, and leave.

"Someone told me to think about my family. They did tell me that, and I didn't think about my family for a second when I was doing those things. Maybe for second... Maybe I should have listened to that. That's the only thing I can ever remember anyone ever saying to me: 'Think about your family. Think about yourself and your family, and who you're going to hurt.' Like, I knew I hurt people, but I didn't care at the time.

"I don't know what I'd say to people to help them, because they wouldn't listen. People like me: they're just not going to listen. They might listen, keep it somewhere in their mind, and then when they're done with the process of getting clean and healthy, then they might think about it like I did.

But I still... I wouldn't know what to say in order to help somebody find happiness, or clarity in the future."
— **William Ashburton**, student, from *The Learning Project*

173. Take care of yourself.

Stresses are like mushrooms: they only make themselves known when they're ready to fruit. For the rest of the time, they incubate, slowly rising to a level of eruption. Learn to recognize the signs of stress before they overwhelm you. The overt signs indicate something's already broken. You want to address these problems before they're disabling.

Stress starts innocuously enough with fatigue, lack of enthusiasm, and distraction. Little things go wrong: your joints hurt, your eyesight is poor, your gums bleed, your sleep is poor, you're irritable, and your digestion suffers. After that, you might hurt yourself by stubbing your toe or straining your back. You'll get headaches, feel periods of dissociation, and find your thinking disturbed.

These are signs of incipient stress, useful indicators of the sources of your problems. The ultimate failure forces you to stop. It acts like the swelling around an injury, immobilizing you. When the crisis occurs— something between a disaster and a really bad day—you may realize there were warning signs that you overlooked.

Don't dismiss the signs. When you feel yourself running down, or being dragged down, that's the time to rebuild your resources, and refill your tank. Don't wait until you're stranded at the side of the road without resources and a situation you cannot handle. Your brain is designed to manage your resources, and that means managing both the short and long terms. Don't let situations grind you down.

"I had a very backward way of looking at myself. I was thinking this negative stuff about myself, and that was making all this negative stuff happen... I realized that I could stop, that I could just stop believing in those thoughts, it was like, 'I can just stop this right now!' It was a huge epiphany."
— **Lotus Bringing**, fashion model, from *The Learning Project*

7 – Behaviors

Growth

As situations evolve, new perspectives arise, and boundaries that separate subjects overlap. Old ideas find new roles borrowed wholesale or adapted in new forms. This has always been the case as it reflects the mutation of ideas across fields. Making conceptual jumps seems to be something humans are particularly good at.

Ideas as fundamental as mechanism, which first appeared in engineering, migrated to philosophy, biology, social engineering, and information processing. Ideas cross disciplines to both precipitate change and stultify other fields. A field beset with problems will explore new ideas, but once a new idea has been accepted, endorsed and an investment has been made, new ideas are not only discouraged, but alternatives are hidden, teaching is biased, and history is distorted to extol the new status quo.

It's hard to see these developments as an outsider because you don't know the real story, and no one on the inside does either. It's hard to see as an insider because your environment is hierarchical, closed to alternatives, and fundamental questions are considered heretical. One needs to be both well informed and independent, and few are. But if you are, then you will see this episodic opening and closing of the collective mind everywhere you look.

As an insider, any efforts to change the status quo will be discouraged, defunded, or outright punished. As an outsider, you have little power to change the status quo. Whatever leverage you do have will be dismissed by the experts, seen as unattractive to the investors, and considered an annoyance to those in power.

Consider some of the major themes operating today which, for the most part, no one is allowed to question: democratic government, taxation, the banking system, fiat currency, modern medicine, factory farming, technology, progress, cities, national defense, separation of church and state, and human rights, just to name a few. These ideas have entered Western culture within the last five hundred years and have grown of their own accord.

Some of these ideas continue to evolve, others define the culture, most have been accepted as defining us as individuals. Some of these ideas are interrelated at the lower level of mechanization and central control, as is the case with digital technology. Some of these ideas are leading us into social, ecological, and health crises. There is much talk, but little of substance is said. Basic questions are discouraged, experimentation is not supported, open dialog is not allowed.

You will not see the benefits and drawback of these socially fundamental issues seriously discussed in any mainstream media. This silence regarding the threats of modern technology led Ted Kaczynski to murder three and injure another 23 people in a revolutionary effort that resulted in the mainstream media publishing his manifesto (Kaczynski, 2018) and his getting a life sentence in prison.

When any of these fundamental memes fail, there is no recourse. The lack of practical options or a basis for discussion results in a spreading chaos. Because we do not exercise knowledgable, insightful discussions, these fundamental memes grow of their own accord, through rudimentary Darwinian selection, and without intelligent design.

Once an idea finds mainstream acceptance, various structures come together to support a wider base. You can see these large themes emerging in the areas of ecology, urbanization, and space exploration.

Innovation is often a casualty of its own success as a steep development curve tapers off to a plateau of adoption and circumscribed improvements. During periods of incremental development, innovation is discouraged as disruptive. Spreading acceptance fuels wider investment which, when combined with accumulating problems or failed promises, generates a growing pressure for improvements.

Abrupt transitions between established and innovative approaches, known as paradigm shifts, are typical when an existing approach exhausts itself, or a discovery opens new territory. These transitions are presaged by periods of resistance, consolidation, lack of alternatives, and crisis.

174. Position yourself in a growing field whose subject deeply interests you.

Few competitors in any field have a deep interest in their work. Most are there to advance the field and gain reward. An innovator has a different personality from those who want to further develop an idea. Innovators are disrupters. In most cases, innovators fail to gain the reward which goes to those to generate wide acceptance.

If you find reward in the work itself and you immerse yourself in it, then you'll become an expert. When the problems are complex, fortune does favor the person whose mind can make the most connections. Being open to disruption versus being inclined to refinement feels like a choice between opposites. A measure of your expertise is your ability to move in either direction.

Talent does not lead to recognition or authority; it is not true that "the cream rises to the top." This has been repeatedly confirmed: those who do the bidding of their superiors excel in hierarchical institutions, and this remains true even for a sycophant whose performance is below average.

A person who is passionate about going beyond what is known is emotionally prepared for changes in their field. A person who is dependent upon what is already known is not prepared for change either emotionally or intellectually. The passionate person is usually the first to hear of opportunities and to know how to exploit them. "Fortune favors the prepared mind," which Louis Pasteur said, is a self-fulfilling prophecy since opportunity is what one prepares for.

Most people believe that experts are innovators, but the opposite is the case. It has been my universal experience, as is substantiated by most innovators in other fields, that experts are about as open to change as the alpha males of any species are open to sharing power. However, in this case, gender plays no role.

I have heard a Nobel Laureate physicist claim that there is nothing left to be discovered, in spite of that fact that this has been said countless times before, and in spite of the fact that we know next to nothing about how or why the universe is the way it is! This also explains why this particular Nobel Laureate is so hostile to the physicist Ruggero Santilli, whose changes to fundamental mathematics threaten to upset all that this Nobel Laureate claims is the ultimate truth, and upon which his fame rests.

Marketing

The notion of bringing something to market encompasses everything from invention to delivery. This world of advertising, marketing, and sales operates explicitly or implicitly in every field and at every level.

I was raised on the misconception that product development was superior to marketing. I believed value was appreciated and good products sold themselves. This is the Overestimation Effect in action; it is the belief that other people think just like you do.

People with a low self-image—which described me when I was young—are attracted to this story. We want to believe our efforts will generate personal value, which is our emotional need. It's a fantasy. Markets provide rewards for their own reasons. In most cases, that means short-term value is rewarded over long-term value. Simply put, people value what satisfies them now, not what satisfies you now or ever.

I was not disabused of this misconception until I went into business to market my inventions. Even then, my experience was filtered by the Halo Effect, in which I felt substantiated by those who agreed with me. I discounted those who did not share my values, and I did not sell to them. You can use the Halo Effect to your advantage to sell to anyone, but that requires a shift to focus on what satisfies the other person.

If you're attracted to the excitement of others, or others are naturally attracted to you, then you have an audience you can play to. Fostering excitement is a skill that can be developed, and you should develop it. Enthusiasm is an important component of rapport.

175. New ideas don't sell.

In order to judge, you have to understand. In order to understand, you have to know what you're dealing with. Asking someone to accept something new is almost a contradiction in terms: you're asking them to render a positive judgment about something they don't fully understand. And if it's really new, then they really won't understand it. In that case—when they can't be confident in their judgment—how can you expect them to embrace a novel idea, no less commit to it? Would you propose marriage to a stranger?

It's uncomfortable to make a judgment about the unfamiliar. You have to apply some understanding based on your past experience, but is this the application of insight or prejudice? A new thing must have some of the things you already want if you're going to want the new thing. Obviously, the new thing will have some unfamiliar aspects. Whoever is trying to sell you this new thing will argue that these unfamiliar aspects make you want it more. You won't know if this is true from your experience, so you'll have to believe them, but taking things on faith is not compelling.

Maybe you know and trust the person who's selling this idea. Maybe you know their thoughts and abilities. They might be your partner, but that alone should not convince you of everything without question. If an idea is radically new, and you have absolutely no experience with it, then there is almost no chance you'll accept it without question. And the question that you'll have, however you might phrase it, will ultimately boil down to wanting proof: you'll want to see it in action. You'll want to gain experience.

Selling a new idea is hard, and that's why so few people bother. Even if you have a new idea, it's easier to sell it if it looks like an old one. This is true even if your teacher, client, customer, target, boss, partner, or investor says they're looking for new ideas.

> *"Forssmann, who was a surgical intern in Germany back in the late 20s, was an interesting guy. He wondered why we couldn't look at the heart using dye. He was told this could not be done because if you put dye into the heart the coronaries would fill up and the person would die.*
>
> *"Well, he didn't buy it. So he took a Foley catheter, which is a thing you put into the urethra for keeping the bladder open, and he stuck it in his antecubital vein, pushed it back up into his heart, squirted himself with dye, and took X-ray pictures of it.*
>
> *"He brings this picture—the first picture of angiography of the heart—to his attending physician, who promptly discharges him from practice for having done this: 'You did the impossible. You're fired!' He later gets the Nobel Prize in medicine for developing angiography."*
> — **George Plotkin**, MD, PhD, engineer, neuroscientist, inventor, from *The Learning Project*

Many of the great inventions we now use were not sold to us, they were forced on us. What was sold was something quite different and usually sold to an intermediary. The population did not make an informed decision to buy the idea of railroads or space exploration on the basis of travel, adventure, or opportunity. These industries were created for the benefit of specific groups, sold to those people, and then implemented by them.

Wars are an even better example: no one in their right mind would support being involved in a war, yet people do, not because they're well informed but because they're misinformed. Wars make sense from the point of view of those who have everything to gain and nothing to lose, but they are the paradigm of a bad idea for those involved in the fighting.

The purchases and investments we're most comfortable with are those we're familiar with. They lack novelty in all the important ways, and the novelty they have is of low-risk. What we buy, then, is not new ideas, but ideas we're already familiar with combined in new ways. We buy believable solutions to old problems.

If you want to sell a new idea, hide its novelty. Sell the secure prospect of satisfying familiar needs. Even better, sell the familiar aspect over which people lust; which is what satisfies their craving. That's what makes for an impulse purchase. Whatever the later judgment, it will form around the seed of the initial emotions.

176. Learn to recognize what other people want.

Our most fundamental emotions rest on attraction and repulsion. At a rudimentary level, you can interpret every action as a consequence of one, the other, or some combination of the two. Once you recognize what others want, it's fairly easy to elicit a positive response from them. Once you do that, you can use the Halo Effect to build other areas of agreement.

The Halo Effect is the positive bias people have toward anything positioned close to something they hold in high regard. The Halo Effect generates support for things that are otherwise entirely unrelated. Politicians use the Halo Effect to buy votes using celebrity endorsements even though celebrities have no expertise in politics.

Recognizing what other people want doesn't mean you're working to become their friend, it means you're working to be seen as someone who provides satisfaction. If you deliver satisfaction, then you can more easily develop friendly relationships. Even if you're not immediately likable, you can still develop a trusting relationship with people who want what you offer. But if you can't deliver satisfaction in some regard, then you won't develop any relationships except with those people who are obliged or depend on you.

177. Nurture and protect what excites you.

If you're a storyteller rather than an innovator—if you are more interested in exhibition than exploration—then you can represent what others are looking to acquire. It's easy to excite other people if you're excited by something they want. Excitement spreads, and the people you excite will excite others.

People want to be excited and they'll tell you what they're excited about if you take them seriously. Distrust is the biggest obstacle to developing mutual enthusiasm. You can assuage a positive person's distrust by being forthcoming and attentive. Unfortunately, many people who carry negative views of themselves, project these views onto the world and onto you. I believe it is best to avoid these people because they drain the energy of others and do not provide positive opportunities.

If I am informed, attentive, and forthcoming and the person with whom I'm communicating is unresponsive, then I write them off. Put your best foot forward and, if that's not enough, step back. To go beyond your feeling of comfort, integrity, and a fair deal is a bad idea. There lies exploitation and manipulation.

Marketing provides the ball bearings that convert desires into action. One must light a fire that motivates the movement of others at each step. In my experience, people who are good at this in one field can become good at it in any field, provided that they continue to be interested and informed.

Personability is a difficult skill to teach as it rests more on charm than content; more on reciprocity than protocol. This generally comes across as collegiality or charisma, which are right-brained skills of recognition, expression, and entrainment.

Personability exists at different levels. There are people who make friends quickly and others who don't. Different people are comfortable with different levels of social etiquette and familiarity. A skilled socializer will quickly navigate the social maze. They'll do this by reinforcing personal boundaries and aligning themselves with social norms. A stranger endorsed by a trusted reference will be given an opportunity, and they may be held to a lower standard, but they still have to pass some basic tests.

Don't be dismayed if you cannot make progress with certain people. Know what you offer, be confident in your intention, and leave the rest to chemistry. If the person you're addressing does not respond, or does not respond positively, don't pursue it. It's their problem, and you'll be better served by finding a more resonant relationship.

Few people are both great performers and great innovators. It's certainly a profitable combination of skills that every successful person hopes to develop to some extent. This combination of skills requires seeing beyond ranks or ratings. Charisma is like humor, it does not accept "No" as an answer. To be charismatic, you must be self-assured; you are not waiting for or in need of anyone's approval.

Ironically, charismatic people often have unpleasant personalities. I am thinking of *Apple's* Steve Jobs and *The Tonight Show's* host, Johnny

Carson, as two examples of publicly well-liked and personally unpleasant people.

This is the realm of the salesperson, performer, humorist, or clown; people who may also be full of self-doubt. These performers seek emotional, rather than intellectual, approval. If you can recognize these different forms of approval, you may be able to tune yourself to resonate with quite different audiences. However, confidence based on the approval of others has no soul. The only permanent ground for confidence is self-confidence.

Tests

There are fair and unfair tests. Testing is typically abused as a rating tool, not a learning tool. The manipulation of tests for ranking, sorting, and behavior modifying has traumatized many of us. These unfair tests range from the poorly explained to the intentionally prejudiced; many tests are guilty of both. There is no such thing as an objective test of knowledge.

We've been bred to fear tests, which arises from being subjected to unfair tests. Unfair tests are those designed to ensure your failure. These tests obfuscate the tester's hidden intention, which is either to hide their ignorance or bestow preference on a certain group.

The most unfair test I encountered was in a graduate course on General Relativity. The test was used to eliminate all but those students who had transferred into the program at a higher level, having learned the material at a better school. These transfer students scored higher. The matriculating students who struggled through the program were eliminated. This was not a test; it was an execution. One simply cannot win in this situation unless you know the game ahead of time.

The highest-ranked students do not have the most success in their fields. They've been trained to follow, and that's what they're good at. They will become managers, marketers, and actuaries. In contrast, CEOs, entrepreneurs, and other high-level leaders often come from the ranks of those who don't take orders and don't finish school. Most tests are vacuous, serve the institution, and their results are of no long-term significance.

178. Don't fear fair tests.

Once you're out of school, no one cares about your grades. Demonstrating that you've survived with your wits intact counts more, and you can survive an educational program, even if you're poor at the tests. Recognize school as a demeaning waste of your time—as it was designed to be—and grow in spite of it. Many do not recognize this and allow their spirits to be crushed.

Most tests consist of a few questions taken from a large area, the idea being that your knowledge of the whole can be inferred from your performance on the parts. But if you need to know certain material, then why not simply confirm it when you learn it? Most tests are tests of memory and how well you crammed for them.

Authentic learning situations don't test or exclude, they teach, and they keep teaching until you know all they have to offer. A fair test is one on which you know how you'll perform ahead of time. You know what you've learned, and you know what's being tested. If there is a discrepancy, the test fails, not you. A fair test does not degrade, it informs. That being said, few tests are fair.

We're trained to think tests measure our ability, but this is not true. Tests are useless beyond the content they contain: the test only tests how well you take the test. Unless performance is being measured by a useful metric, it's not useful.

The fallacy of testing is the implication that passing the test is necessary for progress in the subject. Nothing could be further from the truth. If you fix yourself on a target, nothing short of being denied materials can stop you. You can learn anything you want, and you don't need to succeed in someone else's eyes in order to move forward. Set your own goals, make your own tests, and test yourself.

Practical tests are generally fair, although they can be used in prejudicial ways. If the content is accurate, the exercise realistic, the examiner honest, and the consequences important, then the test meets my standard of fairness. In a larger sense, every real endeavor is a test, and sometimes we fail: we have accidents. Studying these accidents is instructive. Always study your accidents; always test yourself.

179. Recognize the purpose of a test

Courses are not offered for your benefit; school is a for-profit operation—even public schools and especially ideological schools. You're tested because testing is a low-cost way of confirming the product the course is designed to produce. With test results, profiles can be built to expedite selection and exclusion.

Productivity involves more complex skills than can be tested. If you can identify the qualities needed for being productive and demonstrate that you have them, then you'll sometimes be ushered right past the whole testing process.

I took a training course for certification as a Clinical Hypnotist, which was a prerequisite for the subsequent certification as a Clinical Hypnotherapist. My performance in the course so impressed the instructor that I was accorded a higher certification immediately, without taking the next course or the test that went with it.

The publication of work in peer-reviewed, academic journals can be compared to a test. Peer review is a famously arbitrary process which, in most cases, does not involve credible review. Many editors only send out for review work submitted by authors they don't know, or material that makes novel claims.

Those who review are often invested in protecting existing ideas from challenge and in discouraging novelty. As am academic reviewing editor myself, at the *Journal of Mind and Behavior*, I do my best to understand what I'm reviewing, but I find myself reviewing how well I understand the material rather than the authors' ideas. The peer-review process is mostly a process of editing for conformity in which nonconformist thinking is rarely accepted (Smith, 2006).

180. No doesn't mean no.

People speak with many voices, and where power and preference are concerned the same person has voices that can say different things. Our use of language is a thin fabric that often fails to cover the issue. A statement at one point in time applies to a range of other times and circumstances. A yes or no statement is given for clarity, but the world remains as ambiguous as ever.

We're always looking for both meaning and certainty, but they move in opposite directions. When someone says "No" they mean no to something in particular. "No," without further explanation sounds clear even when the situation isn't.

Generalizations like "no always" or "no everywhere" sound definitive but actually add uncertainty. When you ask for a yes or no answer, you're asking for something particular. Recognize the difference between a response that's general and vague versus one that is specific and clear. A "no" is only as clear as the question it answers.

Whenever you get a specific answer, you can wonder if a general answer would be the same. The specific "no" may not apply to the general question. No never means "No, period," it always means "No, and..." or "No, but..." Pay attention to the possible implications and unpack them.

The answer "No, because..." has a lot in common with "Yes, maybe..." You hear them differently, but they have the same implication, namely that they apply with conditions that could reverse them. That first word is a cover to a book, a matter of appearances, or a statement of the party line. It's how the sentence ends that tells you how to use it.

When seeking compliance, recognize the many ways you can be heard. There may be certainty in the present, but every answer has a history in the past and a legacy in the future that hangs in the air like dust waiting to settle. I'm attracted to the larger picture while most people, on the other hand, see things narrowly.

"The police sergeant, who I had been working with to make this all peaceful, came to me and told me that we would have to vacate the stadium... because there was a bomb threat. I kind of paused, and I emptied myself... I did that thing that, for some reason or other, has always worked

with me all my life, which was to kind of empty myself at that point. And I looked at him and I said, 'Look, if I can get everybody in the bowl to search their own seats... then would you let us stay?'

"So when this band that was playing was done I went out and made a little speech. I told everybody what to look for and how to look for it, and everybody looked for the bomb, and nobody found the bomb. And it was done in absolute silence, with absolute discipline in this crowd, and with total seriousness.

"And when it was over there was this moment of complete elation. The whole place had turned into an entirely different group of people who were connected, and who were careful and disciplined and filled with affection for one another. And there was this huge cheer, and it was done."
— **Tom Hurwitz**, filmmaker, from *The Learning Project*

181. Yes doesn't mean yes.

A yes question is a question that seeks affirmation, such as "don't you think..." or "can I..." We ask a yes question when we want a yes response. We'll listen more for the yes in what we hear. We don't ask for a "yes" until we feel entitled to it, even when we're undeserving. We wrap the question in our entitlement.

An agreement has enduring effects and opens future paths. Yes is not just the opposite of no, it also creates an opposing environment. Yes to a project, job, assessment, or relationship opens new dimensions that no does not. Yet, what are these possibilities? Certainly, they're not fully described by a one-syllable word. They exist in your imagination. So how congruent is your imagination with that of the person who says, "Yes"?

"Yes" is a doorway, even if it answers a trivial question like, "Are these my French fries?" Where your mind goes next is up to you. Like a telescope, you dial in your depth of field, looking into the future, and only see what you focus on.

What if you could see both the immediate question and all its implications? If you could, then you would appreciate that the result of affirming the immediate question could be different from affirming all the consequences of it. You might agree to the first question, but you might not agree to the implications of it.

"Do you like me? Do you love me? Will you marry me?" may be a natural series of affirmations in another person's mind, but they may not be a natural sequence of affirmations in yours. The person who asks these question may infer more from your answer than you intend. How certain are you of which question are asked and how is your answer is taken?

A single answer is rarely sufficient, yet one question is always asked first. A given answer rarely means just one thing, yet certain implications are heard first. By the nature of the permission it affords, the answer yes bounces around like the beam of a bright light in a hall of mirrors.

"I wanted to go into a research career because I was, like, 'This is cool! I can do this.' So I got a Post-doc with this guy Stanley B. Kater who was famous in my field. He was one of the top guys in the field and had, like, six Post-Docs and four graduate students and this huge lab. In my naiveté, I figured, 'He must be a really, really good scientist...' He

must be amazingly good if he had that kind of lab. And he offered me a job, and I took it.

"I found that he actually wasn't that great. The reason he had such a big lab was that he was a good salesman. And that was soooo disillusioning to me. I was completely disillusioned. I was like, 'This is what science is about? This is what I have to do to do well in science?' I knew I couldn't do it. I learned a lot about the realities of grant funding and that kind of stuff, but I was very disheartened."
— **Michelle Murrain**, PhD, neuroscientist, computer consultant, writer, activist, from *The Learning Project*

182. Use your eyes.

If you pay careful attention to how you use your eyes and the way others use theirs, and correlate these impressions with other signals that you're getting, then your understanding will expand. The mental process of making sense of what you perceive is called apperception. It's the process of becoming a more astute and active participant in your environment, somewhat akin to learning how to read in a world that's like a book.

There should be a word for doing this in reverse: of putting meaning into how others perceive you. I don't know of such a word, but you still can do it.

Listen to your sentences and use your eyes for punctuation. You will quickly notice correspondences between your sentence, paragraph, interrogative, and exclamation points and the expression of your eyes. You have always been doing this, but, like some lingering speech impediment, you have never perfected it. Start noticing details.

The importance of eyes is highlighted by the reference to the person "who blinks first." It's not really a blink that's referred to, but a micro-movement in the muscles around the eyes. These sorts of micro-expressions occur on the border of our perception, lasting little more than the duration of a single frame of a movie. We don't know what it is that we saw because it happens too fast, but we can feel it, like a quick punch. You broadcast these expressions all the time and, with practice, you can control them. It's done through control of emotion, not muscles.

183. Use commitment to measure insight.

Insight is a deeper view into appearances. When you feel you understand the truth of the situation, you feel greater certainty of what's to come. Commitment is a measure of insight, but that doesn't mean it's right.

Insight is a verisimilitude which is not the same as veracity. Insight comes before veracity and should be respected in its own right. The importance of insight is the associated dawning of a new understanding. As long as there's something new, there's progress. If the novelty is compelling enough to generate commitment, it's something you can bank on. The commitment may be misplaced, but it's got substance you can sink your teeth into.

Lack of commitment reflects a disconnection with any reality. An absence of truth, a lack of presence. False commitment is even worse. Whereas an opinion is a possibility, a commitment is an action. A false opinion is a deception, a false commitment is a failure to deliver: a theft.

Habits

184. Break learning habits.

Be sensitive to habitual thinking and behaviors for which you've been trained. Repetitive patterns develop because people are oblivious to mental habits. The sooner you can see your thinking patterns, the more quickly you'll see the opportunities that lay beyond them.

Holding yourself at arm's length to see your thinking patterns, is like seeing yourself without a mirror: you have to create an image of yourself that you can look at. It's like taking a deep breath, opening a door in your awareness, and stepping into empty space. Looking at yourself without prejudice or pretense is odd, disconcerting, and a bit frightening.

"My sister and I have changed a lot. She and I are best friends now... that just came out of the blue, like I don't know how that happened... It was the day I came back from the treatment center. And she just... she gave me a hug for the first time ever. She had never given me a hug in my teenage years, ever. It felt like she loved me, and I started to cry. I've never gotten a hug from her. So I had to love her back..."
—**William Ashburton**, student, from *The Learning Project*

185. Procrastination isn't a bad thing.

Delaying or hesitating looks like procrastination when you don't have a good reason for it, but if it comes from a particular feeling that something is coming or is needed, then it's a good thing. This is different from disinterest or disrespecting your commitments. That sort of chronic procrastination arises from a kind of depression.

Being pressed to meet a deadline may be necessary for a group endeavor, but if it overrides caution, hurries preparation, or ignores insight, then it will lower the quality of the final project. There are positive aspects to delaying and hesitating. The feeling that something needs to be done won't get anything done by itself, you'll need to act on this feeling to look at or look for something.

It pays to wait until it feels right to do something. This is practically a necessity in creative projects that simply cannot come together until all the parts are "ripe." It's also well known that the pressure of a deadline stimulates action, thought, and creativity. Creative people in all fields frequently do their best work at the last minute.

> *"I also told you that I procrastinate. So a lot of times my public speaking is very fresh, like when I get there it's usually the first time I'm doing it. As everybody else was giving their practice speech, I was sitting in the back of the room writing my speech and trying to memorize it. My Mom was sitting next to me going, 'You should have done this last night! You should have done this weeks ago!'"*
> — **Jessica Henry**, student, from *The Learning Project*

The key is being able to produce work and to overcome inertia. If you still don't feel inspired at the last minute, you should be able to throw something together. It may not be your best work, but it might be. One's best work requires effort and as much pressure as you can find. It doesn't have to be unpleasant, but it does have to be done on its own time. It can't be accomplished just because there's a deadline.

I typically miss deadlines when I need to create an alternative. I want to allow these alternatives an opportunity to manifest. New things happen at the last minute if you keep up the pressure. People behave differently when they're forced to act rather than relying on protocol. People get to the emotional core of the matter when there's no time left.

186. Break up daunting tasks.

Consider anything that blocks you to be a task, and break it down. You don't have to know what you're doing, and you don't have to be right. In fact, it's better if you don't worry about being right, and don't wait until you know what you're doing.

Approach tasks with insight, even if it's a fantasy. Find points of weakness and imagine how this point might yield to your efforts. Find boundaries and break the task into different approaches for either side. Do whatever it takes to reduce the task to something you can hold in your mind as one whole piece.

187. Simplify.

Simplifying correctly can be harder than solving the larger problem, and it is always more important. The fewer pieces at play, the narrower your options, and the broader their implications. The most important ideas are inevitably the most basic. This is why many of the greatest creators appear to be making toys, but they are not toys, they are situations at their most fundamental. They are attempts to see how little you can present and still keep the idea standing.

"Jerry's brother was a concert pianist. When the kids were young, we used to go over to his house and they would lie under the piano while he gave master classes. He would go

over and over the same phrase, looking for the right way to express it—looking for the way he wanted it to sound. That's exactly what this whole thing is about: it's about the process."
— **Maggie Lettvin**, exercise therapist, from *The Learning Project*

We're trained to think problem-solving is about knowing the right solution, but often there is none or none that anyone knows. We're told solving problems measures our intelligence and the smarter person solves complicated problems. The opposite is usually the case. It's the simpler problem that is more constrained, has fewer "free parameters," and applies to more situations. Real understanding follows precisely from understanding the simple case.

"Very often, if you can solve this simple problem, you can add refinements to the solution of this until you get back to the solution of the one you started with."
— **Claude Shannon**, PhD, mathematician, engineer, and inventor

"Do not think that simplicity means something like the side of a barn, but rather something with graceful sense of beauty in its utility from which discord and all that is meaningless has been eliminated."
— **Frank Lloyd Wright**, architect

"Everything should be made as simple as possible, but no simpler."
— attributed to **Albert Einstein**, PhD, physicist

188. Listen to your body.

There is a physical sense of balance that prevails when things are going in the right direction. The direction may not be the direction you want, but you can feel it when you escape from stress and worry. The record of your emotions, vague and rarely journaled, is more trustworthy than a check-list. You can find physical intuition in your body.

> *"Continue to do the things that you do well, but don't forget to use your body... You should really pay attention to all of you. That's one of the difficult things with the educational system I think for some people. I've run into some people who are well educated, who have all of that, and have no relationship to their body at all."*
> —**Christa Dahl**, artist, from *The Learning Project*

There are times I can't sleep through the night and I wake up well before dawn feeling uncomfortable. At these times I explore my internal sensations, my joints and muscles, and the ideas and anxieties floating around me. I allow myself a kind of confusion of ideas and feelings without requiring myself to think straight, as no one train of thought seems to dominate. I rarely find resolution, but I often connect ideas and feelings. Often, but not always, a sense of clarity emerges later that day or the next.

189. We present false personalities.

Few of us are who we pretend to be. Our personalities are a mask for our complicated and compromised feelings. Our character is improvised by necessity, built on memories that draw from experiences of which we consciously recall, as well as symbolic memories constructed from feelings and snapshots from our disjointed past.

The conscious foundation of our personalities are the attitudes with which we feel reasonably comfortable, behaviors we think are reasonable. The unconscious foundations are the impulsive, compulsive, and reflexive reactions worn into us as safe and familiar choices. The subconscious foundations of our personality rest on sunken memories, an archeological past we've been born into, woken up in, and inherited from past generations, abandoned attitudes we thought we had forgotten.

Our stable personality is in line with our values most of the time, though it's normal to have underlying doubts and moments of uncertainty. If you scrutinize yourself, you'll likely find your deeper doubts are pervasive. We repress these for a measure of light-heartedness.

An unstable personality can have a strong presence and a flighty attention, or it may be manifestly ungrounded. Unstable people's sense of presence varies with their audience. Extremely unstable personalities can present themselves in any fashion from being powerful and focused to the complete opposite. They swing between extremes, though you may not witness the full range of it.

190. Don't grouse about the misbehavior of others.

Complaining is a great and useless pastime. When I hear others complain—I won't tolerate it in my conversations, but I often overhear it in the conversations of others—I sense a kind of fear. The fear that the complainer deserves what they received, or are guilty of what they've been accused. The speaker seeks confirmation of innocence and justification for resentment.

This is an emotional infection. Once the feeling settles in, you're infected. Attempts to exonerate yourself from your self-doubt cannot succeed, and attempts to enlist the support of someone who knows only your fabricated personality is pathetic.

If you're guilty, fix it. If you're innocent, ignore it. If those who accuse you are standing in your way, pick another way. Only engage people who are seriously interested in what you have to say.

> *"Grievances are like flowers: if you water them, they will grow. So little grievances grow into big grievances, and it's so unfortunate! Everybody's got problems, and there's sin in the world, but move on and make your life what you want it to be!"*
> — **Phyllis Schlafly,** JD, politician, orator, and social activist, from *The Learning Project*

When others disrespect you, the only well-composed reaction is to recognize these actions for what they are: attempts at injury committed by someone who hopes to gain from it. To accept the injuries or accusations as things you need to explain guarantees you will operate from weakness, and those weaknesses will be your own. In that case, the accusation, disrespect, or misbehavior was well-targeted. You are vulnerable and you do doubt yourself. No amount of social support and no amount of protest to the contrary will clean this infection from your wound.

Recognize your feelings toward yourself, and where you find yourself wanting, recognize that it is this weakness that is being preyed upon. See your accuser or offender for what they are, and recognize that they are not a directly creative force in your world.

191. Respect those who disrespect you.

Those who disrespect you expose personal weaknesses your friends will not confront. These are weaknesses that are carefully hidden outside your social personality. Those who push you in ways for which you're not supported are exposing things you need to fix. They may not be acting out of goodwill, but you should not care: they've given you a gift in spite of themselves.

Not only have they exposed a weakness in you, but they've also exposed their own weakness. In some cosmic way, your weakness and their weakness are connected, and your obligation to improve yourself has some role in fixing theirs. You can't fix another person, but you can help clarify what they see. This is not revenge or reciprocity, so don't expect credit or gratitude. Your respect for their disability is a key component in the resolution of the larger anguish.

If you invite these people to express themselves in minor matters and to small measure, then you may get all you need. It's a matter of being thoughtful, sensitive, reflective, and not defensive. You're welcoming them, not rejecting them. If you recognize disrespectful people before they've done you injury, then you'll better avoid them in more serious contexts where their injuries could be larger, and your gratitude harder to come by.

192. Be a racist scumbag.

The only way to not be something is to know what it is and master it. If you can direct yourself to become a racist scumbag and then not be one—using this term to represent anyone you detest—then you will understand those who don't have the flexibility to shift between the two. Clearly, there is some human reason for this kind of character. If you believe there is a healthier alternative, then it's sort of up to you to prove it. Who else is going to facilitate change?

People don't change, at least not much. And their change is not your responsibility, in any event. This is true on an individual basis, but we are not really individuals, we are networks. Our networks are so interconnected that your effect on one person will have remote effects on other people, times, and places. It's also far from clear what effects you could have. Every person has the obligation to plant seeds, and you probably won't see them sprout.

There are many people I've known who are, for me, iconic racist scumbags. I carry their memory like tattoos, which I wish I hadn't gotten. Only by understanding these people as agents of something else can I begin to forget them.

This is the reason it's important to understand how you could be like them. Once you can do that, you know where they come from and where they're going, and if you want to be involved in fixing those things, then that's where you'll need to go. You no longer need to remember them; they have nothing more to teach you.

> *"If you desire to be good, begin by believing that you are wicked."*
> —**Epictetus**, Greek Stoic philosopher, c.100 AD

193. Don't stop.

Difficulties will slow you down, disappointment will stop you, and depression will make you want to give up. You can slow down and you can change direction, but don't stop, and don't give up.

Always keep some momentum, even if this means just a few moments of each day; always remain attached to your dreams and goals. This is important because there is a rhythm to movement that can turn to stone if you stop. Any effort—as long as it does something—is vastly better than no effort.

The real danger, both to yourself and others, is indifference. Indifference is detachment, a kind of non-living state. If you're part of a system but indifferent to its effects, then you are a contributing to its outcome.

Evil people are presumed filled with negative intention, but in the most severe cases, they're simply indifferent. We'd like to call them psychopaths, but indifference seems to be something you can acquire. Avoid indifference at all costs. Never abandon your vision. Never lose the direction that's most important to you and don't stop working toward it.

The same is true to being creative: keep working even if you're spinning your wheels. You can take a break, a different approach, or a "working vacation," but continue turning the problem over in your mind. Big problems underlie your sense of purpose. They motivate everything and you never stop thinking about them. They don't even demand solutions.

When climbing mountains, you can pause, but you shouldn't stop. You need to maintain your mental state, keep your pulse up, and your body engaged. If you sit down to relax and disengage, it becomes much harder to get going again. You may have to rest ten seconds between footsteps, but as long as you keep making progress, you'll have a schedule and some sense of when you'll arrive. I find this applies to other projects too.

"If you can't fly then run, if you can't run then walk, if you can't walk then crawl, but whatever you do you have to keep moving forward."
— **Martin Luther King, Jr.**, minister and civil rights activist

194. Understand attention.

Focus is the root of learning. How well you recognize patterns will determine how well you recognize relationships and opportunities. Recognition first requires focus, which you develop by reflecting on yourself and your place in the world. What you can't focus on, you can't learn about.

A critical dimension is time: over what period of time are you able to recognize a pattern? Can you remember similarities in shape, color, and texture of things that flash quickly in and out of your field of view? How long can you remember them?

Your navigation through space rests on your recall of location and orientation. This applies to ideas as well as locations since many people are visual thinkers. And because all attention is rhythmic in nature—it cannot be sustained—your ability to manage the rhythms of your attention is crucial.

The attention you pay to faces, body language, and micro-expressions contributes to your skill in appraising character. Prosody, another right-brained skill, is your ability to extract meaning from patterns of rhythm and sound. You can improve these abilities with practice.

"The faculty of bringing back a wandering attention, over and over again, is the very root of judgment, character, and will. Education, which would improve this faculty, would be

the education par excellence."
— **William James**, PhD (1950, p. 424), psychologist

The modern epidemic of attention deficit disorder among school children —a largely nonexistent condition that is cured with counseling in 75% of cases, which is an established truth that has been covered up (Stoller, 2014)—rests on whether the focus demanded by your environment is compatible with your needs.

Focus is as much a skill as a habit; you can change your focus from either point of view: change your habits or develop new skills. There are as many ways to train selective attention as there are things you can select to focus on. You train attention by exercising the systems that you use for focusing: conceptual, visual, auditory, kinesthetic, and so on.

Focus and awareness are related but different. You can develop the ability to focus on things of which you're not consciously aware, but you are aware of at other levels. You can learn to better discriminate facial micro-expressions, even though they are of too short a duration for you to clearly perceive them. You can learn to register them emotionally, but they're gone before you can remember seeing them.

You can develop feelings for things that you're never fully aware of. You can improve your timing through sports or music, or by precision tempo training (Rönnqvist, McDonald, & Sommer, 2018; Ferguson, 2006). We actually do this all the time, but we often overlook it, so we don't develop it as a skill.

Movies are full of these cues, and you will respond to them even if you are not aware of them. Next time you watch a horror, romance, comedy, thriller, or documentary pay close attention to the use of sound, light, color, the intonation of voices, the pacing of scenes and the manner of cutting between them. These are all used to manage your thoughts and attention, and they work at a level that can be just below or far below your awareness.

I monitor my therapy clients' attention by watching their EEG brainwave patterns. It's possible to predict a person's openness to new ideas based on their EEG patterns, and one can learn to reshape these brainwaves. You gain insight by noticing how your thinking is linked to the rhythms of attention in everyday situations. By this, I'm referring to how you're constantly cycling through states of engagement and distraction, which are different states of awareness.

> *"Two approaches to train attention are mindfulness, the faculty of sustaining voluntary attention upon a chosen object, and introspection, the ability to become aware of one's own state of mind... By cultivating them in sequence and balancing and synergistically integrating these qualities you can apply refined attention to everything you do including: raising our children, music, art, business, athletics, science, and inquiry... even observing the depths of your own identity."*
> — **Emma Bragdon**, PhD, therapist, consultant, and teacher (Bragdon, 2013, p. 162).

195. Focus and convergence are entirely different.

Focus is your ability to screen out distractions. Convergence is your skill at thinking along established lines. Conversely, lack of focus means you either become lost or more broadly aware, and more inclusive. Divergent thinking can result in losing one's path and finding another. Neuroscience research suggests these aptitudes, or inclinations, are different.

A person's openness to perceive things that are supposed to be unrelated is connected with their ability to defocus. This seems to characterize highly creative people. It's not that they are thinking outside the box, it's that they are perceiving outside the box. They are making new connections because their systems are able to see—or unable not to see—outside events. (Zabelina, 2015)

Divergent thinking, on the other hand, doesn't imply breadth of perception, but a decision to think differently. A combination of both would suit a creative mind, but the two need not come together.

It is unfortunate that neurological studies assume a lack of volition. Studies showing a person's openness to irrelevant sensory information don't test if this is an innate or developed skill. Part of my therapeutic method is to help my clients develop these skills. Becoming more sensitive is high on my list of skills, and one I always encourage in my clients to refine. It is widely endorsed for expanding one's emotional intelligence.

Divergent thinking can also be cultivated: collect the unrelated approaches and review them together, throwing away objections. This can be done either as intellectual brainstorming or trance-based channeling. Quoting the physicist Neils Bohr, "Your theory is crazy, but it's not crazy enough to be true."

8 – Summary

This volume began with a focus on schools, schooling, education, teachers, and resources. We need to question our learning format because it will form the container for future growth. A seed is not concerned with the shape of the pot, but the pot will determine the shape of the life it leads. Indeed, in the wrong pot, it won't lead any life at all.

An embryo, like a child, contains basic mental nutrients, like a seed carries its initial store of food. Beyond that, we depend on our parents, community, culture, and society to support our basic needs. Few parents provide their children with the best possible support and, as I've argued here, society doesn't either.

You are the only person interested, capable, and free enough to compare your needs with the resources available to you. You must examine each resource, path, agent, and institution, but you are not expected to do this. This process is confrontational because the authoritarian model will resist you. If you are so lucky as to have had an open, resource-filled childhood—and some of us have, to varying extents—then you will know there exists another model in which your learning, growth, and horizons are boundless.

The most frustrating aspect of taking control of your learning is the general lack of good advice or thoughtful insight from any quarter. At times it feels like a horror story in which everyone is colluding to limit you. Every "normal" adult seems blind to your potential and, apparently, their own. Start asking "why" questions and you'll feel like you're trapped in *The Truman Show*, or an episode of *The Twilight Zone*. I'm sorry to say, this prevails at all levels. There is no escape within the institutional context.

The hidden path emerges from the process of becoming aware of yourself. Once you connect with your own sense of life and purpose, you can judge the character and insight of the people you encounter. Once you know what it feels like to get your needs met—even if you don't know the ends toward which you're headed—you gain confidence in your ability to know who your friends are. This is also the starting point for knowing who your friends aren't.

This first volume focused on the essential issue of knowing where we are and what we need. Even if you know nothing else, this gets you started on the project of carving out a space in which to grow. This is the seed's lesson in understanding the pot it has sprouted in. You have the power to change your pot.

The next volume, subtitled *The Inner World*, focuses on how our minds work. It orders our experience into the experiential, intellectual, emotional, and reflexive. It opens us to levels of awareness and our ability to arrange and expand them.

Awareness is the fundamental territory of our minds. It is the pot that contains self-awareness. We will never learn to understand, control, or transcend what we are not aware of. To the extent we lack a full awareness of ourselves, we will remain trapped within these limits.

There is not just one way to expand your consciousness. Your mind is an amalgamation of tools and resources. There are some structural limitations, but most of these limitations are far beyond your current abilities.

Institutions support the easy steps in mind expansion because these require the least investment and yield immediate results. This includes feeding us facts, instructions, and introductions. We are weaned on a diet of palatable knowledge.

To gain greater control of our individual and collective futures will require us to expand into areas of complexity, conflict, and contradiction. Our education system has not prepared us for the feelings of being lost, underpowered, and confused. Yet this is what you'll feel when you venture into the open sea of knowledge, heading toward the edge of the world as it were. Expanding your mind into those areas is not easy.

One of the purposes of the second volume is to make clear just how flawed our unexamined thinking is. We simply are not been taught how to think straight or, to put it another way, we are not taught how to build our own sustainable, independent, communities that are self-sufficient, emotionally balanced, and rooted in spirt.

Clear thinking does not lead to clear results, it leads to increasing complexity, new forms of information, and uncertainty. Learning this territory and learning to be prosperous and creative within this territory is the defining character of supergenius.

THE END

References

Alexander, C. W. (2002). *The Nature of Order, Book Four: The Luminous Ground*. The Center for Environmental Structure.

Bragdon, E. (2013). *Spiritism and Mental Health*. Singing Dragon.

Christakis, E. (2013, Jan. 30). What the Pygmies can teach us about child rearing, *TIME*. Retrieved from: https://ideas.time.com/2013/01/30/what-the-pygmies-can-teach-us-about-childrearing/

Durrell, G. (1977). *My Family and Other Animals*. Penguin Books.

Eby, M. (2010, June 21) Laurie Anderson is bored with the avant-garde, *Salon*. Retrieved from: https://www.salon.com/2010/06/21/laurie_anderson_interview/

Faith, C. M. (2007). *The Way of the Turtle: The Secret Methods that Turned Ordinary People into Legendary Traders*. McGraw-Hill.

Ferguson, S. (2006). Learning musical instrument skills through interactive sonification, *Proceedings of the 2006 International Conference on New Interfaces for Musical Expression (NIME06)*. Retrieved from: https://www.researchgate.net/profile/Sam_Ferguson/publication/221164900_Learning_Musical_Instrument_Skills_Through_Interactive_Sonification/links/5536580b0cf20ea35f125463/Learning-Musical-Instrument-Skills-Through-Interactive-Sonification.pdf

Feynman, R. P. (1965). *The Character of Physical Law*. MIT Press.

Fisher, T. R. (2000). *In the Scheme of Things, Alternative Thinking on the Practice of Architecture,* U. of Minnesota Press.

Goleman, D. (2013). *Focus, the Hidden Driver of Intelligence,* HarperCollins.

Havel, V. (1988). Stories and totalitarianism, *Index On Censorship 3*(88). Retrieved from: https://journals.sagepub.com/doi/pdf/10.1080/0306422880853 4381

Heick, T. (2020, February 15). As the world changes, How should school change? *Teachthought.* Retrieved from: https://www.teachthought.com/education/how-overly-academic-learning-is-killing-education/

James, W. (1950). *The Principles of Psychology*. Dover.

James, W. (2019). *The Meaning of Truth*. Anodos Books. Retrieved from: https://www.gutenberg.org/files/5117/5117-h/5117-h.htm

Kaczynski, T. (2018). *The Unabomber's Manifesto: Industrial Society and Its Future,* Independently published.

Kaufman, B. S., & Gregoire, C. (2016). *Wired to Create: Unraveling the Mysteries of the Creative Mind*. TarcherPerigee.

Lindbergh, C. (2003). *The Spirit of St. Louis*. Scribner.

Nørretranders, T. (1999). *The User Illusion, Cutting Consciousness Down To Size*, Penguin Books.

Pink, D. H. (2012). *To Sell Is Human, the Surprising Truth About Moving Others*. Riverhead Press.

Pinker, S. (2018). *Enlightenment Now, the Case for Reason, Science, Humanism, and Progress*. Random House.

Rönnqvist, L., McDonald, R., Sommer, M. (2018, December 7). Influences of synchronized metronome training on soccer players' timing ability, Performance accuracy, and lower-limb kinematics, *Frontiers in Psychology, 9*, article 2469. doi: 10.3389/fpsyg.2018.02469

Santilli, R. M. (2017). Lawsuit Against Frank Israel and Pepjim van Erp. *EPR Debates*. Retrieved from: http://eprdebates.org/Lawsuit-against-Frank-Israel-and-Pepijin-van-Erp.php

Smith, R. (2006). Peer review: a flawed process at the heart of science and journals, *Journal of the Royal Society of Medicine, 99*(4): 178-182. doi: 10.1258/jrsm.99.4.172. Retrieved from: https://www.ncbi.nlm.nih.gov/pmc/articles/PMC1420798/

Soni, J., Goodman, R. (2017, August 1). 10,000 hours with Claude Shannon: How a genius thinks, works and lives, *Observer*. Retrieved from: https://observer.com/2017/08/10000-hours-with-claude-shannon-how-genius-thinks-works-lives-a-mind-at-play-bell-labs/

Stoller, L. (1987). The Indian's apprentice: Learning to build the dugout canoe, *Wooden Boat Magazine, 4*: 27-33.

Stoller, L. (2014). ADHD as emergent institutional exploitation, *The Journal of Mind and Behavior, 35* (1 & 2), pp. 21-50.

Stoller, L. (2019a). *The Path to Sleep, Exercises for an Ancient Skill*. Mind Strength Balance.

Stoller, L. (2019b). *Becoming Lucid, Self-Awareness in Sleeping and Waking Life*. Mind Strength Balance.

Taylor, E. (2009). *Mind Programming, From Persuasion and Brainwashing to Self-Help and Practical Metaphysics*. Hay House.

Voss, C. (2016). *Never Split the Difference: Negotiating As If Your Life Depended On It*. HarperCollins.

Wright, J. L. (1992). *My Father, Frank Lloyd Wright*. Dover Publications.

Yamamura, M. (2015) *Yayoi Kusama: Inventing the Singularity*. MIT Press.

Yong, E. (2017, October 3). The absurdity of the Nobel Prizes in science, *The Atlantic*. Retrieved from: https://www.theatlantic.com/science/archive/2017/10/the-absurdity-of-the-nobel-prizes-in-science/541863/

Zabelina, D. (2015, January 23). Creativity and sensory gating, Creative people's brains are not good at filtering out sensory information, *Psychology Today*. Retrieved from: https://www.psychologytoday.com/ca/blog/finding-butterfly/201501/creativity-and-sensory-gating

Quotation Index

About the Author

Lincoln Stoller has published work as a physicist, astronomer, statistician, biologist, neurophysiologist, neurofeedback therapist, psychologist, hypnotherapist, computer scientist, software architect, anthropologist, mountaineer, and educator. He has built two houses and has licenses to pilot soarplanes, fly paragliders, and scuba dive.

He holds a PhD in quantum physics from the University of Texas, hypnotherapy certifications from ICBCH and IMDHA, and the patent for the design of a business accounting system which he programmed and supported for 15 years. He is an assessing editor at the *Journal of Mind and Behavior*.

Lincoln has spent 40 years involved with various schools of spirituality and mediation, 20 years with the therapeutic and religious use of psychedelics, 10 years offering EEG brainwave training, and the last 5 years as a hypnotherapist in private practice specializing in medical support, sleep enhancement, spiritual guidance, and business psychology. All of which is to say, he helps people learn things. His previous four books are: *The Learning Project, Rites of Passage*; *The Path To Sleep*; *Becoming Lucid*, and *COVID-19: Illness and Illumination.*

His 22-year-old son Kiran lives with Lincoln's ex-wife in New York, and his 10-year-old son Pythagoras lives with Lincoln in Victoria, British Columbia, Canada, to which he moved for educational and political reasons, and to be closer to mountains, forests, and the sea.

Made in the USA
Middletown, DE
13 February 2021